Seen and Not Seen

Confessions of a Movie Autist

Seen and Not Seen

Confessions of a Movie Autist

Jasun Horsley

Winchester, UK
Washington, USA

First published by Zero Books, 2015
Zero Books is an imprint of John Hunt Publishing Ltd., Laurel House, Station Approach,
Alresford, Hants, SO24 9JH, UK
office1@jhpbooks.net
www.johnhuntpublishing.com
www.zero-books.net

For distributor details and how to order please visit the 'Ordering' section on our website.

Text copyright: Jasun Horsley 2014

ISBN: 978 1 78279 675 6

A CIP catalogue record for this book is available from the British Library.

Design: Stuart Davies
Cover image: Lucinda Horan

Printed and bound by CPI Group (UK) Ltd, Croydon, CR0 4YY

We operate a distinctive and ethical publishing philosophy in all
areas of our business, from our global network of authors to
production and worldwide distribution.

CONTENTS

Part One: The Deconstruction Artist   1

Introduction: Autist or Auteur, That Is the Question   3
*What the book "is." Description of the author's autism, and
how it relates to his early love of movies and creative
immersion, how cultural images provide us with an
unconscious ideology.*

**Self-Engineered Autism: Jonathan Lethem's *The
Disappointment Artist* & the Revolting Development
of Culture**   14
*How movies and pop culture provide conceptual, imagistic and
emotional content as a matrix for self-awareness to grow in.*

**The Soul Searchers: Finding a Sponsor in the Game
of Life**   26
*The socialization process from birth to adulthood, the perils
of imitation, and how movies provide a safe space to test out
social behaviors.*

**Screen Memories & Apple Seeds: Parented By
Pop Culture**   36
Taxi Driver *and* Midnight Express *and the different
approaches to violence, how my attraction to movies began
in the company of my mother.*

**Travis & Me: Why *Taxi Driver* Is the Defining Movie
for a Generation of Lonely Men**   46
*How the Travis Bickle archetype reflects inner "autistic"
qualities and gives a human face to alienation.*

An Imaginal Cloak: The Clint Eastwood Mythos & the Way of Sublimation   57

How to create a persona through fantasy role models, Dirty Harry *and negative identity construction, movies as psychological maps.*

Adolescent Revenge Fantasies: How Hollywood Exploited My Appetite for Destruction   70

How the Hollywood action movie erases the line between propaganda, advertising, and popular entertainment.

"Is it Safe?" The Bottom Line on Movie Violence   81

Breaking open the psychological patterns of family trauma that lurk behind and inside a lifelong obsession with movies and screen violence.

The Soul of the Plot: The Technology of Dissociation   90

How movies provide escape and exploit and exacerbate our learned capacity to dissociate from reality.

Lethem Lives: Hot and Cold Paranoia (An Essay About a Book About a Movie About Alien Mind Control)   100

Jonathan Lethem's social examination vs. David Icke's, paranoid worldviews, and the question of whether the world (and Hollywood) is run by shape-shifting Reptilians.

The Boy Who Cried Polanski   109

The author's mixed motives for writing and the goal of "spiritual autolysis"; almost meeting Roman Polanski.

Part Two: Hollywood Glamor Magic   115

Impossible Objects: *Chronic City* & Jonathan Lethem's Post-Fiction   117

The nature of writing, reality creation, and the crisis of authenticity.

**The Movie Nomad: Getting Lost at the Movies
with Pauline Kael** 131
*An in-depth exploration of Kael's influence, her critical method,
special voice, lack of judgment, and "marriage to movies."*

**Kael Kael Bang Bang: The Kael-Eastwood Feud & the
Lie of the Western Hero** 155
*Kael's stint in Hollywood with Warren Beatty, her feud with
Clint Eastwood, friendship with Sam Peckinpah, and relationship
with her father.*

**Peddlers of Astonishment: Tales to Astonish &
Nostalgia for the Present** 177
*How fantasy trumps reality, comic books and movies as corporate
propaganda, fantasy as self-exploitation.*

**Sympathy for the Damned: Weird Scenes from a Movie
Underworld** 184
*How movie violence helped me to cope with unconscious trauma;
The Texas Chainsaw Massacre and video nasties, Blue Velvet
and the invisible line between exploitation and art.*

**Black Magic Realism: Ironic Detachment, the Naiveté of
Cynicism, & New Levels of Depravity in *The Counselor*** 209
*A story of sin, the American heart of darkness, Jehovah and blood
sacrifice, corporate predation, moral hazard, conditional corruption,
and the extinction of all reality.*

**Crucified Hero: The Mythic Reinvention and Morbid
Self-Destruction of a Dandy** 226
*The gulf between talent and aspirations, a sorcerer's blueprint of
Glaswegian gangsters and early betrayals, serving two masters,
crucifixion as reenactment.*

Sebastian Horsley, R.I.P: Mother Bondage, Ancient Bloodlines, Cultural Plutocracies   **255**
The all-devouring imagination of the mother, the gothic dungeon of desire, dark family heirlooms, Jimmy Savile & glamor magic.

The Dissolving Artist: Or, This Book Will Self-Destruct in T-Minus 20 Minutes   **282**
Clint Eastwood and Woody Allen's art as a cloak for neurosis, why being an artist is an oxymoron, autism again, heroin addiction and moviegoing, why art is the devil's work.

How Did We Get Here? Last Words from the Land of Disenchantment   **297**
Returning whence we started to know the place at last.

Postscript: The Last Word (from Our Sponsor)   **304**
Lethem delivers.

"He would see faces in movies, on TV, in magazines, and in books. He thought that some of these faces might be right for him, and that through the years, by keeping an ideal facial structure fixed in his mind, or somewhere in the back of his mind, that he might, by force of will, cause his face to approach those of his ideal. The change would be very subtle. It might take ten years or so... He imagined that this was an ability he shared with most other people, that they had also molded their faces according to some ideal. Maybe they imagined that their new face would better suit their personality, or maybe they imagined that their personality would be forced to change to fit the new appearance. This is why first impressions are often correct. Although some people might have made mistakes. They may have arrived at an appearance that bears no relationship to them. They may have picked an ideal appearance based on some childish whim, or momentary impulse. Some may have gotten halfway there, and then changed their minds. He wonders if he too might have made a similar mistake."

—Talking Heads, "Seen and Not Seen"

"Entertainment is instruction and instruction is ideology."
—Herbert I. Schiller, *The Mind Managers*

Part One

The Deconstruction Artist

Introduction:
Autist or Auteur, That Is the Question

"Of course, the toxic bullshit of incessant advertising and show biz for nearly a century has stripped us of cognitive abilities for dealing with reality that used to be part of the normal equipment of adulthood—for instance, knowing the difference between wishing for stuff and making stuff happen. We bamboozled ourselves with too much magic."
—James Kunstler

It's ten days before Christmas, 2013. I have just returned from an island retreat (my sixth in two years) in Finland with "enlightenment coach" Dave Oshana. The effect of attending these retreats has been one of accumulative decrease: each time there's less of "me" to comment, or even have an opinion, about the experience. The less of an "I" there is to tell, the less of a story.

Since I was an adolescent, my story included becoming a "film artist" or *auteur*. Ergo, my story is the story of a disappearing artist, unraveling the layers of his fake identity, stitched together out of a movie love that didn't just border on autism but dove all the way *in there*. Through movies I was searching a realm of existence beyond the hell of "I," a way to disappear and still somehow *be there*. Enlightenment.

What happened when I got back to my "life" after the sixth island retreat? A minor incident—I found out my wife had taken up smoking again due to the stress of a new job. In the context of Life Itself the incident was minor. But in the context of my story, it was a *major* trigger which catapulted me right back into the depressed frustration of an old, undying narrative. This *is* my life, damn it, and it's exactly why I go on spiritual retreats: to slowly and diligently take out the garbage, until all that's left is the empty space of being. A blank movie screen.

3

The only possible excuse for including any of this at the start of a book about "movies," besides that it's *what's happening* (or was when I first wrote this introduction), is this. My desire to escape the confines of identity by training with an enlightenment coach, etc., is a *dead match* for why I am drawn to movies. Movies take me out of myself and bring my life-story to a temporary halt. They stop my world.

Movie-watching is a curious addiction, because what movies provide (like heroin?) is *a desire-free state*. Of course the movie in question, like heroin, has to be a *good* movie, uncut with talcum powder or milk sugar; otherwise desire will rapidly creep back in, even if it's only the desire to watch a different movie.

Freedom from desire is freedom from fear. Freedom from identity is what movies provide, for an all-too-brief spell. But since they don't make it better in the long run (they don't help me to clear out the junk of my past), they probably only make it worse; a bit like my wife's smoking.

On the last retreat Dave Oshana said something about how people who are addicted to movies are afraid of living.

Well OK *Dave*; but answer me this: who *isn't* afraid of living?

*

I wonder if that comment could, and should, be extended to people who are addicted to making movies? What drives them? Maybe becoming an *auteur* is a step closer to having total control over living. To not only be able to choose the fantasy worlds which we escape into, but to *create* them and then lure others into them? Like becoming the Wizard of Oz. (There are sinister implications in this which will become explicit by the end.)

For the twelve days leading up to Christmas I have decided to stop watching movies. It's a way to gauge the dimensions of my addiction, a bit like someone who fears he may be an alcoholic deciding to go a full day without a drink. Just to see, you know,

4

how *hard* can it be? How afraid of living am I really?

*

I am only halfway through this "book." I put it in quotes because, until it's finished and published, it's not really a book, any more than a fetus in a womb is a baby. I already have an offer of a contract, but it's a small publisher and I'm not sure it's really good enough. I want to reach a wide audience, to be reviewed by the major periodicals, to end up in the film section of major bookstores everywhere, to be *read, praised,* and *adored.* Of course I do—why wouldn't I? It would make living so much less scary if life turned into a movie. Or so I imagine, in the movie of my mind.

*

Francois Truffaut said: "I demand that a film express either the joy of making cinema or the agony of making cinema." In full sympathy with this decree, I demand that a book express the joy and the agony of its own writing. It should describe the transformative journey undertaken by its author in order to write it. If the act of writing doesn't involve some sort of transformation for the author, why bother? It will never amount to much for the reader.

I'm currently embarked on such a journey with this book about how movies shaped my perceptions of life, the world, and myself. This is my attempt to separate movies from memory (and from identity), and enter more fully into life. Enlightenment comes only when the last of our delusions is over and done. A bold claim. I am writing about movies as part of my decon-struction process—my daily decrease—in the hope, impossibly vain, of an artist who disappears into his art. Which is not quite the same as disappearing up my own—. Never mind, you get the picture. What's the opposite of enlightenment, anyway?

*

It's possible I wouldn't have ever started this book if it weren't for Jonathan Lethem's *The Disappointment Artist*. Before I was halfway through Lethem's book, I was inspired to write the essay that became the first chapter of this "book." "Self-Engineered Autism" is ostensibly about the many surprising correspondences between Lethem's personal history and my own. In the process of writing the essay, however, I made a surprising discovery that became the central exploration of this book: how have I used movies to create a social identity, and how have I become a prisoner to that "image-inary" self? How??

All roads lead to enlightenment, or to the opposite thereof. Movies fulfill more or less the same function attributed to myths. They are blueprints for the soul's journey, "user's manuals" for the world of incarnation. With this in mind I decided to recycle my old writings from *The Blood Poets* into a new, briefer and punchier format. I wanted to focus on the ways movies matched and mapped my own psychological patterns. As soon as I began to delve into the material, however, I found more than I'd bargained for.

In writing about my favorite movies at the age of thirty, I had disclosed all kinds of unconscious information about myself without realizing it. Analyzing the movies I'd escaped into as a teenager and young adult meant exploring my own unconscious reasons for doing so, but indirectly, surreptitiously. If I'd become conscious of what I was uncovering, the books might never have got finished. Fifteen years later, in 2013 and 2014, it felt safe to look more closely at what I'd been doing. *The Blood Poets* was only superficially about movies and cultural studies. Underneath, it was an unintentional autobiography.

This is true of everything anyone writes, ever.

The current work, un-book or not-yet-book, is an attempt to finish what I started with *Blood Poets*. It's a probably foolhardy and certainly compulsive attempt to do consciously what I was doing unconsciously fifteen years ago. There's a risk I'll see things I'm not ready to see, panic, and abandon the book. Probably more likely, I will unconsciously subvert my nobler intentions and skirt around the edges of the unbelievable truth without diving all the way *in there*. In either case the result will be the same. At best I will give up the project in despair and you will never read these words; at worst I will fool myself into thinking I found gold without ever digging all the way through the dirt, to the bedrock. In which case, what you are holding is fool's gold.

If so, don't worry, you will soon know it. Maybe you already know it. My advice if this should turn out to be the case is to put this book down and forget you ever saw it! Don't be a fool! The only reason to read a book is to discover something about the agony or the joy of living, writing, and reading, and *be transformed*.

Transformation is the only real currency. Don't settle for anything less.

*

So now you've been warned, why "movie autist"?

I was forty when I met my wife. She considers herself autistic, and early on she suggested that I might be too. I looked into Asperger's syndrome and found I agreed with the "diagnosis." Not only did it fit my current personality and nature but I found plenty of evidence for autism in my childhood behavior. I was a solitary child to a notable degree. I remember hardly anything from my first seven or so years, but I do know people often referred to how I would go off and be by myself all the time, and that I was seen as an unusually serious child who rarely smiled or laughed. I disliked being touched, or at least kissed, and it was a running joke how I would put my head down whenever anyone threatened to kiss me, offering them only the top of my head.

I was precociously intelligent, like one of the "little professors" described by Hans Asperger when he first described autism in children in the 40s. I even wanted to be an inventor, or "mad scientist," when I grew up. I had night terrors which included bizarre, indescribable sensory perceptions. (One of the primary causes for autistic behavior is unusual perception.) I suffered from what's now called "depersonalization": the feeling that I was unreal or trapped in a dream world/state (or movie?). A lack of a clear sense of self is typical of the autistic experience.

I immersed myself in fantasy worlds such as reading comic books and drawing. I was extremely fussy about what I would eat. As a pre-adolescent I fantasized about being a robot with an on/off switch, as a way to deal with my insomnia. I was a compulsive nose-picker, and remain so to this day. While nose-picking isn't considered an autistic characteristic *per se*, "stimming" is. I now think that nose-picking was (and is) a form of stimming for me, a way to feel more connected to my body. I was a day-dreamer. I lacked body awareness, and I had occasional shocking experiences of cognitive dissonance while looking at my body, as if looking down the wrong end of a telescope.

That pretty much covers the question of "why autist." So what about "movies"?

There's a curious correspondence between the word *autist* and the French word *auteur*, which means "author" (at your service) and was adopted by French and then US and British film critics in the 60s to describe a particular kind of filmmaker whose signature or "stamp" was clearly recognizable in his work.

The simplest definition of autism is self-immersion. As a child I had a huge collection of stuffed toys; all of them had names and super powers, or "special abilities," and I would enact endlessly elaborate scenarios for them, like a film *auteur* working with his actors. I even made my own stuffed animals, and repaired any of my furry friends whenever they began to fall apart.

Not surprisingly, I was deeply involved in the world of Winnie the Pooh. I collected Marvel comics (all of them violent) from an early age, and at around ten I began to write and draw my own stories, inventing my own superheroes and villains. I played with "action men," plastic figures similar to the kind of macho movie heroes I later heavily identified with, especially via the films of Clint Eastwood. Movies gradually replaced comics as my primary method of creating and escaping into a private fantasy world. Clint Eastwood became my role model. I collected every scrap of information and image I could find of him, tried to dress and style my hair like him, and bought a .44 Magnum replica.

Movie immersion was consolidated by an active, creative role and not just a passive one. I used my mother's typewriter to make lists of all the films I had seen in order of preference, the ones I wanted to see, and my favorite actors. I began to review every film I saw, giving them star ratings and arranging them alphabetically in a filing system. This led to the idea of making my own movies. I wrote reviews for the films I would direct, complete with future release dates, and drew thumbnail posters. I wrote scripts (most or all of them violent), and got a super-8 camera for my fifteenth or sixteenth birthday. I was a budding Martin Scorsese. Movies were rapidly becoming "my life."

If all this was my way of making the fantasy real enough to continue to escape into indefinitely, then I was the auteur of my own movie autism. I think one of the reasons I chose to write about film was that I wanted, needed, to confront an injustice in my past that I was unconscious of, and did it the only way I could: by addressing imaginary narratives. I wanted to restore some sort of order to the moral chaos I was born into.

What inspired me to write this book was realizing that the

primary ideology I had adopted related to cinematic standards of excellence. Right and wrong for me are never so clearly identifiable, or so easily asserted, as they are with the question of what constitutes a good or bad film. It's one area where I can feel sure where the ground is. I developed my critical faculties around film from a crucial age, about thirteen to adulthood, the same period my adult persona was crystalizing. To this day I get upset, angry, if a film I consider worthwhile is dismissed by critics (I watched one last night, *Blood Ties*, a wonderful film about two brothers that was largely ignored), and equally so when a crappy or dishonest movie is hailed as a "great." It is as if unconsciously I have been trying to restore justice to the world.

*

In *Autism and Spirituality*, Olga Bogdashina offers an intriguing developmental model in relation to the idea of "movie-engineered autism." Her model has six stages and it's a bit complicated, and since I want to keep this work simple and straightforward I will try and paraphrase without destroying her subtler meanings.

The first developmental stage is between the ages of three and seven, during which the child develops imagination stimulated by *stories* (i.e., movies and comics). The child has authentic "spiritual perceptions" but has neither language nor cultural imagery to represent it. Imagination gets together with those perceptions and sense-impressions to create "faith images." Since culture provides stories (fantasy narratives) during this period, these narratives act like clotheshorses for the child to hang otherwise "shapeless" perceptions and imaginings onto. Hence "the child's worldview can easily be manipulated by cultural doctrines." This is also the period in which the child develops self-awareness.

Self-awareness goes hand in hand with a loss of spiritual

perceptions as the child's experience is *translated into cultural images*, between ages seven and twelve (stage two). In the third stage, from adolescence to adulthood, we start to refer to the past as a way to understand our experience and to make plans for the future. This is the start of continuity, when the "narrative" of identity takes over our awareness. We find our identity by "aligning with a certain perspective ... without reflecting on it critically." We adopt *an unconscious ideology* based on the cultural images—the narrative or *movie*—which best match our spiritual perceptions and allow us to function socially.

Like an actor entering into a movie, we become an image, an assumed role, a false identity, created by the script of our received conditioning. It's an ironic fact that I was escaping into movies—false realities—as a way to try and feel more real, by creating a fake persona that matched the pseudo reality of culture that surrounded me. Movies exist to alert us to the fact that all human existence has been reduced to a movie: a series of frozen images from the past, playing constantly before our eyes, simulating movement, posing as life.

The difference with autistic types is that they don't adopt cultural images to the same degree or submit to an unconscious ideology, so the "mask" of the false movie identity doesn't fit them quite so well. One symptom of this is that they tend to overdo the business of cultural imitation, such as "Trekkies" who dress up as Mr. Spock, or my clumsy attempts to remold myself in the image of Eastwood. Autists don't do instinctive imitation, they imitate the *act of imitation*, and so they get it subtly (or dramatically) wrong.

In *Autism and Spirituality*, the fourth stage described entails leaving "the group mind," which means shedding the fake cultural identity, stepping outside the movie and looking around the theater (or shifting the gaze from the screen to the rear projector). This depends on our becoming conscious of a hitherto unconscious ideology. It implies sorting the seeds of our conditioning to discover which can be planted, and which ones accurately represent our experience, and tossing out the rest. The desired end of this process is relative autonomy—a crucial step towards the ultimate goal of enlightenment.

The book then describes a fifth stage involving "ironic imagination." The now autonomous individual still participates with collective images (movies!), but now sees them as relative rather than absolute: as fiction. The unconscious submission to external ideology has become conscious and is replaced by "the willing suspension of disbelief." Ironic imagination means moving from mere passive recipient, or garbage collector, of cultural imagery, to the shaper of culture—from moviegoer to moviemaker, *autist to auteur.*

*

That's about where this book and its author come in. The sixth stage, I suppose, is the one that corresponds with full enlightenment, whatever that is. But the less said about that the better. After all, that's life *after* movies, and you are here to hear about movies.

We are both still inside the darkened theater. The projector is still turning, the images are still flickering up on the screen. And while we may no longer be captive to them, there is still time, and opportunity, before the lights come up and we leave the theater, to discover just how and why they captured us. To really understand how the movie ends means going all the way back to the beginning.

Describing how this book began is a lot easier than knowing how it will end. I want—*need*—this book to be an account of its own writing. This is no mean feat because writing a book is at least 50% rewriting, and my relationship to the material changes with each new act of writing, rewriting, or not writing.

You can't step in the same river twice. You can't read the same passage twice. Everything is in constant flux. If that doesn't quite make sense, good. Writing a book to find out why it needs to be written is a nonsensical task, like marrying someone to find out who they are.

Come to think of it, I did that too.

Self-Engineered Autism

Jonathan Lethem's **The Disappointment Artist** *& the*
Revolting Development of Culture

"I want what we all want. To move certain parts of the interior of myself into the exterior world, to see if they can be embraced."
—Jonathan Lethem, *You Don't Love Me Yet*

Flashback to three months previous, mid-September, 2013. I'd just written a long piece about Philip K. Dick and autism and I was trying to get people to read it. I'd emailed various names involved with Dick's *Exegesis*, and after some difficulty, I managed to contact the book's co-editor, Jonathan Lethem. I'd heard about Lethem from my wife; she'd recommended *Motherless Brooklyn* months before, but I wasn't much of a novel reader and I hadn't got around to it. I'd found out somehow that he'd written about my all-time favorite album, Talking Heads' *Fear of Music*, so I'd ordered the book and read it in a couple of days. My wife thought Lethem might be on the autism spectrum, and *Fear of Music* seemed to implicitly confirm this. When I contacted him, I mentioned that we had at least these three things in common: Byrne-mania, Dickophilia, and spectrum-dwelling.

Lethem replied promptly and said he'd be happy to look at my piece. I sent it and a couple of weeks later he came back with a glowing response. Thrilled, I ordered his two non-fiction books online, *The Disappointment Artist* and *The Ecstasy of Influence*—naturally I was more interested in reading Lethem now that he was reading me. The books arrived and I delved right into the first, shorter one. *The Disappointment Artist* begins with a short essay called "Defending *The Searchers*." I wrote about *The Searchers* in *The Secret Life of Movies*, so I was hooked at once. Reading the book was like bumping into an old friend whose existence I'd all but forgotten, and then diving right into fond and fevered reminiscences. Before I was even halfway through, I was fired up enough to write a response to it. What follows is that response.

*

What Lethem says about *The Searchers* in his essay:

> Wayne's character, Ethan, is tormented and tormenting. His fury is righteous and ugly—resentment worn as a fetish. It isolates him in every scene. It isolates him from you, watching, even as his charisma wrenches you closer, into an alliance, a response that's almost sexual. You try to fit him into your concept of hero, but ... it doesn't work ... John Wayne's a fucking monster!

What I wrote in *Secret Life of Movies*:

> It *is* possible (or at least once was) to watch the film with only a cursory, peripheral awareness of the lead character's psychotic tendencies, and to see Ethan as merely a more ruthless and unsympathetic version of the standard John Wayne figure. For this is what he is. But *The Searchers* reveals the isolation, fragmentation, and self-loathing at the heart of the Western hero ... With *The Searchers*, the American hero became a psychopath and—most intriguing of all—nothing had really changed.

The theme of the movie, for me at least, was isolation and loneliness. And isolation and loneliness seemed to run like twin streams through Lethem's essay, his book, and maybe even all of Lethem's writing (based on what I'd read so far). But then maybe isolation and loneliness is the theme of *all* real art, anywhere, anytime? All impressions are subjective, but for me at least, there was a plaintive note of isolation and loneliness in Jonathan Lethem's writing that was so sharp and yet so far from bitter that it was impossible not to love it—or him.

In *The Disappointment Artist*, this melancholic note sounds most clearly and brightly in his ode to ode-ious teenage devotion, "13, 1977, 21." The piece describes how, as a thirteen year old in 1977, Jonathan Lethem saw *Star Wars* twenty-one times. Although I was never obsessed with the movie, I did have a poster on my wall as an adolescent—the only movie poster I had during the period (I think I was mostly obsessed with Princess Leia)—and movies would soon become for me what they were for Lethem: a necessary refuge in the face of the incomprehensible trauma known as childhood—in Lethem's case, cruelly punctuated by his mother's death during adolescence.

Reading the passage about his mother was the Turning Point in my relationship to Jonathan Lethem as a reader. It was the point at which I knew he was speaking *directly to me*. My earliest memory of my mother is of watching a sci-fi movie together, *The Day of the Triffids*. I also clearly remember her taking us to see *Close Encounters of the Third Kind*, which came out the same year as *Star Wars* but wasn't released in the UK until the spring of 1978. I didn't sit next to her, but I remember how, in the final moments, as the Mother Ship was landing, my mouth fell open with the required awe-response and she leaned forward in her seat and looked over at me. I could tell she was as moved by the sequence as I was and wanted to check my own response, to share in it. It was a little like the reverse of Lethem's experience of seeing *Star Wars* with his mother in which she didn't "get" the film. But for me at the time (around eleven), I experienced it (or remember it now) as an unwanted intrusion, a bit like being caught masturbating. The Spielbergian bubble of fantasy was burst by my mother's *gaze*.

Still, despite my uncertain boundaries, in later years movies became a kind of shared language for my mother and I: something we could always talk about. I suspect it was because we both shared a need to retreat into the disembodied psychic space of waking dream which movies provide (my mother was an alcoholic, and she continued to drink while I was in the womb). Above all that meant the *shared* dream space of the mother-child symbiosis. (And of course, I was staring at the *Mother* Ship when she leaned over to make sure we were *together!*) We continued watching movies and discussing them right until the last year of her life: they were a way for us to get into that space, both alone and together.

So when it came to describing a formative obsession with fantasy worlds, and how movies become a way to withstand isolation and loneliness, I could write the book on it. Wasn't Jonathan Lethem talking about engineering his own autism— dictating the terms and creating the conditions of his withdrawal into "inner space" by assembling a bricolage of pop cultural borrowings to make the space cozy and inviting and more or less indistinguishable from the "real world"? It was my own story as much as his.

*

Naturally, I wanted to also see this as a Turning Point in Jonathan Lethem's Evolution As A Writer. The moment in which his mother leaves him to watch *Star Wars* a second time (that *day*, actually his tenth or fifteenth time) struck me as a rare snapshot of psychic formation *as it happened*. It was the point at which immersion in make-believe worlds became a conscious necessity and Lethem became a "born" writer—whether he knew it or not. The name Lethem was perfect too, it evoked *Lethe*, the river of forgetfulness. (I knew Jonathan would forgive me for creating my own version of him. It's what all "born writers"—self-engineered autists—do.)

As this stage, I responded much more warmly to Jonathan's non-fiction than I did to his fiction, which left me mostly lukewarm. This opinion was in constant flux and had changed subtly even a day after I wrote it. I suspected my lack of a hot response to Lethem's fiction could be due to my own failure as much or more than his. I felt guilty for having skipped over portions of *The Fortress of Solitude* to get to the stuff that interested me, especially when it really did interest me and made me aware of the bits I'd missed. It seemed like the supreme disrespect of an author's craft. But an hour or two later, I came upon a quote by Lethem online: "I learned to write fiction the way I learned to read fiction—by skipping the parts that bored me." It was like a direct response: as if we had "a moment."

When Lethem spun stories to convey his inner world, I felt almost resentful; I felt impatient of the buffer of make-believe which he put (as every fiction writer must) between his psyche and mine. I didn't want to be kept out with the other neurotypicals. I wanted IN. I wanted total connection, total eclipse, *vesica piscis*, a meeting and matching of lonely souls across space, if not time. (We were very nearly contemporaries—are, I mean—his three-year seniority is a piffle now, though it was a crucial difference back then, or would have been. My own brother, now gone, was four and a half years older than me, and we hardly ever got along. Even so, we were like soul mates who somehow landed on opposite sides of the battlefield. My first movie preferences were largely influenced by him; as an adult, he used to call the movie theater, the "Forgetting Chamber.")

I knew I probably shouldn't let myself be fooled by the arbitrary line between fiction and non-fiction; but there was no doubt in my mind that Lethem had two distinct voices as a writer, and that, while one spoke directly to me, the other (so far) did not. But then, the fiction which possessed me was the sort of fiction in which the author's voice was inseparable from the narrator's: Dostoevsky, Poe, Paul Bowles, Bukowski; either that or the impersonal literary Spartanism of the high-pulp writers, Patricia Highsmith most of all, to a lesser degree Chandler, MacDonald, earlier Leonard.

Fiction has always included autobiographical elements—it would be incomprehensible without it (a bit like Jack Kirby's later period, all gods and no men, hey Jonathan?). What I want, both as a writer and a reader, is non-fiction with all the poignancy, mystery, and suspense of fiction—or better yet, *pulp* fiction! (Pulp non-fiction is what Hunter S. Thompson perfected and called gonzo. Bukowski did it too and it got called literature.) And I want—*need*—it to be about culture, the world out there, as much (*exactly* as much, the balance needs to be just right) as the self *in here*. Know thy culture, know thyself. Auticulture. It cuts both ways.

*

Lots of writers (myself included) have addressed the question of how culture forms us as a collective, culture being a collective outgrowth of values, and so on. As an autist-artist and explorer of my own chronic alienation (an easy definition of "artist," period), my view on Culture, big "C," has always been critical. Culture with a big "C" is something I have spent what feels like a lifetime trying to get free of. Culture is a matrix: it can't tell the artist who he (or she) is. It's up to the artist to transcend culture and remake it. Etc., etc.

The insight I had while writing this piece was this: for all of my perennial cultural rebellion, my distaste and even contempt for collective values whether Christian, liberal, democratic, fascist, Scientologist, or *whatever*, I was still fascinated by and enamored with the artifacts of my own *chosen* cultural conditioning. The comics, pop songs, movies, and books that I "chose" (I put it in quotes this time), and continue to "choose" (who knows what choice is?), as worthwhile representations of my inner world, the furniture and wallpaper to decorate and inhabit it, as aesthetic currency to navigate the outer world, all of that still thrills me to the core to think, read, and write about. I feel like I need to apologize for that last sentence and make amends for it: I am talking about *the stuff I have used to build an identity from*.

Like Lethem, I grew up on Marvel comics. This is probably why I have a low tolerance for fiction: nothing can match the pre- and post-adolescent daze of devouring Marvel comics and crisps (potato chips) and cheddar cheese in my bedroom, alone. This was itself a precursor to my almost total, autistic immersion in movies, which Jonathan Lethem and I also have in common (besides Marvel comics, I mean). Like Lethem, I feel absolute nostalgic loyalty to the formative power—the sanctity?—of that influence. Naturally I feel affinity bordering on love for "someone like" Jonathan Lethem (I have to add "someone like" so as not to get too uncomfortably intimate here), someone who's unabashed about revealing—though *not* without examining, which is a key qualifier here—a similar allegiance. Ditto with movies—I obsessed enough about *The Searchers* to write about it, so I am part of Jonathan Lethem's "private club," whether he wants me in it or not, because greater forces than he or I get to decide such things. *Right Jonathan?* All right.

*

In fact, the discrepancies between Jonathan Lethem and Jasun Horsley are at least as glaring and multiple as the similarities. We both belong to *The Searchers* club, sure. We both had eccentric parenting, and family backgrounds that include a Socialist-leaning grandparent and Quaker roots. We both started writing at fourteen—at least, our mothers both gave us our own typewriters at around that age. We share a passion for Patricia Highsmith (a fact I only found out while reading *The*

Disappointment Artist) and identify with Philip K. Dick (and the piece I sent him about Dick places special focus on 1964, the year Lethem was born). Most striking of all, we have, or had, the same all-time favorite album, and during our formative years looked to David Byrne as a role model. The autism connection is here most nakedly revealed, as is the strange, typically gauche (for autistics, I mean) mirroring that seems to be happening with Horsley, Lethem and, our shared external reference point and the apex of a, possibly imaginary, triangle: David Byrne.

> In a sense *Fear of Music* and I [replace with "Lethem & Horsley" if you like] are like Groucho and Harpo, meeting one night in that doorway that pretends to be a mirror. The false reflection displayed to me a self that was just enough off-register to be completely revealing. Yet this was only possible because we met at a time when we were both wearing the same disguise. [Lethem, *Fear of Music*]

So much for the parallels, so what about the discrepancies? There's a world of difference between growing up in Brooklyn, New York, and Yorkshire, England. I dislike not only Kubrick films (post-*2001*) but Kubrick *fans*. I also have little time for John Cassavetes movies and my favorite Dick novel is *Flow My Tears, the Policeman Said*, which I was mildly appalled to find absent from Lethem's top *fifteen* Dick novels! Already, I was imagining the gory end of a beautiful friendship. Affinity is a funny thing: the more evidence you find for it, the more easily threatened it seems to be. Perhaps this has to do with a suppressed memory of that original "lost body," or shared psychic space—the Mother (Ship) that left and never returned?

A minor confession: this piece was first written before I'd finished *The Disappointment Artist*. Even though the book's only 150 pages long, I couldn't wait to get my thoughts about it down. (That's got to be a compliment to its author, anyway.) So the following passage is one I found only later, as I neared the end of the book, in the section titled (surprise, surprise) "Fear of Music":

Attempting to burrow and disappear into the admiration of certain works of art, I tried to make such deep and pure identification that my integrity as a human self would become optional, a vestige of my relationship to the art ... By ignoring my hunger or need to use the bathroom during a three-hour movie by Kubrick or Tarkovsky I'd voted against my body, with its undeniable pangs and griefs, in favor of a self comprised of eyeballs and brain, floating in a void of pure art. If I wasn't afraid of this kind of dissolution I shouldn't be afraid of death, so I'd be an evolutionary step ahead. I downloaded art into myself, but I was also downloading myself out of my family, my body, and my life, onto a bookshelf of Complete Works or into the ether of music or film. By trying to export myself into a place that didn't fully exist I asked works of art to bear my expectation that they could be better than life, that they could redeem life. In fact, I believe they are, and do. My life is dedicated to that belief. But still, I asked too much of them: I asked them to be both safer than life and fuller, a better family. That they couldn't give. At the depths I'd plumb them, so many perfectly sufficient works of art would become thin, anemic. I sucked the juice out of what I loved until I found myself in a desert, sucking rocks for water.

The words confirmed my fondest hopes about the affinity—the brotherhood of isolation and loneliness —between Lethem and Horsley; and confirmed my worst fears.

Is this irony? Comedy? Tragedy? None or all of the above? What it is is a clue. A clue to a lifelong obsession with embodying the mini-culture which I, like Lethem (who was starting to look more and more like a soul twin) found (and to a degree helped create by consuming it so avidly) so that I could have *some conscious say* in my own psychic formation. But not only that, it's also a clue to my ongoing commitment to examining it to discover *how* that formation happened and—here's the tragedy and the comedy and the bittersweet irony of it—to eventually UNDO it.

Building a false self that's no more than a pop cultural bricolage is a kind of exteriorization of the psyche. It's like projecting one's soul onto a movie screen, into a vinyl record, a set of Collected Works. But the way back isn't *away* from those animated husks but all the way *into* them and through them. It entails reclaiming the force that has animated them, the Silver's Surfer's "power supreme," the love of Psyche for Eros, the Other. It means following the clues, Dick-style, in the "kibble" and clutter of pop culture, like a trail of crumbs that leads *back* to the inner world. It means recognizing the Self by recognizing the Other. Isolation and aloneness is relieved not through brotherhood, but through the self-recognition and self-acceptance that brotherhood brings.

Start with what you know. I can try and try to get at the root of those unconscious influences that shaped me (mom and dad and big brother and sister too), but they will always elude me, at least until I dismantle the "screen memories" of fantasy with which I assembled an inner world (a cultural program) to keep me safe from total alienation, complete isolation, and from a loneliness that cuts so deep it can sometimes even be fatal.

The appeal of those early imprints (that's what they were, not just on paper but on me!), why I still feel a flutter and a buzz looking at old UK Marvel comic book covers online, isn't due to the magical potency of the artifacts themselves. It's not because of their alleged archetypal resonance (though they had it: no one can say the Silver Surfer isn't one of the great creations of American literature without exposing their own snobbish ignorance). The allure and the potency of those things is in *the psyche being imprinted*. Before the comics and movies came along—as if bestowed upon me by a loving God called Consumer Culture—the whole world was magical, potent, in equal parts terrifying and wonderful. This is something I have to *deduce*, though, because I can't recapture the direct experience of it. Can I?

I'm attempting to describe the process of returning to a less cultured, more open and embodied state in which my psyche can simply receive the world, unguarded, wide-eyed, unwashed and somewhat slightly dazed but fully present. And maybe that's what happened while I was reading *The Disappointment Artist*? Maybe by seeing how my "brother" (the Other) did it, and feeling the compassion of that seeing, I could embrace and redeem my own folly? Perhaps I was embarked on a kind of reverse-engineering journey, to emerge from the *faux*-autism of cultural hermeticism (tragi-heroically—nakedly—spelled out by brother Jonathan above), back into a *true* autism: inner-orientation combined with outer receptivity, in which the two are so closely allied, fused, as to be inseparable?

As within, so without? There was Wayne's outcast, Ethan Edwards, framed in the darkened doorway, condemned to leave human community behind and wander the empty desert plains forever—the loner defined by his aloneness. That way was safe, but it was far from full. Someday, Ethan would be sucking rocks in the desert. Then there was Luke Skywalker's way: find the Force and let it guide you. *True* interiority that neither depends on nor leads to isolation or alienation, but which cancels them out forever. Where the Force *is*, we are not alone, and never can be.

For a child's psyche, those fantasy worlds were a way—maybe the *only* way—to keep intact at least *some* innocence in the face of an adult-assembled nightmare of depravity, savagery, indifference and neglect, a nightmare called Culture. Like an adolescent boy hiding in a movie theater, forgetting, just one more time, what's waiting for him on the outside—a Death Star world, an Empire that never ends—the nostalgic pull of the past isn't so much in those fantasy artifacts as *behind* them. They are both doorways and gatekeepers, inviting and forbidding our passage back to that garden of earthly delights, the lost body of childhood. The wonder of a still relatively embodied psychic existence in which everything was imbued with the sort of mystery and magic that, slowly and inexorably, over time, would become attainable to us only via comic books, pop songs, TV shows, and movies—artifacts which in turn, tragicomically, became more noise to block the signal, until the fantasy utterly obscured the reality, the gods were forgotten, and we were finally—tragically, comically—"men."

And as the song of innocence was drowned out by the increasingly terrifying experience of living, naturally the artifacts of escape had to keep up with that revolting development. I went from Winnie the Pooh to *The Wild Bunch*, and the rite-free passage was invisible to me, utterly mysterious. Both fantasy worlds—that of pristine innocence and scabrous experience—are equally dear to my soul, but perhaps only because they belong to the same self-protective engineering process. I still love Winnie the Pooh, and *The Wild Bunch* still competes for my "number one spot" of cherished movies.

Probably the strongest reason for that has nothing to do with the brutality and destruction which first drew me to it, however, or even with the way it one-ups *The Searchers* by exploding the Western mythos and portraying "men's men" as lonely, loveless misfits, bent on their own destruction. It's rather because it revealed *why*. Most of all, I think it's because of a line which, for me, continues to say it all:

"We all dream of being a child; even the worst of us. Perhaps the worst of us most of all."

The Soul Searchers

Finding a Sponsor in the Game of Life

"It's not easy to like something you know nothing about."
—The Man with No Name, on "peace," *A Fistful of Dollars*

Unless you count Elvis, my first role model was Clint Eastwood. The first, and I think strongest, impression he made on me was as the Man with No Name in the Spaghetti Westerns. I dimly remember a time—I was ten—when my older brother was watching *A Fistful of Dollars* on TV and I briefly viewed it over his shoulder. I wasn't curious enough to carry on watching (Westerns weren't my thing yet), and it wasn't until a year or two later, when my brother and I were watching *Where Eagles Dare* on TV together, that my obsession with Eastwood began.

It's an odd fact that the first memory I have of going to the cinema is of *the same movie*. I don't know how old I was (*Where Eagles Dare* was released in 1969, when I was two, though I certainly wasn't that young), but it's possible I was young enough for our father to have still been with us (he left when I was seven). If so, then it's the only memory I have of seeing a movie with my whole family—and I can't help but note that the letters in the movie's title spell "WED."

Be that as it may, how is it that the first movie I remember seeing at the cinema was also the movie that, several years later, ignited a lifelong passion for movies? Let's just say I was being *primed*. (Eastwood even resembled my father.)

*

The key to Eastwood's "No Name" in *A Fistful of Dollars*, more than anything, is his *silence*. The essence of his power, his

26

deadliness, seems to reside in an almost supernatural restraint. He's a serpent that sleeps, or appears to sleep, until the moment he's trodden on. While the invulnerable Eastwood might appear an odd choice for an Aspergerian adolescent to emulate, he did possess at least one autistic quality: he was largely nonverbal. And his silence relates to containment—like many autistic types, No Name and the other Eastwood incarnations kept their inner worlds to themselves—and that containment was the secret of much of their power. It was mostly seen as "superhuman cool," but looked at from only a slightly different angle, it can also be seen as *a deliberate lack of human connection.*

The most appealing thing about No Name for me wasn't his brutality, or even his speed; it was his *intelligence.* His silence wasn't surliness or boredom, it was the silence of a thoughtful and calculating mind, busy at all times, carefully observing everything around him.

*

Generally, the safest form of behavior is imitation. Imitation (something autistics are extremely bad at) reduces the number of variables and therefore the chances of "getting it wrong." Socialization is largely a process of trying out various kinds of imitative behavior and, through a process of elimination, settling on the ones that "work," that adequately represent our inner experience while allowing us to be received—to function—in the outside world. This is tantamount to saying that we can only become as authentic as the world permits us to be.

When I was growing up, the person I was naturally drawn to imitate, the one who was most obviously similar to myself, was my older brother. The trouble was that he hardly tolerated my presence at all, much less my copying his behavior. When I was eight or nine, I remember sitting at the kitchen table and tapping my foot to a T-Rex song he was playing. He stamped on my foot under the table and scowled at me. This was *his* music and I wasn't allowed to like it.

The first time I made it into an "X"-rated movie (the UK-rating for mature audiences, back in the 1980s), I wore my brother's army coat to make myself look bigger and older. I was twelve or thirteen, and the movie was *Dawn of the Dead*. When the two women at the box office asked for proof of my age, I presented them with my brother's passport, having fixed a photo of myself over his image. They saw through my ruse but, amused, let me in anyway. My fascination for horror movies was adopted straight from my brother, so it makes sense that I impersonated him as a way to gain access to that forbidden zone.

If my brother's hostility didn't stop me from trying to mold myself in his image, it did make me more secretive about doing so. Growing up under his unforgiving gaze, I couldn't win. If I was too much myself, he felt threatened by my individuality and tried to crush it. If I responded by trying to be more like him, he liked that even *less*. Yet through his relentless intervention, I was getting to experience the world in microcosm. It may have been the best preparation I could have been given.

*

As a teenager I knew John Ford's *The Searchers* was supposed to be a great movie. I knew it had influenced one of my movie heroes, Martin Scorsese. But the first time I saw it I found it pretty boring. I still do, actually, and if it weren't for the final image of the film, which slays me every time, it probably wouldn't mean half as much to me as it does. The movie fascinates people; actually, it mostly fascinates men, witness Jonathan Lethem's description of his frustration with his girlfriend's indifference to the film, in *The Disappointment Artist*.

I think the appeal (for men) of *The Searchers* has to do with the way it reveals the isolation, fragmentation, and self-loathing at the heart of the Western hero, and by extension, of western men. The film parallels the external, dramatic conflict of "cowboys and Indians" with an internal, psychological conflict at the heart of its protagonist. John Wayne's tormented psyche is seen to reflect, not just vaguely but precisely, the genocidal hysteria taking over the US in its "formative" years. I'm not American, but I suffused myself in US culture via movies, comic books, and pop music during my own formative years. Inevitably, I was drawn to works that mirrored my own internal psychological conflict.

The passage from childhood to adulthood is a process of "taming the wild." It creates a split deep in the soul that leads to a lifetime's searching. But what searches and what is being sought? Maybe they are the same thing? That loneliness and longing, and the apparent nobility of it, is what made the Western hero so appealing to me, as one of a legion of lonely, alienated adolescents. It's also a Hollywood crock.

*

Movies are a way to "try on" social behaviors in a risk-free environment. When I entered into the world of a movie as a youth, I got to watch people acting in relation to others. By identifying with movie protagonists, I could test how those behaviors matched my inner experience; better yet, I could see how well those behaviors were likely to be received by others. If I watched movies with family members and friends, I could also get an idea of how acceptable the protagonist's behavior was to those around me. This is the theory, at least, but it depends on movies representing our reality, which of course they don't— until they *do*. (It's also relatively *safe* to *imitate* the behavior of movie characters—provided we're discreet about it—since unlike my brother they won't react to what we're doing by stamping on us and telling us to "find our own music.")

*

The critical reputation of *The Searchers*, over and above almost any other Western, isn't because it turned the genre inside out and upside down. The movie has psychological significance—it's *relevant* to us (men) in direct and highly personal ways, even private ways. My own experience eventually led me to an insight which Wayne's Ethan never reaches, one that isn't easy to admit to even now. Because my early, formative experiences of home life were so traumatic, what I was consciously seeking (companionship, union, integration, wholeness, belonging) were the same things I was running from!

For the traumatized psyche unconsciously chasing its own tale—locked into a pop cultural identity as the loner, avenger, self-sufficient wanderer, *whatever*—the search never ends, because what is seeking and what is being sought are *the same thing*. Like a dog's tail, the more fiercely we chase it, the more it flees us.

*

My whole life I have searched for one thing: a way to feel safe enough to be myself. To discover and express my inner experience and be received. But the self doesn't appear to be some fixed, finished entity trapped inside us, waiting for the right circumstances to come out. It appears to me more as if the self only comes into existence *via the act of physical expression*. It's a bit like how a character in a movie is created, through the actor's portrayal. Until then, it's only words on a page. If we don't find the right social environment—the right people and surroundings—to express the innermost self and discover who and what we really *are*, we will remain an unrealized project, lingering our lifetime away in development hell.

We will have no sponsors, no backers, to help bring our soul project into being.

*

"Things always look different from higher up."
—The Man with No Name, *A Fistful of Dollars*

I was drawn to violent movies from a very early age—as early as eight or nine if you count Hammer horror movies (which my brother was obsessed with). That soon led to a more consciously developed interest in psychopathic and self-destructive behavior (serial killers and the like). My identification with the Man with No Name and *Dirty Harry* slowly gave over to a more troubling (but also more self-aware) identification with Travis Bickle of *Taxi Driver* and Sam Peckinpah's heroes—and eventually with Peckinpah himself. (Actually the first film book I ever owned was about Sam Peckinpah. I stole it from Hull library before I'd ever seen any of his films. It was called *Crucified Heroes*.) I was raised by two alcoholic parents, and up until my thirties I wanted to become a filmmaker, so it's no mystery that I was drawn to explore the inner workings of Peckinpah—an alcoholic film director whose artistic genius was inseparable from his self-destructive addiction. The self-destroying gene that killed Peckinpah also decimated my family, in one way or another, so of course it was active in me. Understanding it was more than just an intellectual interest. It was a question of survival.

*

I didn't really think that much of *The Wild Bunch* either the first few times I saw it, as a teenager and young man. Its subtleties were lost on me, and it seemed like little more than an extremely violent Hollywood Western. I don't remember when my point of view changed, but I guess it was a gradual process. Somehow, around the time I turned thirty, I developed an obsessive interest in Peckinpah. I learned everything I could about his life and wrote a 200-page screenplay about him. After a while I wasn't able to separate the tragic, self-destructive characters of *The Wild Bunch* from Peckinpah's own self-destruction. Later I turned the epic script into an epic novel. While I was writing it, my computer was infected by a strange virus that entered the Word document I was working on. Everywhere the words "Sam" or "Peckinpah" appeared, it replaced them with the word "I."

True story.

*

Finding the right sponsors isn't easy. A sponsor is someone who has gone before us and who managed to develop a reasonably authentic way of being in the world without becoming *of* the world, someone who has managed to express their inner selfness and be accepted for it. Finding a sponsor has been essential for me in leaving developmental hell and coming of age in the world, entering all the way into my life and body. My parents and older siblings were supposed to sponsor me; they couldn't because they didn't have their own sponsors growing up, and the one thing they couldn't show me is the one thing I needed to be shown: how to authentically *be*. After that the search was on to find my sponsors *out there*, in the world. But how could I do that when I hadn't developed an effective way of entering the world? It was like trying to make it in Hollywood—where you need an agent to work but you have to find work to get an agent. Catch 22.

Thus the hero's quest begins, though of course it's not the hero who quests but the quest that makes the hero. The search for embodiment can only be embarked upon from a place of disembodiment.

I think this is why I was always drawn to established artist personalities. I was hoping to find a like mind and kindred spirit to sponsor me. If Scorsese or Polanski, Bowie or Byrne, could express their bizarre, perverse, and disturbed inner experiences to the world and be accepted, there was still hope for me. Connecting to such fellow travelers as I groped my way through the mythic underworld became my life's mission, one which I still haven't completed, especially if seen in the context of Hollywood, where I first imagined, vainly, my soul-sponsors would be found. (Actually it was in Finland.)

*

A theme throughout my adult life—it runs through my taste in movies like bloody pigment—is sympathy for the devil, an affinity for violent, psychotic characters. Long before I discovered Dostoevsky, I was drawn to Polanski, Scorsese, and Peckinpah, and nurtured through their work a desire to see past the destructive exterior of seeming "bad men," into the suffering souls underneath. The presence of *Crucified Heroes* on my book shelf (my first film book) was evidence of an unconscious affinity which only became fully conscious after years of reading, viewing, and writing. Now, whenever I return to *The Wild Bunch*, I find new meaning, new poignancies.

The Wild Bunch are like wayward children—not maladjusted but refusing to adjust at all. Like Peckinpah himself, in his futile attempts to defy the movie industry, they have taken their devilish games far beyond their power to control them. But there's an innocence, even a purity, to these "children" that somehow redeems them in Peckinpah's eyes. When the old Mexican tells Pike how we all dream of being children again, he expresses all the mystery, the melancholy and the poignancy of Peckinpah's (i.e., the human) dilemma. The film acknowledges, implicitly, that sadness is at the core of all violent men—and by inescapable extension, all *men*.

The Bunch are involved in a romance with death and with each other. Death is the end and brutality is the means. Besides the desire to make a score, this is pretty much the only thing that unites them. It's also the only measure of respect they have for each other, and the only measure of manhood—of life—which the film allows them. Women have no place in Peckinpah's fantasy world: they are only mothers to leave behind, wives to avoid, or whores to enjoy, briefly, between bouts of killing.

It's one of the beautiful ironies of the film that children are spoken of as symbolizing innocence yet are pictured—in the opening shots and the film's most painful scene, in which Indio is tortured—as representing the "original sin" of primal, sadistic impulse. Peckinpah yearned to return to innocence but was unable to believe it ever really existed (rather like my brother). What did that leave but glorious, nihilistic self-destruction?

*

If Dave Oshana is my spiritual sponsor, Jonathan Lethem is probably the closest I've yet come to finding the worldly kind: someone whose inner experience seems to be a close match for my own but who has managed to convey it to others in such a way as to be received, and to have achieved unequivocal worldly success. It's no wonder I felt so inspired by *The Disappointment Artist* (or even how it inspired this present work). Even the title speaks to me. Finding Lethem felt a bit like finding the older brother I was "supposed" to have been met by at birth, though of course, if we'd actually been brothers it would have been a different story. Even as it is, I am nervous about stating it so boldly, for fear of jinxing the mojo.

A good sponsor is someone whose experience matches one's own while still being sufficiently different for there to be meaningful exchange, and for camaraderie instead of rivalry. A sponsor must also be sufficiently further on down the road to be able to assist one's own advancement, even if they also may be stuck, or lost, in other ways. On his mythic journey, the hero invariably finds allies without whom he couldn't proceed, allies who are often freed or redeemed in some way by the act of giving their assistance.

Sponsoring is always a two-way arrangement. A younger sibling always has things to show the older one, even if it's simply by seeing that person in new ways. We can only advance in the game of life by helping those who come up behind us. Personal success can't be an end, only the means. An authentic expression of the soul's special meaning (also known as art!) provides vital information for those who come after, and even those who came before. As a young filmmaker Scorsese was "mentored" by Michael Powell (inspired by his movies); in later life, the roles were reversed and Scorsese brought about a revival of interest in Powell's work, thereby transforming the director's final years.

What goes around comes around. Birds of a feather may wind up in far distant nests with no idea of their common ancestry or destiny. But eventually, if they follow their inner orientation faithfully, they *will* flock together. Nature always trumps nurture.

It occurs to me as I write these words that *here* is the "private club" which Lethem refers to in *The Disappointment Artist*. The Soul Searchers—men for whom art is the only way to assuage their alienation, whose defining dream is to become as little children again.

Even if it means we have to battle with monsters first.

Screen Memories & Apple Seeds

Parented By Pop Culture

It's around 1972 and it feels like late night but probably isn't. I am around five years old. I'm sitting on a large bed in one of the spare bedrooms of our giant mansion house, High Hall, with a friend, Nick Fenton (he's now an award-winning film editor). My mother comes in with two shiny green apples, one for each of us. She turns on a small, black and white TV set and the movie begins: *The Day of the Triffids*. This is a clear memory, and it's also the only one I have of my mother from the first few years of my life. (I only have one memory of my father from that time too, dead drunk on the bedroom floor in his underwear; but that's another story.) What does it say about me that my first memory of my mother is of her handing me an apple before watching a movie together? A mythic narrative!

Movies made an impression on me, sometimes even before I saw them. Not only do I remember when I first saw *Taxi Driver*, I remember when I first *heard* about it. I was twelve or so and I was sitting in the back of a car (a taxi cab?), driving through Boston, in the US. It was 1980 (four years after *Taxi Driver* was released) and my brother, who would have been seventeen or just turned eighteen, was describing to me the pistol-mechanism which Travis Bickle (Robert De Niro) rigs to his arm halfway through the movie. For some reason, I thought my brother was talking about an old movie and I pictured the scene in black and white. Why do I still remember such a trivial detail when so much of my past is forgotten?

I first saw *Taxi Driver* a couple of years later, at around fourteen or fifteen. It was one half of a double bill with *Midnight Express* which played for (what seemed like) years at a small repertory cinema just off Leicester Square in London's West End.

I had travelled all the way from Yorkshire to London, alone, on the early morning train (what my stepfather called "the sparrow's fart"). I remember making these trips frequently during my adolescence. To begin with I went to London to buy Marvel comic books at the Forbidden Planet shop on Denmark Street. Later, once I was old enough, I also took overnight trips to see movies. This was back in the early 80s, before the arrival of the video cassette. I was living in a small town with no repertory cinemas for three hundred miles, and movies were like coveted treasures which bestow knowledge and power on the mythical journey—like Jason's Golden Fleece. This quest was not for the faint of heart or weak of will. It was only for the most dedicated of seekers and I had to proceed with patience, sweetness, ruthlessness, and cunning to achieve my goals.

Somehow my mother allowed these trips, probably because I would have thrown a fit if she hadn't. I was an incredibly willful boy, and it was rare for me not to get what I wanted, by hook or by crook. Although I don't remember this part, I would have spent the night (or a couple of nights, maybe the weekend) sleeping at my brother's apartment in Chelsea. My brother was four and a half years older than me, and at that time he was living with his girlfriend (later his wife), attending St. Martins art school.

While I was writing what became the first chapter of this book, about Jonathan Lethem's *The Disappointment Artist*, I hit upon a reason why movies imprinted me so deeply. It occurred to me that they (along with Marvel comics and the books I read as a child) intercepted an early formative process in which I was struggling to make sense of the world and became integral parts of the identity I was assembling. Movies, comics, and books (and pop songs) provided cultural images to represent my inner experience and give it conceptual, linguistic, and emotional form. They were like a matrix for self-awareness to grow inside. Before I even had sufficient memories to assemble a sense of a self—a linear narrative of "I-ness"—I found these essential pointers, cues, and inspirations outside of me, in the world. The so-called real world overlapped with the fantasy world of popular culture, those symbolic narratives with which I unconsciously created an operating system for my "hard drive." But because I mixed elements from pop culture up with direct experiences, my memories became a kind of cultural implant, or *screen*. Figuring out which is which is roughly what this book is about.

When my mother and I watched movies together (and when my wife and I do today), we became one mind with a single focus (and afterwards we had something to talk about). Like tribe members telling stories around a fire or witnessing/participating in a shamanic ceremony, movie-going is a bonding ritual. At the very least, it's a way to create a safe communal space. My mother's focus certainly wasn't always, or even primarily, loving, and that went double for my brother, who was almost always hostile towards me (except when we ganged up on our sister). My father was mostly indifferent and his gaze rarely fell on me at all (and when it did it was rarely sober). My guess is that, to be focused on the TV or movie screen rather than on each other was a way to enter a psychic dreamspace together. Securing that space, completing the fantasy, meant having the same responses, laughing together, gasping, crying. This is what my mother was checking during *Close Encounters*, when I felt violated by her gaze: "*Are you with me? Are we together?*" Right up until her death I could always tell what sort of reaction she was having to a movie—and I didn't even need to look.

*

Just as I first heard about *Taxi Driver* from my brother, I first heard about *Midnight Express* from my sister. I was eleven or twelve, making her eighteen or nineteen. She'd seen the movie at college and loved it, and with great enthusiasm she recounted the story to me one evening, while we were sitting in the living room with our stepfather. She began with the opening sequence in which Billy Hayes (Brad Davis) goes through Turkish customs with several kilos of hashish taped to his torso. He's sweating profusely and his heartbeat is audible on the soundtrack. It's a visceral sequence that identifies us, as intimately as possible, with the hero—literally putting us inside him. The heartbeat is probably the first sound we ever hear in life, so the movie was tapping into something primal in the viewer. I saw the movie shortly afterward (a year or two before I saw it again in London), at the local cinema where they didn't much care about letting minors in to see "X" movies. I loved it.

In both of these cases, *Taxi Driver* and *Midnight Express*, I was *primed* for the viewing experience. "Priming" is a big part of what caregivers do. My being given an apple by my mother while watching *The Day of the Triffids* is a good example of priming. It suggests that, ever since that time, I've unconsciously associated movies with nourishment, and with the nurturing presence of my mother. In the case of *Taxi Driver* and *Midnight Express*, I associated each of the movies with one of my siblings, and with the specific circumstances in which I first heard about them, meaning that my perception of those two movies was to some extent informed by those initial experiences. The contrast between my brother's "method" and my sister's is obvious: my sister recounted pretty much the whole movie, while my brother only gave me one significant detail, which, like a hook, eventually reeled me in. My brother's account of *Taxi Driver* was mostly neutral, and made me aware of the movie without selling it to me. At the same time, everything that my brother was interested in, interested me. My sister's gushing retelling of *Midnight Express* didn't just make me want to see the movie; it was as if I had already seen it *through her eyes*.

The cultural images I received growing up came *via* family members. They were the people I most trusted to guide my development, so naturally I was open to their influence. The way I received and perceived movies and other cultural artifacts was inevitably informed by who brought my attention to them, and how (and why).

*

Superficially, I have a lot more in common with Billy Hayes than Travis Bickle. I am from well-to-do parents and I started smoking hash (with my sister) at aged seventeen. I never went to Turkey, but I lived in Morocco, homeless and penniless, in my early twenties, and wound up associating with a Belgian Mafia-troubadour transporting hashish across the Spanish border. A couple of years earlier, I spent a few days in a Mexican jail (in Oaxaca) after being in a car accident. It didn't take long for me to bribe my way out, but while I was there my cell mate was taken away and had his testicles hooked up to an electrical device (he came back weeping). Being a foreigner—and unlike Billy—I managed to avoid getting the same treatment. After I got out, I paid another "fine" so my cell mate could get out too. I was sure he was innocent, just as he said he was.

While *Taxi Driver* has gone on to become a classic, *Midnight Express* has been largely erased from the collective memory by the passage of time; with its brazen hostility towards the Turks, it's become somewhat of a cultural *embarrassment*. The obvious thing that linked these two movies together, that made them a seemingly logical double bill, was also the thing that attracted me to them: they depicted men trapped in an experience of alien-ation and powerlessness, expressing their rage the only way they could—through violence. If I was drawn to movies of this sort it was because my own rage as an adolescent was mostly unexpressed, and movies provided the opportunity *to enact my suppressed anger through fantasy and identification* (i.e., catharsis).

I identified with Billy Hayes because the filmmakers forced

me to, from the pumping soundtrack on. The way *Midnight Express* presents him, Billy Hayes isn't really a character—there's no sense of his inner life—so much as a virgin sacrifice for all the atrocities which the filmmakers can pile on top of him. His blankness is his only virtue, but Billy isn't really innocent—he's indisputably guilty—and the only thing that distinguishes him, finally, is that he's an *American*, who has fallen into the hands of evil Turks. The film forces us to identify with Billy in the same way *Dumbo* forces kids to identify with a baby elephant torn from its parents—by tapping into primal fears and exploiting them.

Taxi Driver approaches its subject matter in a very different, even diametrically opposed, way. It's an odd kind of inversion of the racist-jingoistic fantasy of *Midnight Express*. Travis is an American too, and he's also weirdly innocent, even slightly autistic. A Vietnam vet who returns to civilian life, he finds himself totally disconnected from his fellow citizens. Travis's *experience* of New York is quite similar to Billy's inside the Turkish prison: he's surrounded by incomprehensibly corrupt and slightly monstrous strangers. *Midnight Express* surrounds its American "hero" with such depraved "otherness" that, even though he's guilty, he seems by comparison pure, even heroic. *Taxi Driver* places its protagonist in contrast to his surroundings also, only here Travis's "innocence" is what makes him the "other," unable to relate to anyone around him, seeing only enemies to be destroyed. (Maybe Travis's experience in Vietnam was equivalent to Billy's in Turkey?)

Taxi Driver offers the inverse model to *Midnight Express*. It shows how the desire to take control, the refusal to be a passive victim (which drives Billy to do what *he* does), leads to psychotic acts of destruction—acts that can easily be misinterpreted as heroic. Like Travis, I was unable to find a way to connect to others. I was dreaming of rescuing maidens from dragons but unable to do anything about it besides give into helpless fits of rage and escape into solitary writing (and movie watching!). *Taxi Driver* became a part of me because, even before I saw it, it already *was* a part of me. It spoke to me and reflected my inner experience, like a mirror which, when I gazed into it, also gazed back. *Midnight Express* was more like staring into a toilet. If *Taxi Driver* was about the powerlessness (sexual and spiritual impotence, and social alienation) that underlay the rage eating away at my insides, *Midnight Express* showed what *pseudo-empowerment* (ego inflation) looked like—psychotic rage that's psychotically justified by the demonization of an "other"—not by the character but by *the filmmakers*. It was as if the tabloid mentality which at the end of *Taxi Driver* turned Travis's act of desperation into heroism, and made pulp fiction out of tragedy, was extended to a whole movie.

The first few times I saw it (true to my priming), I adored *Midnight Express*. One thing that probably had an influence on my changing viewpoint was Pauline Kael's review of the film, "Movie Yellow Journalism," which is included in the first Kael book I ever read, *When the Lights Go Down*. Like *Crucified Heroes*, I came across the book (at about fifteen) at the Hull library. I can still remember standing in front of the shelves, seeing *Carrie* and *Taxi Driver* listed on the cover, and thinking, "I'll *have* this!" I hid it under my topcoat, took it home, and read all the bits that interested me, then went back and "liberated" copies of *Deeper Into Movies* and *Reeling*. So I would certainly have read the piece on *Midnight Express*. Here are a few of the highlights:

The film is a like porno fantasy about the sacrifice of a virgin. [It] rushes from torment to torment, treating [Billy's] ordeals hypnotically in soft colors—muted squalor—with a disco beat in the background. The prison itself is more like a brothel than a prison ... *Midnight Express* is single-minded in its brutal manipulation of the audience: this is a clear-cut case of the use of film technique split off from any artistic impulse. Parker

seems almost vindictive in the way he prods the viewers—
fast, efficiently, from one shock to the next ... Billy is
conceived as a victim, [the filmmakers] deify weakness ... The
film is a crude rabble-rouser: like a wartime atrocity movie, it
keeps turning the screws to dehumanize Billy's jailers ... At
the same time, it's sanctimonious about Billy's victimization.
[It] may be something close to an all-purpose fantasy ... an
ultimate romantic horror show ... this picture is not only a
full-scale fantasy for the drug culture but the cautionary tale
that parents have been waiting for. It has been a long time
since middle-aged people could say to their kids, "You don't
know how lucky you are to be Americans, safe and
protected." ... *Midnight Express*, with its sadist sexual current,
is a there's-no-place-like-home story, of a very peculiar
variety. Hysterically sensual on the surface but with a basic
honor-thy-parents-and-listen-to-them glop at the center, it
manipulates cross-generationally.

Kael's searing denunciation of the film also pointed out how the
movie portrays the Turks' drug laws and treatment of prisoners
as barbarically regressive, without addressing the fact that the
US put pressure on the Turkish government to keep dope out of
the States, and how it gave Turkey an assistance program in
criminology and trained its customs officials. The review also
zeroes in how the film's final scrawl states that, 43 days after the
film was shown at the Cannes film festival, the US and Turkey
"entered into formal negotiations for the exchange of prisoners."
Kael cuttingly observes that these negotiations had been going
on for *several years* before the film's release, and that nothing at
all had changed in those "43 days." The film was spinning the
facts to elevate itself to cultural and political significance.

When I re-read this review a few weeks ago, while I was
working on a chapter about Kael, I didn't have any conscious
memory of the examples she cites of the rank hypocrisy of the

film; but *at some level* it must have entered my awareness *the very first time I read the piece.* Whatever my visceral response to the movie had been, part of me was already alerted to the fact that *Midnight Express* was a multi-level scam. What's the opposite of priming? Kael, the fairy godmother (fair and good mother), had "set me straight" by letting me know that something was rotten—not only in Hollywood, but in my own home environment. (And the link between false family values and sexual sadism will become apparent as we proceed.)

*

I opened this piece by describing an early memory of watching a sci-fi movie with my mother and a friend and eating a fresh apple. I said that I have next to no other memories of my mother from these first few years. Why not? My mother had two sides to her. Some of the time she was a loving and nurturing presence, as indicated by this seemingly harmless memory. But my mother was also a heavy drinker and a depressive, with very little control over her fits of irrational rage. Her other face was one I lived in fear of, and I never knew when it would appear. It was vicious, poisonous, deadly, and cruel. I have plenty of memories of this side of her from my adolescence and adulthood, but none from those first few years. Yet I know I was exposed to it, so I can only deduce that it was too terrifying for me to consciously assimilate, and that those early (and most formative) experiences of domestic terror were swallowed up by the river of forgetting.

If life is but a dream, expect symbolic meanings. The first face of my mother was the green apple: pure, nourishing, comforting. The second face was a Triffid: devouring, ferocious, alien, toxic. My fear of her demonic face was probably the primary source of my own unexpressed rage, unexpressed because it wasn't *safe* to express it. So then is it that my childhood fear of my mother, and the rage it stirred in me, is *at the root of my attraction to violent movies?!* Like Eve with Adam in the Garden, with that apple (and that movie), did my mother initiate me into knowledge of good and evil?

It wasn't only my mother and father (and brother and sister) who raised me but the greater "tribe" of pop culture. For better or worse, those cultural images (which are representations of the social community) had an active hand in my psychic formation, one that I am only now choosing to look at. Without getting overly conspiratorial about it, this is probably part of an intentional phenomenon, at least to some extent. As Kael's observations about *Midnight Express* make fairly explicit, movies are tools of propaganda, and the State will do what it can to influence (or sabotage) the development of its members, to turn them into efficient workers in the system—prisoners for life. Honor thy parents, take your beatings, and eat your glop: and don't forget how lucky you are.

Travis & Me

Why Taxi Driver *Is the Defining Movie for a Generation of Lonely Men*

"I don't believe that one should devote his life to morbid self-attention. I believe that someone should become a person like other people."

—Travis Bickle

The appeal of *Taxi Driver*'s Travis Bickle is an archetypal appeal, meaning that the aspects he mirrored (to a specific subset of the male population) were *inner* rather than outer ones. When I first saw the film, as a double feature with *Midnight Express*, I didn't think, "That's me!" But something about the film got under my skin. I'm not the only one—in fact we are legion. But the sorts of guys who relate to Travis aren't obviously Travis-*like*; they're not groping, inarticulate, unsophisticated rubes, and Travis himself would never have gone to see a movie like *Taxi Driver*, much less dug it (he only ever went to porno flicks).

This is what I wrote about the film in 1999, in *The Blood Poets*:

> *Taxi Driver* unfolds with all the force and inescapable logic of an authentic nightmare. It makes a sense beyond sense. It puts us squarely and wholly inside the point of view of its steadily deteriorating protagonist and drags us ever deeper into his feverish dementia. Pauline Kael cited Dostoyevsky's *Notes from Underground* in her review of the film, and both Scorsese and Paul Schrader (who wrote the script) were admirers of Dostoyevsky when they made the film. Dostoyevsky, like Scorsese, was a deeply religious artist with a genuinely apocalyptic vision of suffering. He saw the criminal mind as having a twisted relationship—or affinity—with that of the saint, and

he used madness as his subject because for him it was the most fertile ground in which to plant his ideas about humanity. Like Scorsese (and like Travis, who lacks an artistic release and becomes a killer instead), Dostoyevsky saw the world as a kind of madhouse, an everyday inferno in which we are all burning, alone. In "Underground Man," Pauline Kael wrote: "part of the horror implicit in this movie is how easily [Travis] passes. The anonymity of the city soaks up one more invisible man; he could be legion." For Travis, isolation and anguish are one. He isolates himself primarily in order to suffer, and yet he suffers above all because he is alone. Travis is alienation incarnate, and when he's up there on the screen, we don't feel disgust or superiority—our hearts go out to him. The irony is that Travis is both a nobody and an Everyman. He's an archetypal stereotype.

This is what I wrote in December of 2013, the night after a four-alarm fire almost burned our apartment building down:

I spent most of my life up until my mid-thirties alone. I used to claim I never got lonely, but it was a lie. If I opted for isolation at a young age, my guess is that it was a way to avoid the pain of being unable to connect to those around me. To begin with I chose isolation as a way not to suffer, but over time it became a way *to* suffer. Isolation had a numbing effect, and in the end I needed to be alone so I could delve into the suffering of my aloneness and feel *something*. Being a writer was the perfect path for me: not only does writing require solitude, it *condones* suffering, immersion in pain, as a means to plumb the depths of the soul for the raw material of "art."

Taxi Driver comes closer than any other "work of art" that I know of to representing my experience. It was made from the fusion of three male psyches, each in their thirties at the time, weaving together their shared obsessions, neuroses, and preoccupations, part sexual, part religious, wholly existential. The suffering of the solitary (male) psyche as it struggles to find some way "in" to the world—to connect the inside to the outside, the soul to God (the body to a woman) without being rejected—*damned*—in the process. Curiously enough, Travis Bickle's struggle is not only the artist's struggle to turn his or her demons into something constructive, into a currency which the world will recognize as having *value*; it's also the *autist's* struggle to communicate with a world which he has no way of understanding, because an abyss stands between them.

1999: "The idea had been building up in my mind for some time: true force. Here is man who would not take it any longer. Here is a man who *stood up*..." Right before the words "stood up," the film cuts to an overhead shot of Travis, curled up fully dressed and fetus-like on his bed. He looks like a catatonic rag doll, drained of all vitality, dignity and purpose: a lost soul. All his bravado and his newfound sense of direction are reduced by this image to an insane man's desperate reaching for sanity, a drowning man's last grasp at the straw that will break the camel's back. Travis is split in his moral outrage and his nausea. He can't decide whether to strike at the top or the bottom of this irredeemable hellhole called "society." Lacking the clarity and the courage (and the honesty) to identify the enemy within himself [his own morbid self-attention], Travis redirects his destructive energy outward, at a more or less random target, as a way to bring about his own death. But when Travis attempts to end his life after the carnage of the finale, his guns are empty. He is left stranded, *huis clos*. No exit. He has become of the world, as his only way *into* the world.

2013: Travis displays many of the tell-tale signs of autism. For one thing, his social awareness is practically zero. In the opening scene, he applies for a job as a taxi driver. When the interviewing manager finds out Travis was a Marine, he instantly warms to him and tells him he was in the Marines too. Travis doesn't so much as grunt or nod in response—clearly he knows nothing about small talk or social repartee; he appears to have no clue that this found affinity will help him to get the job. When one of his fellow cabbies asks Travis how he's doing, Travis's answer is to talk about a recent, random act of violence against another cab driver (half his ear was cut off). It is as if he doesn't have a life to comment on. And not only "as if."

As a soul in search of identity, Travis is caught in a double-bind. His lack of a self makes him incapable of connecting to others, and his inability to connect to people only deepens the vacuum inside him. Self can only be fully experienced through expression, and it can only be expressed in relation to others. Travis has no idea. He seems incapable of recognizing that others even exist outside of his own inchoate projections. He lacks "theory of mind." He is caught inside a fevered dream of relating, with no way out (no way to awaken) save through violence.

1999: It's particularly intriguing (and disturbing) to look at Travis's two attempts at relating through violence— his failed attack on the presidential candidate Palantine and his murdering Sport and the other hoods—in relation to two real-life events that followed *Taxi Driver* and which appear to have been inspired by the film (in the first case directly, and in the second case only indirectly). First off there is John Hinckley, Jr.'s assassination attempt on Ronald Reagan. Hinckley claimed to be haunted by the film and to have fallen in love with its adolescent heroine, Jodie Foster, who plays the underage prostitute, Iris, inadvertently "rescued" by Travis's acts of mayhem. In a truly uncanny (and somewhat suspect) case of life imitating art imitating art imitating life (an endless loop, mirrors inside mirrors), Hinckley was allegedly "inspired" (coerced?) to imitate a movie "hero" (really a psychopath) who was loosely based on the diaries of Arthur Bremer, presidential candidate George Wallace's would-be assassin.

I don't know about Bremer, but Schrader's Travis seems to have been inspired—albeit unconsciously—to act out his own fantasies of violence by a culture gorged on infantile ideas of heroism, as propagated by John Wayne films and the like (*The Searchers* being the key exception, and the template for *Taxi Driver*). The trail of accountability goes from Hinckley to Bickle to Schrader to Bremer to Wayne and then out, to the larger culture that summoned forth all these images of "sacred violence" to begin with. (We won't mention the CIA or whatever agencies are usually found lurking behind real-life "random" assassination attempts. [Except that we did!])

Regardless of the true meaning or motive to the Hinckley affair, it proved one thing beyond all doubt—*Taxi Driver* was an uncommonly powerful film, the kind that affected people deeply, and, if the media was to be believed, could incite them to attempt murder. If Hinckley was "archetypally possessed," then Travis was the archetype that possessed him. Who'd have guessed he had it in him? The everyman-nobody became the ultimate somebody.

2013: Travis gets the idea to buy a .44 Magnum (Dirty Harry's gun) from a demented passenger in the back of his cab who fantasizes about destroying his wife's vagina. The passenger is played by Martin Scorsese. That this only transpired when the actor Scorsese cast fell ill proves, if proof were needed, that supernatural forces had a hand in the making of *Taxi Driver*. The film would have been incomplete without this act of *deus ex machina* in which the divine Demiurge entered into the creation and directed the action *from the inside*. With this scene, Travis is not merely inspired by the movies but by *the intelligence behind the movie that is his life*. Scorsese's presence in the film is satanic intervention and demonic inspiration combined. It allows Travis's fantasy (movie) self to come fully alive. Recall that Scorsese is the man who once said "Movies are my life," a walking encyclopedia of cultural images whose primary ideology, unconscious or otherwise, comes from the cinema. What possible better *fiat* for Travis' movie possession could the film possibly provide?

1999: The Bernard Goetz case established something even more remarkable about *Taxi Driver* than the Hinckley affair. At the ending of the movie, Travis's explosion is interpreted, by tabloid journalism, as authentic heroism. Travis is not only exonerated but emerges as a modern-day crusader—a crime fighter along the lines of *Death Wish*'s Charles Bronson or the Batman. This was received by some critics as an implausible resolution. With Bernard Goetz, however, those critics were forced to eat their words. Goetz exploded one day on a New York subway car, drew a pistol and shot down several young black men he claimed were trying to rob him. The young men denied this claim and at least one of them sued Goetz for damages. Whatever the provocation, it seems likely that Goetz, like Travis, simply snapped one day and started shooting, out of personal rage and frustration and more or less at random. The media and the general public, however—apparently fed-up with the (alleged) increasing crime rate and street violence of New York—reacted with (only slightly qualified) approval. Here was man who would not take it any longer. Here was a man who *stood up*. (Goetz was charged with illegal possession of firearms and nothing else.)

2013: Cultural images that provide lost souls with an unconscious ideology and allow for a temporary sense of identity, lead to drastic action that in turn feeds back into the cultural trends (those of the violent urban crusader, the Western hero transposed into a modern setting) and enlarges them, making them brighter, gaudier, more vital, but also more nuanced and ambiguous. *Taxi Driver* offers a homeopathic cure (awareness), which, if administered wrongly or in excessive doses (as in the case of poor Hinckley, whether or not he was "managed" by covert agencies), can end up exacerbating the condition being treated.

1999: In *A Cinema of Loneliness*, Robert Philip Kolker called Travis "the legitimate child of John Wayne and Norman Bates."

> [T]he more deeply he withdraws, the more he comes to believe in the American movie myths of purity and heroism, love and selflessness, and to actuate them as the grotesque parodies of human behavior they are.

Travis's (and Hinckley's) insane fantasies might not be so aberrational as they seem. They may be the inevitable product of the society and culture in which they exist. Logically, to the extent it shared in and even seeded such fantasies, society would accept, and even embrace, Travis as the hero he imagined himself to be. Whatever our feelings about the film's ending, the Bernard Goetz case put any doubts to rest as to its plausibility and proved that truth is indubitably stranger—and more twisted—than fiction. When the movie slips into outright fairy tale in the last scene, when the ice-angel Betsy "comes back" to Travis, the fantasy is complete. No doubt these closing images fanned the flames of Hinckley's own delusion of an equally improbable denouement with Jodie Foster. Travis, Goetz, and Hinckley (and Bremer) are like rival siblings, reared by the same "movies."

2013: Travis is so clueless about the culture he lives in that he has never heard of Kris Kristofferson and doesn't know that porno movies aren't the only movies to take a girl to. The absence of visible cultural influences on him strengthens the feeling of his isolation, and the influences become conspicuous by their absence. Travis's lack of a clearly defined sense of self, his cluelessness about how to be and act in society (and in his own life), leaves him with no other way to express himself save by becoming an unconscious parody of "Hollywood," i.e., of American fantasy ideals of maleness. He is indeed the bastard son of John Wayne and Norman Bates, of *Walking Tall, Dirty*

Harry, and *Death Wish* (all films released shortly before *Taxi Driver*). Culture infects its members even when they aren't directly exposed to its products, by osmosis. My own "autistic" fascination with movies may, ironically, have been an instinctive way for me to *reduce* their influence on me by making it more conscious. I didn't imitate Travis Bickle, I imitated Paul Schrader (who was also a film critic).

1999: Travis is crucified by his own fear and loathing, a martyr to modern alienation, a suffering phantom with no chains to rattle (the soundtrack rattles them for him). The tragedy of *Taxi Driver*—and of maybe all solipsistic sociopaths driven to violence—is that Travis only becomes real (to himself and to a world of indifference) when he kills.

2013: You would think that spending time in the Marines would have given Travis at least a rudimentary idea about social etiquette, such as what kind of movie to take a nice working girl to on a first date. But, like many autistic souls, Travis (who may be suffering from post-traumatic distress) exists inside a cultural vacuum. He really has no clue. Since he has seen couples at the porno theaters he frequents, he assumes it's the place to take Betsy. "Are these the only kind of movies you go to?" she asks. Travis seems bewildered: are there any other kind? His lack of cultural savvy is one with his isolation and naiveté. Somehow, even the world of Hollywood has passed him by. It's reasonable to suppose that someone like Travis would go to ordinary movies, maybe not to Goldie Hawn rom-coms but at least to Charles Bronson and Clint Eastwood shoot-'em-ups. The way he's been conceived, however, he's too unsophisticated even for moviegoing. He doesn't seem to watch porno for sexual arousal, either, and the closest we get to seeing him having a response is when he points an imaginary gun at the screen. Sex seems unthinkable for Travis; even the casual sex of porno requires *some* kind of intimacy. Watching sex movies, he may as well be at biology class studying a mysterious process. (The movie he takes

Betsy to has weird documentary footage of sperms surrounding the ovum.)

The sense of Travis's complete isolation extends to his own body, which he fills with junk and then worries about getting stomach cancer. He is left with no means to connect save violently.

1999: Travis's hell of loneliness and enforced celibacy comes primarily from his incapacity to connect with women. Either he wants to be saved by them, as in the case of Betsy, or he wants to save them (Iris). In both cases, there's no real possibility of understanding between them. Travis feels betrayed when these women don't act according to his fantasy-view of them. He says of Betsy, "I realize now she is just like all the rest, cold, distant. Many people like that; women for sure. They're like a union." Travis experiences women as gathered together against him, refusing him access into their world. But Travis is so isolated inside his own fantasy that all his efforts at communicating—at sharing—are doomed to failure. Only when he literally blasts his way out of his shell and into the world does the world sit up and take notice. And when Betsy returns to Travis in the final scene, it is Travis's ultimate fantasy fulfilled. He has not only slain the dragon, he's won the maiden. But since he is above such earthly desires, he gets to reject her (gently), thereby proving his own superiority, his righteousness. She is "in Hell, like all the rest"; now that she realizes it and comes back to him, it's too late. He has moved beyond her. She cannot touch him. Iris, on the other hand, since she always knew she was in Hell and only needed a little reminding, was capable of being saved.

2013: This whole area of anima-projection/soul rescue is so rich and wormy that I'm loathe to even touch on it for fear of getting sucked into a dark vortex. Suffice it to say that my own fantasies of being a knight-in-shining-armor/sex shaman, rescuing lost damsels from their own misguided folly and the corrupting influences of debased male lust, began as a pre-adolescent and continued all the way into my thirties. The only way I was able to connect to women, by and large, was by seeing myself as their spiritual savior, someone who, by definition and like the knights of old, was not required as a sexual partner but, *au contraire*, as a paragon of sexual purity, a sexless (infantile) brother/father/son figure, an idealized image made not of flesh and blood but of some other substance altogether. *Taxi Driver* shows how the inevitable side effect of assuming such an impossible role—of saving the maiden from male lust in the delusional hope of satisfying one's own desire—can only lead to that disowned lust coming out *as violence*. The impossibly pure savior becomes the very dragon which he is saving the maiden from.

1999: In his self-imposed hell of ascetic isolation, Travis has been gazing into the abyss for so long that it's all he sees. He sees dragons—venality, corruption—everywhere, "all the animals come out at night—whores, skunks, pussies, buggers, queens, fairies, dopers, junkies." His inner hell—his suppressed, insufficiently sublimated libido—has spilled out into the world around him. Travis's internal conflict—the tension and dread—is so intense, so overwhelming, that (in lieu of a woman) he *needs* a visible enemy to provide a means of releasing and directing the pressure. The bloodbath, when it comes, is a baptism. The final orgy of killing in *Taxi Driver*, while anything but pleasurable, is strangely orgasmic. It offers the only relief that Travis, and by extension the viewer, can get. The random massacre is not only Travis's redemption and damnation in one, grisly package; it's his solitary sexual consummation. As Pauline Kael wrote in "Underground Man," it's "the only orgasm he can have."

2013: Revisiting this material has cast my lifelong identification with Travis in a new, more ironic light. I didn't just identify with Travis's isolation, his social awkwardness, his rage and despair, his feeling of being shut out and rejected by women, his fumbling attempts to connect with them, and his inevitable, maudlin retreat into violent (sexual) fantasy (not to mention his journal writing and his autistic self-immersion). I also identified with a less obvious but more fundamental characteristic: *his lack of identity and his need to find cultural images* (the Cowboy and the Indian) *to identify with.* Travis was the "autistic" movie anti-hero whose identity is cobbled together out of the unconscious ideology of movie heroism. I was the autistic moviegoer, unconsciously constructing identity out of *anti*-anti-heroes like Travis. It was a seemingly never-ending, repeating loop of isolation, fantasy, sexual frustration, rage, and despair.

Yet the scene that affected me the most in *Taxi Driver* is devoid of any real violence. Travis is watching a tacky soap opera on his cheap black and white TV set. A young couple are talking about their relationship. Travis pushes the TV set slowly away from him with his cowboy boot until it topples over backwards and explodes. He leans forward and puts his head in his hands, holding the .44 Magnum against his face. "Damn," he says, over and over. The scene haunted me as a teenager. Travis has no way of understanding, much less expressing, the nature of his condition. His confusion is complete because he has no reference point outside of it to refer to, no model of authentic ("heroic") behavior that isn't a lie. When he looks inward for a self to give meaning to his despair, he finds only an abyss. That's the true horror: the search for an authentic self that turns up nothing, that can only conjure from the abyss an expression of its infinite emptiness.

Travis wasn't as lucky as I was. He only had daytime soaps to rub the salt into the wound of his endless social alienation. He was stuck in a one-bedroom apartment, staring at non-people he couldn't ever relate to, in a make-believe world he could never hope to enter, while striving to be one of them. Travis couldn't find any mirror to stand in front of that didn't turn him into a parody of manhood. At least I had the looking glass of *Taxi Driver* to gaze into.

An Imaginal Cloak

The Clint Eastwood Mythos & the Way of Sublimation

"The 'realism' of *Dirty Harry* is that of dreams. It harks back to a simpler, more primitive time, when black was black and white was white, and saints and dragons still walked the Earth."
— *The Blood Poets*

When I was twelve—and caught up in the terrifying disorientation of adolescence—I discovered Clint Eastwood. It was through the portal of that one, all-consuming focus that I became the movie autist I am today. As a teenager, just looking at images of Clint gave me a kind of dreamy bliss. It was a strange kind of love. I didn't desire him, I wanted to disappear *into* him, to *become* him. There was a huge, coffee table book on Warner Brothers in our local bookshop. Whenever I passed the shop I went in, opened the book to the page that cited *Dirty Harry*, and gazed at a small black and white photograph of Harry on a sandy strip of land (the site of a murder, I eventually found out), in his Paisley jacket, holding a walky-talky. Not counting this one, I collected every image I could find of Clint and pasted them into scrapbooks. I bought a replica of a .44 handgun. I decided I wanted to be a cop when I grew up. What? How? It was about as far from my actual destiny and character as it's possible to imagine, but the spell of movies was so strong it blotted out my reality. That was the idea.

There's a Talking Heads song, "Seen and Not Seen," about someone who chooses a particular face and concentrates on it until his own face begins to resemble it. I did something similar with Clint. When a schoolmate mentioned having seen a preview for an upcoming Eastwood movie, I was skeptical and asked if he knew what Clint looked like. "Sure," he said, "Like you, only better-looking." It not only made my day, it made my year. In certain photos (usually when I'm smiling broadly—a rare event), it's true that I slightly resemble Clint. I am tall and lean (actually rail thin) with a high forehead, heavy brow, often a beard, and brown hair (seriously thinning). The resemblance is only superficial; I look more like an alien than a cowboy, and where Clint is monolithic, earthy, I am ethereal and vaguely vampiric. I would probably be cast as a villain in his movies, or as a jittering junky who gets blown away in the first scene.

*

In the section from *The Blood Poets* on Clint Eastwood, I began with a brief essay on "movie brutes" which referred to Robert Mitchum:

> Pauline Kael described Robert Mitchum as "a lawless actor" and commented that "His strength seems to come precisely from his avoidance of conventional acting, from his dependence on himself; his whole style is a put-on, in the sense that it's based on our shared understanding that he's a man acting in material conceived for puppets."

The desire to be someone else is central to the appeal of movies. Movie stars make a living pretending to be someone else. A successful movie star turns him- or herself into a public figure, a celebrity, and, in Clint's case, a living icon. To have an idol means to focus your attention so ardently on it that it blot outs your own identity. Seen and not seen. Like ancient man offering himself up to the gods, we want to be consumed by our idols and remade in their image. But if a movie star is little more than a glorified marionette, who's the puppet master? Popular wisdom assigns the role to the directors and writers. But if Clint was embodying my adolescent fantasies, in a sense he was dancing to *my* tune.

Watching a movie allows us to *become* our idols by identifying with the characters they pretend to be. We are on a level: Clint is no more Dirty Harry than I am. We enter into a complicit agreement to suspend disbelief: my belief completes the actor's fantasy, and without it there's no consummation. Reality is in the eye of the beholder.

*

A Clint Eastwood movie always features Clint Eastwood as Clint Eastwood—that's what people come to see. It isn't necessary for Eastwood to act in order to fill out his role. In *Dirty Harry*, for example, we never feel we are seeing a real San Francisco cop but only a Hollywood idealization of such a cop, all our fantasies (and fears) embodied in a single icon.

The above (from *Blood Poets* chapter three, "The Year of the Anti-Hero") is somewhat overstated. Eastwood certainly acts; he feigns anger, sympathy, and humor according to the script's dictates. But the main body of his performance, unlike method actors like Dustin Hoffman or Robert De Niro, *is* his body: his physical presence. Eastwood's efficiency as a performer comes down most of all to his ability to relax in front of the camera. He is *cool*. As a recipient for the viewer's (in my case adolescent) fantasies, the blanker a slate he is, the better.

Considering that Eastwood really doesn't do much acting he is a devilishly engaging screen personality. Like Gary Cooper, he fulfills Hitchcock's primary requirement of the movie star—he does nothing, impeccably. We have only to see him striding down the street or munching a hot dog to feel all the excitement, apprehension and delight that we come to the movies expressly to get.

Here I was speaking personally, of course, while using the royal "we" (something I borrowed from Pauline Kael) to disguise just how personally I was speaking. In transference, the more neutral a presence the therapist is, the easier it is for the client to project his or her father, mother, brother, *whatever*, issues onto them. Having a movie mentor or a fantasy role model is similar. As a teenager, Clint to me was like Humphrey Bogart is to Woody Allen in *Play It Again, Sam*: a perennial witness, advisor, confidante. Throughout the day, at school, at home, or in-between, I would curl my lip in that special Eastwood way or speak in a whispery growl and feel like I *was* Clint. The image projected outward around me was an imaginal cloak—movie armor.

The space which the movies opened up for me was a space I could feel absolutely safe inside. Like a womb, perhaps?

*

Why exactly I needed armor, what sort of wounds I needed to cover and protect, and what kind of dragons I needed defending against, is something that can only be deduced, for example by mapping the sequence of my infatuation—which films I saw first, and so on—*if* I can remember it. As mentioned, I first saw *Where Eagles Dare* at the cinema as a very young boy, and then—the turning point—on TV over Christmas holidays, in 1979. A week or so later, having pored excitedly through the Christmas editions of *Radio Times* and the *TV Times* for any more Clint movies, I saw *Paint Your Wagon*. Both these films are about two men on a mission. In *Eagles*, Clint and Richard Burton sneak into a Nazi castle to rescue a British captain; in *Wagon*, Lee Marvin's character rescues Clint from a wagon crash in which Clint's brother is killed, and they partner up to find gold. The films were made back to back, *Where Eagles Dare* was released the year after I was born and *Paint Your Wagon* the year after that, when I was two. I saw *Where Eagles Dare* first with my whole family, and then, the crucial viewing, with my brother.

The first Clint movie which came out at theaters after my great infatuation began was *Escape from Alcatraz*, based on the true story of three men escaping from a maximum security prison. The movie is also a sort of parable (like *One Flew Over the Cuckoo's Nest*) about how the Establishment crushes the artist's spirit, somewhat improbably equating Clint's criminality with the creative spark. The next Clint movie (if memory serves) which aired on TV after my obsession began was *Thunderbolt and Lightfoot*, in which Eastwood also plays a criminal and which is also about two men (Clint and Jeff Bridges) on a mission, this time to find money which Clint stashed inside a schoolhouse, after a big heist. I was only able to see the first five minutes of the movie because I had to go to bed at 9:30. My brother was watching it, and I caught the opening scene in which Clint, dressed as a preacher, runs through a wheat field chased by George Kennedy with a gun. No amount of imploring could persuade my mother to let me stay up, and I was forced to leave my brother to watch the rest—no doubt fueling the intense envy I had for him at the time (envy that continued through into adulthood, and even up until his death), as well as strengthening the association of movies with forbidden, hence doubly desired, fruit.

I think the next film I saw was *Play Misty for Me*, which I watched on TV with my mother on a Saturday night (I was allowed to stay up on weekends). We both loved the movie and found it terrifying. Clint plays a DJ who sleeps with a female fan; she becomes obsessive and turns into a psychopathic stalker. Eastwood (who directed the film, his first) used Roberta Flack's "The First Time Ever I Saw Your Face" in the movie for a montage in which Clint makes love to his "good" girlfriend. I remember how, after I saw the movie, I listened to Elvis's rendition of the song and felt immensely sad. At an educated guess, I saw *The Beguiled* next, a key movie in Clint's *oeuvre*, being the only one in which he dies (until *Honkytonk Man* in 1983), not in a hail of bullets but at the hands of possessive females (they give him poisoned mushrooms). He plays a soldier wounded in the civil war and sheltered at an all-girl's school, where he sleeps with three generations of women. Before the women dispatch him, he has his leg amputated; the film is an obvious castration anxiety parable.

The first theme that emerges from this cursory breakdown of my adolescent Eastwood initiation is: men as brothers, missioning/rescuing/getting rich together; women as dangerous predators, possessive, murderous, and not to be trusted. There are very few sex scenes in those early Clint movies (not counting the ones about the dangerous females, in which sex leads to death). One exception is *High Plains Drifter*, the first Eastwood movie I owned on video cassette (I stole it from a local rental shop). In the first fifteen minutes of the film, Clint's "Stranger" rapes a high-born woman. The woman (Marianna Hill) challenges him on the street and berates him in a "motherly" fashion, questioning his manhood and criticizing his lack of "manners." He responds by telling her, if she wants to get to know him, she should just say so, adding that she's the one who could use a lesson in manners. He then drags her to the barn and has his way with her, which the film makes clear is what she wanted all along.

The first Clint movie I saw at the cinema (unless it was *Alcatraz*) was *Every Which Way But Loose*. I saw it with my childhood friend, Adam, who shared my Eastwood obsession. Clint plays a bare-knuckle fighter who lives with an orangutan and falls for a heartless female (Sondra Locke). At the end of the movie, Clint throws the fight he's about to win, realizing that, if he becomes the bare-knuckle champ, everyone will want a piece of him; so instead of entering the big-time, he opts for defeat. After that, and after Clint escaped from Alcatraz, he made *Bronco Billy*, which marked the beginning of a new, more "sensitive" and whimsical direction for him as actor and director. This was a source of great disappointment for me, his number one fan. I wanted Clint violent, punching horses and women, not as some small-time, benevolent father figure guy.

Throughout all of this, the one Clint movie I was most desperate to see was *Dirty Harry*. I actually had a chance to see it in 1980, while I was holidaying in Maine with my family and heard that it was playing at a local repertory cinema. My brother and I both wanted to see it but it was an R and we would need an adult to accompany us. Our stepfather refused to play this role, no doubt further compounding my disillusionment with him. Perhaps he sensed that Clint was a rival influence as I began to make my way through the undiscovered country of adulthood, one he could never compete with? I certainly didn't look up to my stepfather or want to be like him. It was a warrior I wanted to be, and neither my father (a material sensualist) nor my stepfather (a spiritual sensualist) fit that bill.

When I finally saw *Dirty Harry*, it was under my own power and by my own initiative, just as it was supposed to be. I remember sitting with bated breath inside the Notting Hill cinema in London, waiting for the double bill of *Dirty Harry* and *Magnum Force* to begin. *Dirty Harry* became my favorite movie instantly. When my mother got me a video recorder, a short while after, I rented the movie over the weekend and watched it over and over again during those two days. I *absorbed* the movie, lived in it and invited it to live in me. It was an alternate reality, like dreaming awake. Harry Callaghan was everything I wanted for myself: he possessed total assurance, total cool, total control. He stood in opposition to everyone and everything around him, and his oppositional stance was the proof of his *individualism*. In 2013, when I was working on a long piece about autism and the media, I learned the term for Harry's stance. It's called a *negative identity*.

*

Harry is "anti" all right, not merely indifferent, like No Name, but actively hostile towards everyone and everything. He is a loner, like No Name, but, unlike the wandering stranger, Harry also appears to be lonely. There is an aura of isolation, almost of melancholy, that surrounds Eastwood's impeccable cop and gives him an almost saintly glow—a halo. He is selfless in the best tradition of saints and martyrs, and seems to be motivated by nothing other than sense of duty. The way the movie presents him, he's practically a force of nature.

Three qualities overlap in the above definition: Harry's hostility towards everyone around him; his isolation and melancholy; and his selflessness that translates into an almost superhuman power. Much more than his brutality, or even his cool, these were the qualities (not counting the superhuman selflessness) I identified with, and which still somewhat describe me today, or at least how I see myself. There was another element to Harry which I emphasized in *Blood Poets*: his lack of sexual drives.

Where No Name was asexual, Harry is merely disinterested— celibate. Harry is like a fighter who never knows when the next big fight is coming: the sexual gratifications sought by other men seem to be beneath him. Harry was once married, and his wife was killed in a senseless road accident. This piece of information is not given us to deepen Harry's character or as any kind of motivation, but simply to add an extra dimension of pathos. It makes his loneliness seem noble, his silence deeper. Instead of being simply surly or sulky, Harry's silence is stoical: it's the silence of graceful suffering.

Now I would say that the detail about his wife *does* deepen Harry's character and add nuance to it; it even suggests, quite strongly, that his lack of warmth towards others, his outsider status, is the result of *pain*. Maybe, like Bruce Wayne's Batman, it's this pain that has driven Harry to embody the archetypal role of protector-avenger (a force of nature), a role that makes sex, love, and companionship—which would also be the most threatening things to him—"mere" distractions to be avoided. Clint's manly mission, in other words, was only superficially about finding/rescuing the "gold" or killing the bad guy. At a deeper level, it was a way to avoid duplicitous females, and the terrifying intimacy which they invite, or demand. As with Travis Bickle, Harry's violence was the result of *sublimated sexuality*.

*

The purpose of deconstructing my semi-voluntary movie conditioning (following Clint through a violent cinematic underworld of sublimation) is to help me see the original trauma-conditioning which I was trying to oppose. It was early traumas which drove me to seek compensatory immersion in fantasy in the first place, so the nature of the fantasy being escaped into indicates, in a series of subtle correspondences, the shape of the reality I was trying to escape from. My parents and siblings fucked me up because, being fucked up themselves, that was all they knew how to do. Movies helped me adjust to that by finding my "own" value system, a value system that hasn't served me any better than parental conditioning because it was a reaction *against* it. Eastwood was the anti-father. Emulating him didn't decondition me, it *re*conditioned me. It gave a name, a face, and a shape to my rage.

> *Dirty Harry* is one of the most ruthless and persuasive arguments for police brutality ever put on the screen, but also, ironically or tragically, one of the best police dramas ever made. The director Don Siegel's technique is so gripping and

exciting that even liberals can have a good time watching it: they may even come out feeling they've had their ideas strengthened! After all, Harry may not be everyone's idea of a perfect liberal (for the bureaucrats in the film, much as they begrudgingly respect his efficiency, he's their worst nightmare come true); but he's certainly an individual spirit.

The emotional center of *Dirty Harry* is Harry's indignation at the indifference of the political system which (in the film's view) protects the rights of the criminals at the expense of the victims. It's that indignation—a combination of compassion for Scorpio's victims and hatred for Scorpio—that drives Harry and the movie forward. The film is bookended by Harry's famous "Do you feel lucky?" speech. It's delivered first with cool, rather sadistic aplomb to a wounded black bank robber. Since Harry knows his gun is out of bullets, and since all he has to do is reach down and grab the guy's shotgun, he's really just toying with the criminal, like a cat with a mouse. Maybe this is what a saintly cop does for kicks? When he gives the same speech at the film's climax to Scorpio, Harry *knows* he has one bullet left and *wants* to put it inside Scorpio (how's that for sublimation?). Clint/Harry delivers the lines with all the wrath and indignation that's been building inside him (and the audience) throughout the movie. Harry's ironic detachment has become righteous, wrathful engagement. "Now it's personal."

This is all good melodrama, and the mechanics of the Hollywood Revenge Fantasy in action. But it's also the moral of the movie. Harry was probably the first in a line of emotionally-driven, "beyond-the-call-of duty" cops who throw the book away and resort to extreme prejudice in order to get the job done. The question these movies all ask is the question finally voiced, in the pulpy *Year of the Dragon* (loosely based on a real-life cop and written by Oliver Stone—who wrote *Midnight Express*—and Michael Cimino, who made *Thunderbolt and Lightfoot* and co-wrote *Magnum Force*), by Mickey Rourke's Stanley White: *"How can anybody care too much?"* The real question is *why* do Harry and the others care so much? The filmmakers want us to believe it's because they are heroes and heroes care about doing justice and protecting (or avenging) the innocent. Yet they also want to provide the emotional, quasi-sexual satisfaction of *personalized*, revenge-driven killing—without which there's no catharsis. The only way to square that circle (since only the bad-guy is supposed to enjoy killing) is to elevate the hero to an implicitly divine moral status. Governments (especially the US government) do the same thing, which begs the question: how much is Hollywood influenced by government, and how much is government influenced by Hollywood? The easiest—though not necessarily right—answer is that government *is* Hollywood, and vice versa.

Dirty Harry exists, historically speaking, as a sort of watermark, indicating America's return, after a brief and brutally curtailed foray into idealism during the '60s, to an almost medieval kind of totalitarian thinking. The irony is that Harry is the free individual, the "rebel," while the "liberal" system has become the Establishment which this rebel opposes. (The villain Scorpio gets this liberal system to work *for* him, which is more than Harry ever manages.) So the transformation of outlaw-rebel into renegade cop, made of the anti-hero—a reactionary!

Politics is all about muddying the picture by rechanneling primal rage into national policies; I want to try and trace this subli-mation process back to its origins. If *Dirty Harry* falls back on the obvious, archetypal sublimation methods of fairy tales, knights and dragons, etc., then it's implicitly mirroring the environment in which those narratives were first required, namely, childhood. My father ran a very poor, "under-policed," overly liberal home environment. One key result, for me, was that I was bullied by my older brother. My parents (the bureaucratic, liberal system which Harry is pitted against) either looked the other way or simply couldn't see what was going on through the alcohol haze. If *Dirty Harry* is an archetypal narrative, it's also a deceptively mundane one.

This subtext of domestic dysfunction is much more evident in *High Plains Drifter*, which Clint made two years after *Dirty Harry*. In *The Blood Poets*, I quoted this description of *Drifter* from Robin Wood: "the Lone Hero rides in from the Wilderness not to defend the Growing Community but to reveal it as rotten at its very foundations before annihilating it." In a further twist, the Stranger is the ghost of the former sheriff (absent father) of the community, *avenging his own murder*. Clint (who resembled my father, though I didn't recognize it till I was forty) represents the avenger-protector which every child needs while growing up but which so few get. Admiring Clint's anti-hero and choosing him as a role model was an unconscious way for me to give the finger to both of my male parental figures. (My father was a liberal pacifist, my stepfather a spiritual seeker and Yoga-doer.) The liberal values that came from my parents weren't my values (they weren't even *their* values), and in an attempt to deprogram myself, I unconsciously adopted the *opposite* values (not political but emotional and aesthetic ones) from movies: a love of violence and strong-arm tactics.

My father was the opposite of a disciplinarian; not because he was soft but because he was indifferent. There were no rules in our house and certainly no punishments, strong-arm or otherwise. One result of this "liberal" (overly permissive or "loose") home environment—the one that most counted for me— was that when I was bullied by my brother, no one stepped in to prevent it and administer "justice." As a result I developed my own protection system. I donned the imaginal cloak of Clint and became an "outlaw rebel"—opposed to everyone and everything—a "reactionary." My brother was like Scorpio: he managed to get the system to work for him. He did it at home, by charming our mother into believing he could do no wrong. He did it at school, where his rebellion was always covert (unlike me, he never got caught). And he continued to do it, as an adult, in "the world," becoming a minor celebrity with his memoir *Dandy in the Underworld*, which told a tale of our shared childhood that I could barely recognize. That was *his* sublimation process, and unfortunately, inevitably, I was roped into it and got the brunt of his otherwise unexpressed rage.

At the same time, since I didn't have a strong paternal figure to make my home environment safe for me to develop my own masculinity within, I had to find a way to sublimate my sexuality in order not to be overwhelmed by it. Violent movies—and identifying with violent men—became that way of sublimation.

Adolescent Revenge Fantasies

How Hollywood Exploited My Appetite for Destruction

"Advertising is a form of psychological warfare that in popular culture, as in politics, is becoming harder to fight with aboveboard weapons. It's becoming damned near invincible."
—Pauline Kael, "On the Future of Movies"

Pauline Kael writes that "The dirtiness on Harry is the moral stain of recognition that evil must be dealt with; he is our martyr—stained on our behalf." The idea of taking on the "dirt" of the community is an old one. The job of the "sin-eater" or shaman is to negotiate with the dark forces of the tribe (its sickness, corruption, etc.) and act as a mediator between the social realm and the archetypal one, the underworld or the community's unconscious. In my early twenties, the shaman's path took over from my Hollywood aspirations and I went from wanting to be a cop (Harry), to wanting to be a filmmaker (the intelligence behind characters like Harry, the original sublimators), to wanting to be a sorcerer like Carlos Castaneda. The Hollywood makeover of the sin-eater distorted a metaphoric process and literalized it, turning shamanic cleansing into police brutality. It was the sublimation process in deterioration. As Sylvester Stallone's unintentional *Dirty Harry* parody, *Cobra*, had it: "You're the disease. I'm the cure." But when the shaman becomes a crime-fighter, the saint becomes a psychopath.

Harry is a warrior so disposed to violence that he seems to actually seek it out: wherever he goes, he finds a war. Pauline Kael called him "the hero of a totally nihilistic dream world." He carries his .44 magnum at his side with the nonchalance that other men carry their briefcases and umbrellas, and he makes explicit what was only suggested in the Spaghetti Westerns—that violence is his one and only means of expression, his passion, and the only pleasure he allows himself.

Reading that last line was a bit like hearing an unconscious confession. The reason I wrote *The Blood Poets* was because I wanted to write about my greatest passion, movies. To write about the movies I cared about the most, I focused on *violence*, since that was the common thread running through them all. So were movies my passion, or were they the pretext?

*

Because of the four-alarm fire in late December, 2013, our building was evacuated and I spent the day in the back of the local bookshop, where my wife has an office. While I was working on "Travis & Me," she came into the back with a local author, W.P. Kinsella, to introduce us. I knew Kinsella was local, and I'd heard of him because his book, *Field of Dreams*, was made into a Kevin Costner movie in the late 80s. I had hated the movie so much it made the number one spot of my list of worst movies ever made. My mother had liked it, and I'd worked long and hard to convince her that she had been conned. This was back before the mainstream press had been entirely declawed and defanged, and some periodicals (*Rolling Stone* was one) had excoriated the movie for being a concealed paean to Reaganomics. (Pauline Kael called the movie an "opening salute of the Bush era"—its message was "Play ball.") After my harangue, my mother watched the film a second time and this time didn't like it. She said I must have been "whispering in [her] ear" the whole time. I didn't mention any of this to Kinsella, I just asked him about his experience of the movie. He said it had been a good one and that he was happy with the result. I asked what he was working on now and he said he was no longer able to get published by mainstream publishers.

In 2002, the director of *Field of Dreams*, Phil Alden Robinson, made *The Sum of All Fears*, with CIAsset Ben Affleck, about a terrorist nuclear attack on the US, confirming my suspicions—if confirmation were needed—about the earlier film's political allegiance. The thing to remember about propaganda is that, if it's really effective, it doesn't look like propaganda. It looks like entertainment.

*

Since the line between political propaganda and so-called ordinary "advertising" has become pretty much invisible, popular entertainment, advertising, and politics all seem to overlap into one blurry mess of mind control. One can only trace the trends and map the parallels. Movies are (inarguably?) one of the primary mediums of American advertising, and the Hollywood Revenge Fantasy is the primary form which this advertising takes.

These lines, or variations of them, first appeared in *The Blood Poets* in 1999. It was the first book I published and I hoped it would pave my way into the Promised Land of Hollywood, a land I'd been dreaming of entering since my adolescent obsession with Clint Eastwood first began, in 1979. During the genesis of this present book, I revisited a chapter called "Hollywood Über Alles: Here Come the Designer Fascists," thinking to rework it into a new piece. What follows are the highlights I found, muscled up and pared down by my current sense and sensibility, and interrupted by present-day observations regarding the author's "journey"—the one that *didn't* take him to Hollywood, and which he now accepts never will (since he has neither the desire nor the ability to become a CIAsset, like Ben Affleck or Phil

Alden Robinson).

*

The Hollywood Revenge Fantasy is dedicated to building up audience emotions to such a state that they need and *demand* an act of violence as the only possible (and just) means to relieve that tension. It both instills and satisfies in audiences an "appetite for destruction," *a lust for blood*. Hollywood movies— most especially the action/blockbuster variety—are not made by individuals (regardless of the names on the credits) but by groups or factions (the studios or the conglomerates behind the studios) with a specific agenda to follow. This agenda, though primarily commercial, is also political.

It's no secret that psychological research plays a central role in the "art" of advertising. It's not unreasonable to suggest it also plays a not-insignificant part in the creation and direction of movie trends, and even, to an extent, the construction of the movies themselves. If the CIA now has a fully operational Hollywood wing, the indication is that what was once covert has now become fully overt. Movies are the largest American export after weapons. This should tell us something about the relationship between movies and politics.

The last two lines were added in 2013. Back in 1997, when some of this material was first scribbled down, it wasn't widely known just how deeply the CIA and the US military were involved in Hollywood product. It probably still isn't. One thing about this material that surprised me while going over it is how political it is, even to the point of having a slightly indignant, liberal tone. I never thought of myself as a political writer, and certainly not a liberal one, so this can only be a case of parental conditioning showing through. My father despised right-wing values and, perhaps not coincidentally, had zero tolerance for violent movies. (He liked to tell me how he hid under the theater seat while watching *A Clockwork Orange*.)

Now I'd say there's an unvoiced conflict in this material, one that undermines it and that needs to be addressed. I was writing about violent movies because, unlike my father, I loved to watch them. But here I was writing about movies as *a tool for psychological warfare* without considering how my own (writer's) sensibility had been shaped by that tool. Having revisited the material on a seeming whim (after a blogger tweeted about his moral objections to certain movies), I am now feeling obliged to look at the material more closely and honestly than I was able to back in 1997-9.

I was infected by the Hollywood virus from an early age, and more than thirty years later I am still displaying the symptoms. I am still writing about Hollywood, trying to get "its" attention (I tweeted to Matthew Modine the same day I started this piece). Hollywood hasn't managed to take over my psychic system entirely (probably because I've never managed to establish myself there), but nor have I succeeded in completely expelling it. Every time I try, it grows back and then there I am, courting its favors again. Not only that, but courting it by denouncing it as corrupt. Could I possibly *be* more divided?

*

"Some of us Americans are tired of having our nervous systems raped."
—Pauline Kael, *Conversations*

Over the last forty years (since *Star Wars*, roughly), Hollywood movies have become every bit as much of a science as an art. They probably have a closer affinity to advertising than we would care to admit, and certainly than they do to any other art-form. (Marshall McLuhan called advertising the greatest art form of the twentieth century.) Advertising relies upon sexual stimulation to "open those neural floodgates" (a line from *Videodrome*), arousing audience interest and attention and invoking specific responses and feelings—and even actions. Hollywood action movies use violent imagery to create a state of emotional tension and excitation and to make viewers vulnerable to suggestion. Certain values or meanings can then be introduced. This is evident in the way violent movies so often include extremely inappropriate and sentimental moments of grief, exaltation, or such (any kind of emotional outburst will do), as a release for the tension created. Audiences then associate the values or meanings inherent in these "affecting" moments with *relief* (i.e., pleasure), and hence identify them (unconsciously) as *positive* values. Often the release itself involves images of violence, which serve as a "cleansing" or cathartic culmination to all the prior images. The "climax" of action pictures is a kind of sexual or quasi-sexual climax. It appeals to the Travis Bickle in us all.

The Hollywood Revenge Fantasy is *the* basic model for the action movie because emotional content is required for catharsis, and rage is the easiest emotion to invoke. Two hours of violent imagery serves to build up the suspense, emotional tension, anxiety, apprehension, and hatred which, in the last moments, can then be released.

*

As a teenager, I had a preference for watching scenes of sexualized violence and violent sexual imagery. Now I know that the rage and hostility I felt towards my mother had to come out somehow, and that this was the safest way I found. You don't have to be Freud to figure this out (even if it took me twenty years). Back then I thought there was something wrong with me and naturally I kept it to myself (until I wrote *The Blood Poets*, more or less). My infatuation with violent (nonsexual) action movies, on the other hand, especially ones featuring Clint

Eastwood, seemed perfectly normal and I didn't try and hide it. Yet today I no longer see the two interests as separate.

I had a lot of rage trapped inside me which it wasn't safe to feel, much less express. Movies provided a way to at least connect to that rage and rechannel it, by identifying with both the violent heroes and psychopathic killers (or sexual predators) of movies. "Hollywood" — in the widest sense of the word — provided me with all the fodder I needed to do this. I identified with Clint Eastwood because he was everything I wasn't at that time: he was tough, cool, ruthless, efficient, he was in control, he was *his own man*. The politics never occurred to me — at least until I read Pauline Kael, but even then I didn't really care. I intuited, rightly I think, that Eastwood's appeal went beyond politics. It was primal, which is exactly what made it so appealing, and so dangerous.

Apart from the opportunity which the Hollywood Revenge Fantasy provides for explosive action, it exploits a basic male desire to "get dirty." A capacity for violence and the ability to make violence as gory, intense, cool, exciting, amusing, and aesthetically pleasing as possible. These are the qualities required of the modern action hero. It's hard to think of an American leading man who *hasn't*, at some point in his career, played the maverick lawman or spy (or more recently Super-Hero) with a tendency to take things personally. Many of the top (male) box office stars have made a career out of variations on this stereotype. Anger is perhaps the easiest thing for an actor to play effectively, and revenge fantasies are almost invariably popular with audiences (including internationally). The tough, brutal but *"sensitive"* crime-fighter hero is both flattering to the *"orgastically impotent"* (Wilhelm Reich) male ego and arousing to female libidos. All in all, judging by recent cinema history, playing crime-fighters on a revenge ("justice") mission is the easiest possible route to fame and fortune for a male actor. It's especially telling that revenge and justice are more or less interchangeable here, because, to the American (political) sensibility, they *are* interchangeable.

*

"[T]he writers and the directors no longer create different emotional tones for the deaths of good and bad characters. The fundamental mechanism of melodrama has broken down."
— Pauline Kael, "Killing Time"

Hollywood came up with the revenge fantasy in the late 60s and early 70s, not as simply another twist on the action film (much less as a psychological drama), but as a new (sub)*genre* in itself. This led to a change not only in movie content but also in style. A personal incentive on the part of the crime-fighter is essential to the tawdry, relentless intensity of the revenge fantasy action movie. This allows the plot to do away with "the line of duty" and highlight the personal element, accentuating the hitherto incidental violence until it becomes the *raison d'être* of the film. Perhaps even more than the Clint Eastwood *Dirty Harry* films, *Death Wish* (1974) was the model for the Hollywood Revenge Fantasy. The general feeling that this new genre played upon was a growing urban dread and paranoia that things were coming apart at the seams, and that *someone had to do something*! Enter the lawman, and lately, as problems have become more global, the technologically enhanced secret agent and/or Super-Hero.

It's an ironic fact that, although "Dirty" Harry Callaghan (the fantasy right-wing avenger) would, if true to his character, have hunted down and blown away Charles Bronson's vigilante architect from *Death Wish*, the two figures are essentially the same. Both *Dirty Harry* and *Death Wish* exploit the same "civilized" fears of anarchy and social collapse. Both are calls to increased surveillance, control, police action, etc., and both feed and exploit public unease, insecurity, anger, indignation, and other non-rational responses by presenting an exaggerated, grossly simplified, or just plain *false* picture of the ways things are.

When George Bush, Sr's scriptwriters turned Sadam Hussein into an Iraqi Adolf Hitler, and later, when possibly the same scriptwriters working for his son turned Osama Bin Laden into a real-time Bond villain, what was it but the Hollywood method extended to foreign policy: the tail wagging the dog? *Zero Dark Thirty* was Hollywood's 2012 account of "the greatest manhunt in history," the alleged tracking and killing of Osama Bin Laden, and the film's director, Katherine Bigelow, and her team were (reportedly) given access to confidential information which the mainstream media was denied. At this point how can we tell the difference between Hollywood's cynical exploitation of people's desire to escape into fantasy, and the government's manipulation of information to keep the public in the dark? What's the difference between spoon-fed "entertainment" and political manipulation? *Approximately zero.*

In the midst of all this confusion between fantasy and fact and good and evil, the apparent *social* need for order/justice in America has somehow—in movies at least—become inextricably mixed up with the more emotional desire for revenge, or *blood*. 9/11 was a catastrophic, collective enactment of this moral mix-up. The primary, central message of Hollywood action movies is: "There's nothing wrong with killing as long as the right people get killed." The same can be said for US foreign (and domestic) policy (except it doesn't even matter if they are the right people, so long as they are the right color/class). Now breaking arms and heads to solve problems has developed a dark nuance, as systematized torture has become a central set-piece in so many movies and TV shows, almost always shown to be *justified*.

*

I once read an interview with the author Umberto Eco in which he was asked why he writes. He replied with one word: "Revenge." While that's certainly not the whole story, it's a central strand *in* it. Powerlessness is the primary, primal experience for everyone (what could be more powerless than a baby?), and writers and artists tend to be people who had it especially bad and who were compelled to deal with the alienation and trauma creatively. My goal to "make it in Hollywood," my desire to write, my identification with Clint Eastwood, and my attraction to violent revenge fantasies, are all part of the same "complex," a complex that has pulled me to (re)write this present piece, to try and arm-wrestle that psychic octopus one more time and get it *under control* (make rational sense out of it) *once and for all*. The name of the complex is sublimation. The tragic irony of this current work, this book-to-be, is that its subject matter is one with its method: the sublimation of sexual violence through writing—specifically *writing about movie violence*.

Of course I have failed again. I will never be the conquering hero in my life because the conquering hero is a myth, and worse than a myth, state-funded propaganda. But I *am* one step closer (one less tentacle to go) to seeing the psychosocial patterns of control that drive me, and to recognizing how the imaginary solutions I dreamed up as a child and adolescent (violent fantasies included) will never solve the crisis I was born into. But also, to seeing how they don't need to. It's already over. I already won; I survived my own Vietnam.

The Hollywood Revenge Fantasy presents a world teetering on the brink of moral chaos and social anarchy, a "state of emergency" due either to crime, terrorist action, drugs, free speech, or whatever, with only a single individual prepared to resort to *extreme measures* (martial law, rendition, torture) standing between us and anarchy. This individual—whether cop, vigilante or Super-Hero—represents the American Hero, and by extension, America. Perverse as it may seem for a collective governing body which depends on increasingly totalitarian control to function, the American State, via Hollywood, has chosen the lone individual "frontiersman" to represent it.

The Hollywood Revenge Fantasy not only mythologizes the past but romanticizes the present. More covertly, it shapes the future by imposing old traditional black-and-white values that never really existed (or never *worked*) on an increasingly confused, morally ambivalent, all-too gray world. In the Wasteland of the twenty-first century, the values that serve to reassure audiences are the values of Hollywood movies, which are themselves the collective fantasies of those same audiences, still wrestling with the amnesia of original trauma. The appeal of movies is that they allow us to forget. The danger of movies is that those who forget the past are condemned to repeat it. Life becomes an endless series of reruns, remakes, and crappy sequels, because the trauma constantly seeks its own reenactment in order to be healed. But whatever is being sublimated invariably leaks through and colors the sublimation, like blood through a bandage.

The field of dreams covers mountains of bodies. It's not the poetry that moves us: it's the blood.

"Is it Safe?"

The Bottom Line on Movie Violence

When I first put together the first volume of *The Blood Poets* in 1998, I began with a quote from the author Paul Bowles:

> It's unsettling to think that at any moment life can flare up into senseless violence. But it can and does, and people need to be ready for it. The process of life presupposes violence, in the plant world the same as the animal world. But among the animals only man can conceptualize violence. Only man can *enjoy* the *idea* of destruction.

I got to know Paul Bowles in 1992, when I threw away a family fortune and moved to Tangier to live on the street, in a somewhat irrational response to the end of a romantic relationship. One of the reasons I chose Morocco as my destination was that I knew there was a good chance I would get killed—that "senseless violence" might flare up at any time. For a time I enjoyed the *idea* of my own destruction. Ironically or poetically, as you like, meeting and spending time with Paul Bowles was like an island of light within those dark waters. The Bowles quote juxtaposes two seemingly contradictory ideas: the unsettling awareness that life can become violent at any moment (and the need to prepare for it); and human beings' capacity to enjoy *conceptualizing* violence.

If movies are collective fantasies, violent movies are collective fantasies of violence. Why do we spend so much time fantasizing about something that most of us are careful to avoid in real life? Is our enjoyment in imagining violent scenarios an unconscious way to prepare for them? If so, the sword cuts both ways, because imagining something is also a way to *make* it reality (like filmmaking), and the chances of our enjoying it when that happens are probably pretty slim. Unlike sex, violence is something most people only enjoy vicariously. For the thousands of people who watch boxing and wrestling matches, only a small portion go out and get into fights for pleasure. In movies, things are more complex.

Violent acts define us, usually as a criminal or psychopath and at best as out of control, but very rarely as heroic. Violence is also what imprints us during our formative years. Whether it's physical violence or "only" the emotional or psychological kind, it's the brutal and shocking experiences that impact us the most. On the first page of *The Blood Poets*, I wrote this:

> [A violent movie] must on the one hand present it unflinchingly in all its horror and brutality, and on the other poeticize it, make it beautiful to us, in order to establish its terrible allure. Above all, the script must itself be a meditation on this violence ... The filmmaker and his film must, like the audience, be manifestly ambivalent about violence in order to present it honestly to us.

It's this same ambivalence that caused me to write three books about violence (including *The Secret Life of Movies*, which looks at more internal forms of violence), and which has brought me back to the subject fifteen years later. One reason for this ambivalence is obvious: we need violence in order to survive. It's a form of defense, and not only physical defense. "Enjoying the idea of destruction" is probably one of the ways I learned to adapt to living in a climate of psychological violence, by creating an "inner landscape" that matched it, a bit like creating a map to navigate the terrain. The reason fairy tales are so dark, grotesque, and violent is because this is how an unformed psyche experiences childhood. To a hyper-sensitive, highly vulnerable soul, the world of adults *is* a dark, grotesque, and violent affair. Fairy tales are the result of sublimation (authors working out their own trauma and redirecting their damaged sexuality), and they provide a sublimating function for the children who read or hear them. This is true also of the adult fairy tales of movies.

I grew up in a home environment in which nothing was certain. Both my parents drank heavily, and I couldn't be sure they would even be conscious. One thing that *was* certain was movies and TV. *Those* worlds were constant, reliable, and safe, no matter how violent they were.

Violence—along with sex—is the subject about which we are all, artists and laymen, most uncertain. It seems, and is, an intrinsic, inevitable part of life: and yet (like sex), we can't help but wonder what it's there for. Our pleasure in violence is a guilty pleasure; but it is not necessarily an immoral or transgressive one.

Here the author (my past self) was presenting an argument in defense of violent movies, at least when they were "art." At an unconscious level, something else was going on, something which my present self, revising and editing words from the past, can see more clearly. Those words from my past now look like a veiled confession. I did wonder what sex was for. Although I was turning thirty when I wrote *The Blood Poets*, I had only just begun to figure it out. I also had difficulty separating sex from violence, not in my daily life but in my psyche: when most teenagers were discovering porn, I was immersing myself in the world of the video nasty and jacking off to scenes of women being brutalized.

I'd certainly prefer not to have stated that as baldly as I did, but what's the alternative? If you are going to pull off a Band-Aid, just do it. By revisiting this material I am coming clean about my past sins; there's no way it can be pretty. When my past self writes that enjoying violence is a guilty but not an immoral pleasure, he is surreptitiously, sneakily, asking for mercy from the bench. I was testing the waters of the world's forgiveness. Could I come clean about my transgressions and still be accepted by others? More importantly, could I fully own that self-destructive aspect of myself and not be destroyed *by* it? Was it safe?

Is it safe?

*

The phrase "Is it safe?" occurs repeatedly in the 1976 movie *Marathon Man*—a movie I saw in Paris in or around 1982 and which became my "number two" movie for a while. (*The Omen*, which I saw on the same trip, was no. 1.) The words are spoken, over and over, by Laurence Olivier's Nazi dentist as he tortures "Babe," played by Dustin Hoffman. The dentist is trying to ascertain if it's safe for him to come out of hiding and sell his diamonds on the New York market. Babe has no idea: as his name suggests he is an innocent who has been drawn into something as a result of *his older brother's shady associations*. (I added the emphasis because of the parallels with my own story.) His torture is completely pointless, except that it turns Babe into a *revenge-driven killer* who eventually brings about the dentist's death. Something of the kind seems to have happened in my own psyche, or to be happening now, in the "torturous" process of uncovering all of this.

In *Marathon Man*, Babe's father suicided (when Babe was young) after being investigated for his Communist leanings (leanings my own father had); when Babe is tortured, the Nazi mocks his father's weakness. Babe's big brother isn't able to protect him—on the contrary, Babe needs protection *from* his brother, or from the violence which he brings down on both of them. Babe takes the heat and is repeatedly traumatized until (like Hoffman in *Straw Dogs*) he snaps and becomes a man of violence. Pauline Kael called the film "a Jewish revenge fantasy," and like *Midnight Express* (though not quite to the same extent), *Marathon Man* is a violent movie I once thought highly of but which I no longer care for. The film's director, John Schlesinger, said that the film "is about [Babe's] survival in a grim and hostile world. In our present age of anxiety we can all identify with characters who are not trying to get ahead but simply to survive." Schlesinger doesn't mention what Babe has to do to survive, however, or that becoming like his tormentors is the only way for this "innocent" to feel safe.

There's a phrase in the introduction to *Blood Poets*: "A cat will toy with a mouse in what appears to be sheer sadistic glee, but is actually a manifestation of the hunter instinct." As a young boy (about eight), I was allowed to take two gerbils home from school for the weekend. At one point, I took them out of their cage, wrapped them up in a sweater, and threw them across the room. The creatures were terrified, though not physically hurt. I was sexually aroused by the act. I had no idea at the time why, or why I was doing it. I just knew it was "wrong" and that there must be something wrong with me for doing it. I have memories from this same period of my first sexual experimentation (with a girlfriend), and of being kicked in the stomach on the stairs by my older brother. I also have a memory of being woken up late at night on my (ninth?) birthday to watch the Hammer horror movie *Prince of Darkness*, starring Christopher Lee as Dracula. Lee was one of my brother's heroes and pictures of him (along with other Hammer movie characters) were pasted all over the walls of his bedroom. Somehow all these memories seem interconnected. Those were dark times in my life.

*

The pleasure we take from sex is, for an animal at least, a secondary side effect of what remains a natural, programmed function. The pleasure would seem to be a sort of incentive (or even consolation?) to ensure that the animal keep at it, do its best, give its full attention to the act, etc. In sex and in violence, the organism comes fully alive, to attention, because there's no other way to do justice to the act.

I don't think I really knew what I was talking about here. It sounds logical enough, and it was *somewhat* experience-based. But it's all head-stuff, divorced from any sort of visceral or body sense. Ironically, that's kind of the point: masturbating to sexualized movie violence appealed to me because it brought me into my body, if only briefly, and in ways that were so stressful or troubling to me that, in the long run, it probably did more harm than good. Teenagers who cut themselves seem to be doing something similar—they are trying to *feel* something. Above all, I think they are trying to feel real. I know I was; ironically, I was using fantasy to do so.

Being dissociated/disembodied was a way for me to feel safe in a hostile environment. The price was that, being disembodied, I never *really* felt safe because I couldn't even *get* to my body to protect it—or to be protected by it.

There is no getting away from this fact: man has violence within him, and, willy-nilly, it must come out. Hence there is no denying that movies (like sport and wrestling and all the other pastimes, including sex) may serve as catharses by which this violence can be experienced, vicariously, and hence released.

This sounds deep and meaningful, but did I really know what I was saying? It would have been better if I'd said it like this. There's no way for me to get away from the fact that I have violence in me, and, one way or another, it's going to come out. Apparently movies (unlike sport or wrestling and other pastimes which I have no interest in, and in the absence of sex, which I am not getting) serve as a cathartic way for me to experience my own violence, vicariously, and possibly to some degree, to release it (without terrorizing small, helpless animals).

Had I written *The Blood Poets* like this, however, I doubt I'd have found a publisher, and my grand plan to conquer Hollywood and wreak revenge on an indifferent/hostile world would have come to nothing. It didn't come to anything anyway, because my lack of upfrontness or honesty was the result of being divided in myself, unable to look more closely and unflinchingly at the subjects I was discussing. I was writing the book as a way to complete the construction of an identity—as "movie shaman"—which began in adolescence, to establish myself in the world. I wasn't (consciously) trying to take that identity apart, and the Hollywood dream along with it, as I now am.

My tolerance for people who flinch from screen violence, and insist that they have no time for violent movies, is extremely low. It seems to me nothing other than moral squeamishness, which is one of the most contemptible weaknesses there is. Yet this weakness is, to all intents and purposes, presented to us as virtue.

These words were addressed indirectly to my father. I was certainly aware of it at the time I wrote them, but not aware enough to acknowledge it, either at the time of writing or with my father afterwards (man to man). My father read the first volume of *The Blood Poets* (and some of the second) and was proud of me for writing it. He didn't say this to me, exactly, but others close to him told me, and I knew he kept the books in the communal toilet to be sure any visitors would see them. As a young man, he'd aspired to being a writer but his dream died after he married my mother and entered his father's business.

According to Robert Bly, a male child who doesn't receive the father's blessing suffers the equivalent of an axe blow to his soul, a wound that never heals. My father wasn't even around to give his blessing, and when he was he mostly communicated indifference and discomfort. (When I visited him at weekends he spent most of the time hiding behind his newspaper.) The closest I got to his blessing was when I was published, but it was far too little, too late. The first book I published included, in the first few pages, an open if indirect expression of contempt for him. He was the man who flinched from screen violence and presented his "moral squeamishness" as virtue. That was the paternal program I was fighting against, and it's no coincidence that the unconscious "catharsis" I found to release my own violent rage against my mother took form as, or through, my father's shadow: an immersion in film violence. Maybe I wrote the book so he would know?

If movies can serve to bring us closer to understanding our feelings about violence, our fear and our fascination and our loathing of it, then they have served a useful, essential purpose, a social function no less, and deserve to be tolerated, as does all art, no matter how shocking or "immoral" they may ostensibly be. This is apparently the bottom line on all questions of censorship.

This is what I read between the lines of this passage today: if what I communicate, or what I *am*, can bring you, the big other — the *father* — closer to understanding your feelings about violence (or about *me*), then haven't I served a useful, essential purpose in your life? Don't I deserve to be tolerated, no matter how shocking or immoral (or worse, insignificant) I may appear to you? This is, palpably, the bottom line of all questions raised here. Whatever hypocrisy I recognized in my father — and to the extent that it caused contempt in me — exists in me. The sublimations of the fathers are inherited by the sons. I suspect that my father's own capacity for violence, which came out in passive aggression towards our mother and impatience with us, was mostly rechanneled (sublimated) into his remarkable success as a business mogul (at one point his business included the slaughter of livestock!). But besides this, whatever aspects of his character my father rejected in himself were inevitably picked up by his sons—and both of us adopted negative identities which quite openly *enjoyed* the *idea* of destruction. It was what innocents did to feel safe.

When I went to Morocco, it was because I wanted to go somewhere where "everyone would be really nasty to me." Was I unconsciously seeking to recreate my home environment? It was my own internalized violence (self-harming) that made me feel constantly *un*safe. Going to Morocco, where I would *really* be unsafe, and having to deal with the possibility of externalized violence breaking out at any time (which it occasionally did), was, ironically, a way for me to find a measure of internal peace. It wasn't myself but my negative identity—my father's shadow side and unlived life—which I wanted to destroy. How fitting that it was a *writer*—Paul Bowles, whom my father probably never read—who validated that self-destructive side; and how fitting that I had to go all the way to darkest Africa to find for myself a positive father figure.

When I first met Bowles, I told him why I'd come to Morocco: "I was looking for adversity, before it came looking for me." He nodded, apparently understanding all too well. "Oh, if adversity comes looking for us," he said, "we're sunk." Sometimes the only way to survive is to try not to.

The Soul of the Plot

The Technology of Dissociation

"Through a circle that ever returneth in
To the self-same spot
And much of Madness and more of Sin
And Horror the Soul of the Plot."
—Edgar Allan Poe, "The Conqueror Worm"

From *The Blood Poets*:

> There is a largely unconsidered dimension to film criticism
> cum cultural studies, and that is the subject of cinema as a tool
> for "social engineering." This idea is far from a new one, but
> it is one little indulged by most film critics, convinced as they
> seem to be that movies remain a 'harmless' and largely diver-
> sionary form of 'simple' entertainment. I would agree with
> this assessment, of course, up to a point, for it is just such
> escapist qualities that attracted me to movies (as opposed to
> other art forms) in the first place. And yet... The power of the
> image should never be underestimated.

When I wrote this back in 1998, what I wasn't disclosing was that
I fully subscribed to a paranoid worldview and saw history as
nothing less than a sequence of vast, sinister conspiracies of
cosmic dimensions. My *weltanschauung* was Phil-Dickian, and
probably best encapsulated by the John Carpenter B-movie *They
Live* (at least until *The Matrix* came along, just before I handed in
the final draft of *The Blood Poets*). Now, in 2013, my *weltanschauung* is post-paranoia. It's not that I no longer believe history
is a sequence of vast, sinister conspiracies of cosmic dimensions;
it's that I no longer consider it so important. If what we take for

reality is a matrix, then *everything* is metaphor, including the idea that reality is a matrix. What interests me nowadays is how I unconsciously, instinctively constructed an *internal* matrix in my early years, as a defense against reality, and how that constructed identity keeps me imprisoned, Rapunzel-like, inside a 24-hour movie playing on the inside of my mind. More specifically, how I allowed (or used) movies *to tell me who I am.*

In the passage quoted above, I juxtapose the seemingly "harmless" nature of movies as escapist entertainment with their more covert and sinister function for brainwashing or behavior modification. Now I'd say that movies' power to provide escape—to both exploit and exacerbate our learned capacity to dissociate from reality—is exactly what makes them so effective as tools for social control. At the risk of repeating myself, it's now increasingly obvious to me that writing *The Blood Poets* was an unconscious attempt to undo this programming by exposing the inner workings of it. I only went halfway; while I deconstructed most of my favorite movies (the violent ones), I didn't take the next logical step and look at the inner workings of my own crucial fiction as moviegoer, movie writer, and aspiring movie shaman. *The Blood Poets* not only has a paranoid tone but a cautionary one. I didn't understand that the most compelling and persuasive cautionary tale we can tell is our own, because that's the story that made us paranoid to begin with.

*

The fact that the director, if he knows what he is doing, becomes a kind of "mind-controller," not only of the individual but of the mass, should in no way be underesti- mated. Hitchcock may have been a "master"; but if so, he has a thousand disciples.

When I was a teenager, a film director was the ultimate goal to aspire to, the supreme achievement in life. For whatever reason, perhaps because he was an obvious misfit, I chose Polanski as my identification figure. His films (the early ones, and the first I saw) were raw and trancelike exercises in film-as-dissociation; of all filmmakers, Polanski's life, starting in the Nazi concentration camps and reaching a dark zenith in 1969 with the murder of his wife and unborn son (followed by his flight from the US for statutory rape charges in 1977), was unmistakably traumatic, and his movies, both pre- and post-Manson, reflected that trauma. Polanski was a little guy who was also an artist, a unique sensibility who, against the odds, attained the most desirable status (to me) possible in the Western world. I imagined the same great destiny for myself, minus the tragedy and trauma. Like many people I had blocked most of my own childhood out of memory. All I knew was I wanted to become a master of the fates of others and to be adored for it. To be an artist with worldly power, what could be grander than that? What could be safer?

I was born in 1967, in the Spring of Love, four weeks after Ira Levin's instant best-seller, *Rosemary's Baby*, was published, and exactly one year after *Time*'s "Is God Dead?" cover (which appears in Polanski's movie of Levin's book). These might seem like minor details, but not to me. At fourteen or fifteen I had a copy of Barbra Leaming's *Polanski*, and reading it was probably the first time I gained more than a passing acquaintance with the Manson family. Looking back on it, my guess is that, since I was disturbed by my own peculiar sexual propensities, I took comfort in knowing that Polanski had been embraced, not despite but *for* his perversity (until he wasn't). His work was proof that it was possible to turn madness into method. My fascination with Polanski as a teenager was later validated when I became immersed in researching Satanic conspiracies and mind control in my twenties. I didn't know it at the time, but by going so deep into Polanski's life and work in my adolescence, I was unconsciously acknowledging an affinity which would take me all the way from movies to occultism, conspiracy lore, Ufology, alien abductions, and finally (in 2013) into the psychology of trauma and dissociation. And now the circle has returned in to the self-same spot.

In *The Blood Poets*, I presented Polanski's story as a cautionary one. Success in Hollywood, I implied, required a figurative (maybe even a literal) deal with the devil, exactly as Guy Woodhouse (played by Jonathan Lethem's hero John Cassavetes) makes with the witches in *Rosemary's Baby*'s. Once upon a time the evidence for a similar reading of Polanski's unlikely success story proved compelling to me, maybe because my own fear was that success invariably leads to (or is the proof of) corruption. In good Poe fashion, my contempt for success was maddeningly combined with an obsessive desire for it, an internal conflict which can be sourced, like everything else, in early childhood. My father was a successful businessman who had no time for his children: like Guy Woodhouse, he sacrificed his duties as a father for worldly ambition. Maybe this was partly why he seemed to regard his success with disdain bordering on contempt? Certainly, it would explain why *I* do.

Those who are mind-controlled want to control others. That's the nature of the beast. Trauma infects the psyche and tries to pass itself on, down the generations. Making movies about trauma and dissociation as Polanski did (as *all* of my favorite filmmakers did, pretty much) is a way to exorcise those demons without becoming a psychopath or a pariah. The trouble is that, if demons animate the art, eventually the artist will become both dependent on and vulnerable to those demons. Hitchcock's mastery of the film medium was cruelly shadowed by his impotence (perhaps literally) as a husband and a father. As various books and two recent movies suggest, he tortured his actresses not only to create his "art " but out of unconscious hostility towards his mother. The two drives, creative and destructive, were one obsession. To be a master of the world means, above all, never letting one's guard down. It means allowing the inner guardian to master you, because otherwise, the Master Plan will come all unraveled.

*

"All this filming isn't healthy."
—Blind mother from *Peeping Tom*

In the first draft of this essay, I tried to describe the ways in which movies could be used for social engineering, but the subject proved too large and complex for me to make sense out of it. Then I remembered how I wrote about *Peeping Tom* in the introduction to *The Blood Poets*, and how the film's story pretty much encapsulates the themes of this present chapter. *Peeping Tom* came out in 1960, the year after Polanski graduated from film school and the year Hitchcock released *Psycho*. The film is about a young photographer, Mark, who is tormented as a child by his father (played by the film's director, Michael Powell), a sadistic scientist obsessed with "fear and the nervous system" who subjects his son to perverse experiments, including constant filming. Mark grows up under the permanent gaze of his father's eye, represented by the camera, and he is formed in this "image." As an adult, he takes to murdering young women and filming them in their final moments: using a camera mounted on a tripod, a steel spike attached to the end of one of its legs, a mirror attached to the camera to allow the victims to witness their own deaths.

The film is obviously a metaphor, and it traces quite clearly how the desire to control others, the sadistic impulse, and the urge to make (and watch) films are all inextricably intertwined. Probably the most interesting thing about *Peeping Tom* (which is quite ineffective as a movie, it's not even that scary) is how it was received by the public and the effect it had on the director's career: it more or less ended it. This is what I wrote in *The Blood*

Poets:

Audiences and critics balked fiercely at being made accomplices to Powell's perverse vision ... Powell is confessing—in the most public manner possible—to his own sense of complicity in, and fascination for, the acts of perversity which the film portrays. *Peeping Tom* is a more "serious" work than *Psycho*, and that's exactly what makes it less successful. It sets out to do what no single film ever could—to trace the lines between fact and fantasy, between the act and the imagination, and in the process it shows those lines to be fuzzy indeed. [T]he film portrays [Mark] as a victim throughout, driven and tormented by his own obsession. This is presumably how Powell himself felt at the time, and *Peeping Tom* may well be so popular among filmmakers because it amounts to every director's worst nightmare of himself—a voyeur who preys on human weakness and fear. [But] *Peeping Tom* [has] an abyss at its center. Finally, it appears to be the camera itself—or the impersonal act of filming (or even looking)—that becomes the antagonist. So where does that leave us? *Peeping Tom* is a metaphysical tragedy without a metaphysic: it raises questions that it can never hope to answer, and it leaves audiences feeling exposed, violated, disturbed. In a world where looks kill and no one is innocent, there seems little else to be *but* disturbed. *Peeping Tom* was, I suspect, a kind of exorcism for Powell, and as such it was certainly effective—his demons are all up there on the screen, and the film effectively ended his career in cinema. Is it any wonder his public turned on him? You can't unleash your demons on your audience and expect them to love you for it. Making *Peeping Tom* may have been a cathartic experience for Powell (he described it as a "nice film" about "memory"); but, for the rest of us, watching it may be closer to hearing confession.

Was Powell deliberately committing career suicide with the film? Was he coming clean about his sins, knowing exactly how it would be received but determined to make peace with himself at any cost? What's it say about the film industry that, where Polanski could break the law and flee justice but still go on making movies and eventually win the Oscar, Powell couldn't get away with making *a movie* that exposed our complicity with film violence? The only thing I can think about it is that, however unsatisfying *Peeping Tom* might have been as a work of art, Powell's thesis was sound. So if movies are murder, what exactly is being killed?

*

"Just on the basis of the technology itself, the invention, the moving picture, it's … not sure what the word would be, you can say 'rank' but fucked up is just as accurate. So what if a moving image has been achieved? You see moving images if you just open your eyes. Things are moving all around you. So what if you can artificially evoke a 'moving image'? To then start making 'movies' out of it, demanding people's attention, the shit starts there. Even if you're just watching those first images of a train arriving in a station, why not just jump up and say "Sure, interesting, but why the fuck am I sitting here watching this on a screen?"

—Phil Snyder, in text chat with author

Why are we sitting here watching a simulation of reality on movie screen? Because reality is what we want to escape from, and to do that, the simulation needs to be convincing enough for us to mistake it for real.

Movies are like artificial, collective dreams. Virtual reality is obviously the next, crucial step; but if, for the sake of argument, we think of a cinema audience as being hooked up to the screen, sharing in a dream and leaving the theatre with this dream forming an intrinsic and inseparable part of their psyches (both consciously and—far more insidious—unconsciously), we may start to suspect how profound the effects of even the most "forgettable" movie are. [E]ven a mediocre film, so far as it successfully suspends our disbelief and ushers us into its "reality," achieves a hypnotic power over us, at least for as long as we give in to it. Movies cast a spell, and this is above all what accounts for their charm, their magic, their lasting appeal, and, what is far less acknowledged, their insidious power to sway us.

None of this has prevented me from watching more and more movies—including mediocre ones. What is the definition of addiction? Is an alcoholic addicted to alcohol or to the experience of numbed out, blissful, dissociation which it gives him (or her)? If I'm addicted to losing myself in fantasy worlds, and if my own inner state has become a fantasy world built in imitation of those fantasy worlds, how can I ever get clear of that addiction? Can I even try without entering a still deeper layer of fantasy?

Movies show us the machinery of our dissociation. We spend months, years, and millions upon millions of dollars, organizing individuals and groups, creating technology, giving out awards, feeding an industry whose primary purpose is to help us *forget* our existence for a brief time and escape into an imaginary life where we can enjoy the relief of *not being ourselves*. When Woody Allen said "My only regret in life is that I wasn't born someone else," he voiced the message that defined the medium (advertising): the promise of a new, socially engineered identity. When a movie fully engages us we say we're *absorbed* by it. We lose ourselves into the narrative and the words and images effectively take over our consciousness. If we are totally absorbed in a movie then we are also possessed *by* it. Our soul *becomes* the plot, and vice versa.

The filmmaker-as-father-sadist-scientist of *Peeping Tom* creates a monster out of the misguided attempt to understand and control fear, using film and his own offspring to do it. The film's director did roughly the same, fathered a film about fear that became a monster and that, like Frankenstein's creature, "destroyed" its creator (his career anyway). When we take refuge in images (dreams) as a way to escape the terror of reality, there's always the danger we will wind up lost in the most terrifying realm of all—the disembodied realm in which thoughts are things and looks can, and do, kill.

In *The Pervert's Guide to the Cinema*, Slavoj Žižek said, "We escape into dream to avoid a deadlock in our real life. But then what we encounter in the dream is even more horrible, so that we literally escape from the dream into reality." How does this work? Why is Horror the Soul of every Plot? The best I can come up with for an answer is that, when we use dream to escape from reality, we take refuge in the unconscious, and the unconscious is where trauma goes to "die," and hence where *the real horrors lie*. If we are *lucky* we are shocked out of dream (now nightmare) and back to reality. If we're not so lucky, our dreams become reality. In Powell's case, he made a confessional movie about his trauma and how making movies was *his* way to escape it and the price he paid for that (becoming the villain of his own movie). He then paid the price in real life, when the public rejected his offering and him along with it, by becoming the villain (scapegoat) and losing his career. In Polanski's case, he dreamed his way from a Nazi concentration camp to Cielo ("Heaven") Drive, Beverly Hills, making a movie about a "Guy" (Cassavetes, also a filmmaker, an anti-Hollywood one!) who cuts a deal with the devil and gives up *his unborn son* for success. Lo and behold, success was his (*Rosemary's Baby* was Polanski's breakthrough hit in Hollywood). The following year, his wife and unborn child were murdered. And because the event seemed so uncannily like something out of one of his movies, the mainstream media (portions of it at least) *blamed Polanski* for what had happened.

Of course they were wrong, just as the critics were wrong to condemn Powell for *his* fantasy life. But at the same time, were they also *right*? When the suppressed trauma that drives us into the dream-life bubbles up to the surface and storms our heaven—when reality turns inexorably to nightmare—it's our own unconscious that's directing the show. It's the technology of dissociation come to life.

Lethem Lives

Hot and Cold Paranoia (An Essay About a Book About a Movie About Alien Mind Control)

"Sleepwalkers, leave other sleepwalkers alone!"
— Jonathan Lethem, *Chronic City*

While first planning this book, after devouring *The Disappointment Artist* in a day, I ordered and read Jonathan Lethem's *They Live*. It provided an interesting, not-unwelcome, challenge for someone whose primary ideology pertains to pop culture. In the second volume of *The Blood Poets*, I wrote that, if morality is little more than a matter of taste, taste becomes nothing less than a question of morality. The first thought I had after reading *They Live* was: How did Jonathan Lethem manage to write an entire book (admittedly a small one) about John Carpenter's 1988 B-movie *They Live* without once using the word "ludicrous"? I don't think I could write a first *sentence* about this movie without it (I didn't, anyway). The word seems to have been *made* for the film; or maybe it's the reverse, and John Carpenter's movie generously provided the context for the apotheosis of the word "ludicrous"? Whichever, Jonathan Lethem is a serious guy, with I think only a few ludicrous bones in his body, and if he takes *They Live* seriously enough to write a (small) book about it, then, damn it, so will I.

*

The next word I want to present to the reader is actually a phrase, once popular in certain circles: "cognitive dissonance." It's a handy phrase here, now, because *They Live*, the movie, in its supremely ludicrous fashion, is "all about" cognitive dissonance.

But that's not why I wanted to introduce the phrase. That was because reading Jonathan Lethem's *They Live* caused far more cognitive dissonance in me than watching John Carpenter's *They Live* ever could. Here's a sometimes brilliant writer, with whom I recently discovered an unexpected affinity and have been enjoying an embryonic relationship via email (a medium in which relationships can stay embryonic for years without ever being born), here's Jonathan Lethem, a man with many fish to fry, books to write, tours to do, lectures to give, emails to read and write, children to raise, and so on, spending who knows how long writing a pretty-good-but-not-great book about a movie which, for all its David-Ickian paranoia and maybe-just-a-little-ahead-of-its-time-ness, can't, in my mind at least, be fully divorced from the word "ludicrous."

Then again, a lot of people would say the same about David Icke. Hmm. What was the question again?

*

I think the answer has something to do with paranoia. How we (Jonathan and I, and anyone else) explore it, express it, digest it, assimilate it and disseminate it. One of the most surprising things to many people about Jonathan Lethem is that he's paranoid, not in the clinical, "Should-I-be-worried?" sense, but in the hip, socio-politically aware sense. So now the question inevitably surfaces in my own mind, like a creature from the black lagoon: which is David Icke? More to the point, what does Jonathan Lethem think of David Icke? I find myself wondering if, in any of the interviews he presumably gave for *They Live*, this question ever came up. Lethem and Icke seem to exist in separate worlds, yet they are worlds which I have frequented, and even represented, not only as a reader but as a writer and researcher.

They Live (the book) would seem to be a very tangible—and functional—bridge between them.

*

Paranoia.

Next I find myself wondering if Jonathan Lethem has any time at all for David Icke. And how about Slavoj Žižek, who talks about Carpenter's *They Live* in his new film, *A Pervert's Guide to Ideology*? I suspect not. I suspect (though I'm only guessing) that's partly why Lethem and Žižek treasure a movie like *They Live* (which *does* have its moments, maybe I will get to them), because it allows them to briefly hang out in Icke-land without feeling too … icky. If so (and it's only a guess), I don't blame them. I have spent my time in Icke-land (full disclosure: though I never went to one of his presentations, I have listened to quite a few of his interviews and even read one of his books all the way through), and I can't honestly say it was all that edifying. Not as edifying as Jonathan Lethem's *They Live*, anyway, or Žižek's *Pervert's Guide to the Cinema*; but also not nearly as ludicrous as John Carpenter's *They Live*.

It would seem there are two kinds of paranoia—*cool* paranoia of the playful, postmodernist, academic or pseudo-academic, Marxist or quasi-Marxist, Lethemic and Žižekian paranoia; and "hot" or *un*cool paranoia of literal-minded whistleblowers of *actual*, nuts-and-bolt occult global conspiracies, such as Icke and his ilk.

*

"My parents were Vietnam War protesters; I grew up in the era of Watergate; the first president I remember is Nixon. I remember being instructed as a child that I shouldn't go to school and blurt that Nixon was evil. Not that we didn't *know* he was evil at home, it just might not be such a good idea for me to say it. I felt he was evil like Dracula. It was like being taught not to curse when you go to your grandmother's. So when I found that Rod Serling and

Philip K. Dick and Thomas Pynchon also agreed with me that the president was probably an evil robot programmed by a computer, it was merely a matter of pleasurable recognition that someone was naming the world. In that sense, I'm a native. When you say I don't appear paranoiac to you, I figure you mean I don't traffic in the thin membrane of social paranoia. Why bother? We live in a fallen universe. We can at least be kind to one another and not jump on one another's slightest errors or moods. In a desperate situation, pick your battles."

—Jonathan Lethem, *Paris Review* 2003

When I was a teenager, a few years before the fall of the Berlin Wall, my mother bought me a T-Shirt with "I Heart Gorbachev" on it. I wore it for a couple of years, not so much because I loved Gorbachev but because I despised conventional political ideologies and I thought it was cool and subversive to have a Russian premier on my chest. That was the first and last time I ever endorsed a political figure.

While I have never known quite how literally to take David Icke's view that the world is run by shape-shifting blood-drinking Reptilians disguised as human beings, like Lethem (at least Lethem circa 2003) I accepted it as a useful metaphor. I still think it is probably closer to the truth than the common view that political leaders are just people like you and me, only a bit more corrupt. To this day I (sort of) see the world as controlled by nonhuman agencies that use the *appearance* of humanness (or simply use human beings) to further their unfathomable aims. I am, from the common perspective, paranoid. But it's not a social paranoia and I don't watch news clips of politicians trying to count how many times they blink per minute. I just leave the question open and am careful not to assume anything when it comes to global events, public figures, and so forth.

Icke's list of Reptilians masquerading as human beings includes some celebrities: Kris Kristofferson for example, who was in Scorsese's *Alice Doesn't Live Here Anymore* and, obliquely, in *Taxi Driver*, when Betsy quotes his music to Travis and Travis naively buys her the album. Kristofferson even plays a Reptilian-like insider in probably the best (most sinister) scene in Richard Linklater's *Fast Food Nation*. I don't really know what to make of all this, but I do think that something is far from right in the world of the power elite, and that, while it may not literally involve scaly skin and blood drinking rituals, if we knew the truth we might be no less shocked by it. One of the figures Icke named a decade or more ago was Jimmy Savile, who, it recently came to light, was behaving in ways more easily associated with a Vampire or alien predator than the harmless talk show host we took him to be when I was growing up. (More on Savile in Part Two.)

This is the world I have mostly stayed out of, besides long-distance research which many would consider lunatic-fringy; yet at the same time, I have put a great deal of energy and effort trying to gain access to it. Not the world of politics, that is, but of show business. And since it's widely accepted that politics *is* show business, it's only a matter of time before the penny drops and we realize that show business is also politics.

So what does this have to do with Jonathan Lethem? For one thing, because Lethem feels like kindred, and based on all appearances, he has accessed "that world." So my interest in him is both professional *and* personal.

*

The first book I ever saw with Jonathan Lethem's name on it was *The Exegesis of Philip K. Dick*. At the time I didn't know Lethem from *Lethal Weapon* (I didn't know dick about him). Since Dick was my unwitting introduction to him, the idea that the best-selling, award-winning author, McCarthy-fellowship receiver, and Disney Professor of Writing, might at heart be *one of us* (the

Reptilian resistance—only kidding!) was always a given to me, never a surprise. The surprise was how square he might seem based on his more "high-profile" work and status. An outsider like Icke (or Dick) he ain't. Lethem immersed himself in Dick-land (alas, not a rhyme for Icke-land) from an early age, and so far he has managed not to go insane, become a paranoid messiah *à la* Icke (or Dick *almost*, in the last years), or convert to Christianity. Based on this, it seems like he has a high tolerance for paranoid awareness, even if he draws the line at... certain subjects we won't talk about.

The difference between Dick and Icke is that one was a sci-fi author of high intelligence who explored beguiling philosophical and spiritual questions about the nature of reality while writing ground-breaking novels (a bit like Jonathan Lethem, potentially at least?), and the other, well, why be cruel, the other does something else (something distinctly more *L. Ron*-like). David Icke takes himself and the whole *They Live* scenario just a little bit *too* seriously for anyone of discerning intelligence (like Žižek or Lethem) to want to take Icke seriously, at all. Nonetheless, the fact remains that the only thing—to my mind— which can really account for (I won't say justify) Jonathan Lethem's abiding fascination for *They Live*, the only thing that redeems it from the adjective every artist most dreads having applied to him or her work, or him- or herself, is that, like *The Matrix* after it and at some as-yet-undisclosed-how-metaphorical level—*it's all true*. And that you don't have to be a Marxist to say so.

*

Lethem's *They Live* is fun. It's a lot more fun than the movie, which I rewatched for the first time since it came out in preparation for reading the book. But is it really subversive? If the medium is the message, maybe for Jonathan Lethem (best-selling award-winning author, McCarthy-fellowship receiver, and

Disney Professor of Writing), writing a book about a ludicrous little movie that only geeks, Marxists, and full-blown paranoids could possibly take seriously for the ninety minutes it takes to watch it (much less the time it takes to write an exegesis on it), maybe that's a more *subversive* act than touring the world and Spreading the Truth About Our Reptilian Overlords could ever be? Frankly, I don't see David Icke as doing anything really subversive, at all, even *if* it's all true. I think it's all part of The Plot. So maybe I just answered my own question? Maybe the best kind of subversion is the kind that doesn't seem all that subversive, at all?

So what would have drawn me to Jonathan Lethem to begin with if he *weren't* a subversive author? Because for me, art is either subversive or it's just helping people pass the time on the way to their graves (i.e., all part of The Plot), which is why I could (once upon a time) write something as seemingly incendiary as "taste is as important as morality." Which leads me to a more pertinent question: what's the good in being subversive if no one reads you? Or if the wrong people do? Maybe Lethem's kind of subversion entails disguising his subversive intentions well enough to join the system he means to subvert? A dangerous question indeed. But if so, it's a bit disappointing he didn't let his *true* paranoid pedigree shine through more in *They Live*.

Philip K. Dick's *Exegesis* is a thousand-page exercise (culled, I presume partly by Lethem, from a million-page exercise) in making subversion into an art form, albeit a very *private* art form since Dick never intended his notes to be read by anyone. So Lethem is no slouch when it comes to getting a hundred percent *behind* someone else's subversive vision. But is he *hiding* behind it? Whatever else it is, *They Live* is a very funny book, a chuckle-out-loud book. It has to be in order not to become as ludicrous — or as paranoid — as its subject matter. It's hard to say what Lethem is making fun of, however — the movie, its paranoid worldview, or himself for being so drawn to them. But in the right context —

the world being an illusion to disguise the fact that we are enslaved to inhuman intelligences, just *say*—humor *can* become a subversive act. Not too many chuckles at a David Icke presentation, are there? And if it really *were* all true, wouldn't the only possible *sane* response *have* to include laughter?

*

Actually the first half hour of *They Live*, up to the "cheese dip moment," which is the point when Nada starts hurling muscle-brained insults at the ghouls, is pretty good. The movie could have ended there, with the line, "It *figures* it would be something like *this!*" and we wouldn't have lost much. The only thing we'd have lost, really, is the infamous back alley fight sequence, by far the best of what's left after the movie "dives into the cheese dip." The reason the fight sequence transcends the rest of the action is that, once the movie becomes fully self-aware and owns up to how ludicrous it is, we are freed from the seat-shifting, skin-squirming, eye-rolling experience of "Did he/she/they *really* say/do/expect us to *believe that?*" Even better than the fight sequence is the aftermath, when Nada and Frank stagger like zombies to their fleapit motel room, whether to lick their own wounds or each other's, it's never fully divulged.

*

Returning to cognitive dissonance. The real dilemma for me isn't how paranoid Jonathan Lethem may or may not be. It's how can he possibly say *They Live* is a good movie, and can I still respect him in the morning? I am sinking to (self-) satire now, because it's the only way to admit that, for some of us (me), the assignation of value to pop culture is an ideological question just as important as distribution of power and wealth. In the same way, someone's integrity and trustworthiness as a human being can sometimes seem to depend upon such a question. It's crazy I know, but all ideology is, and no one is immune.

If *They Live*, at some, who-knows-how metaphorical level, is all true, if human beings are just livestock sleep-stumbling like ex-Wrestlers making a pathetic attempt to break into screen acting through an alien-controlled screen-reality with no clue what's really going on behind the scenes (and only the Ickes, Dicks, and John Carpenters of the world to clue us in), *who the fuck cares whose movie is better*? If any of this *were* true, then the truth would make what we previously took for reality appear *utterly ludicrous*. So maybe being ludicrous is part of the point? Maybe what we think of as reality looks like *a really crappy B-movie* once we are through to the other side of the "screen"?

Isn't a movie that *tells it like it is*, no matter how ludicrous, better than a masterpiece that doesn't (say Sam Peckinpah's *The Wild Bunch*, which Lethem compares *They Live* to on three occasions)? If it's all fake, is a movie that forces us to endure the hell of a crummy, 2-D, totally unconvincing sham of a simulation of a good movie (never mind reality) providing a more authentic and *useful* service than one that casts a magnificent spell over us and makes us believe it's not only as good as but even *better* than "life"?

I am tempted to answer, with Nada-like bravado, "Fuck NO!" But I'm afraid it would sound as hollow and ludicrous as Nada's bubblegum battle cry in the face of an alien apocalypse.

So I will just leave it open for now.

The Boy Who Cried Polanski

"All Thinking is Wishful."
— Jonathan Lethem, *You Don't Love Me Yet*

Movies are manufactured visions. Once upon a time I went on vision quests to see certain movies which I believed would grant me special knowledge and power. Now I know I was deceived, that what I was seeking wasn't on the screen but *behind* it, so to speak. It's as if Dorothy went to Oz but forgot to take Toto with her and the curtain never got drawn aside and she came away believing she'd really got to see the Wizard, knowing, deep down, that something wasn't right. Eventually she would *have* to return, to peak behind that curtain and see for herself what was or wasn't there. I am compelled, too, though I know it might mean the end of all my stories.

In a book called *Spiritual Enlightenment: the Damnedest Thing*, Jed McKenna describes something he calls *spiritual autolysis*. Autolysis is self-digestion, and basically what "McKenna" (a pseudonym) proscribes is deconstructing the false identity by writing. McKenna, the author/character of the books, claims that's how he got enlightened, by writing. Isn't that just what a writer *would* say? I don't believe it's possible to totally digest oneself until there's nothing left but truth, not by writing anyway. Yet I live *as if* I believed it. It's my "true goal" (i.e., the one I most want to believe in), even after all my small successes and massive failures have proven, time and time again, that I will probably never achieve it. I can say that I write because it's my way of deconstructing the lies of my false identity and getting to the bedrock of my experience. But chances are, that's only what I tell myself because the false identity *needs* to write to keep itself going. Like an alcoholic with his alcohol, I use writing to keep the hazy cloud of unknowing intact, to keep reality at bay.

I am a deconstruction artist. I never tire of finding still deeper layers of "text" to break down to their constituents and find out what's beneath them. I also never seem to cease believing that, someday, I will reach the "ground"—pay streak. But I also write to get the world's attention. I write in the hope it will provide me with a platform from which I will receive a never-ending stream of admiration, and this desire never seems to go away. Either way, writing provides me with a feeling of engagement, purpose, and meaning, whether it's with my inner world or the outer one. There's process and there's product, and you can have process without product (write with your finger or invisible ink, write and then delete it all), but you can't ever have product without process. *Ex nihilo nihil fit*, nothing comes from nothing. The means must always justify the end.

As I sit here, the only part of me that's moving are my hands and arms. My attention is on rows of keys and on the small characters on a computer screen. That's it. What's engaged most of all is my so-called mind. The architect of illusions. The controller of worlds, a mere chimera, a collection of snowflakes posing as a snowball. I am writing another book about movies. I write about movies because I love to watch them. Movies are an escape from my thoughts. Of course I am still thinking when I watch a movie, but if it's good enough I'm thinking about what's going on in the movie instead of (so much) my own life. In that sense, a movie is a transcendental experience, it allows me to transcend, momentarily, my identity. A bit like alcohol, but like alcohol, after the spell is over my identity comes back, as petulant and resilient as ever.

I have few illusions about movies; I watch them as a way to unwind and zone out of physical-mental existence. It's like sleeping with my eyes open, a ready-made dream to download. On the other hand, because it's mentally relaxing for me, it's possible I am more in my body when I'm watching a movie than at other times. Not with my awareness (I don't focus on my body when I watch a movie), but in some sense I may be more aligned with my body, more settled into it. When we sleep we certainly are, and even drunks are said to fall down stairs better than sober people. (By "better" I don't mean more frequently or rapidly but without harming themselves so much.)

My goal is to write with the total body. To write as a means to become embodied, and to allow the process of embodiment to inform what I write and give it substance, blood, *body*, so the reader can receive a literary transfusion and become more embodied too. As I write, hour after hour, week after week, and year after year, I am waiting. I am waiting for that final break-through, the epiphany in which all the pieces come together for an instant and I see the method of my madness and let it all go, watch my identity disperse into nothingness and nowhereness, leaving only the echo of an unraveled life. The moment it all comes to an end and I am finally *done*. At the same time, part of me hopes that the moment I find that authentic core, my true voice, I will produce something so profound that the curtain of anonymity will draw aside and I will be shuttled onto the world's stage, an audience of millions wildly applauding.

I know this is all crap. The internal breakthrough, if it's real, won't leave me holding a Pulitzer Prize but be the end of my story forever. An empty stage, with no audience, no performer, no prizes, *nada—No hay banda*. The self-digested author. The part of me that's motivated to pursue the process of writing to create a product that will launch my career doesn't understand this. The catch of spiritual autolysis is that no one ever reads it. I can't be totally honest if I am writing to be read. I can't even be totally honest when I'm *not* writing to be read, when it's only me, myself, and mine. We are bullshit to the end.

The desire to make a good impression and the desire to get clear of the false identity (which only cares about the impression it's making) can't co-exist. It's one or the other. If I really believed

I could write myself to freedom, I would stop writing to be read and get down to it. But I'm afraid that then I'd stop writing at all.

*

The writer is working on another book, and already looking for ways to get it published. He (that's me) is already "dreaming" of holding a shiny artifact at the end of all his labors, with great satisfaction. But I've already published seven or eight books (I first typed "boobs" there, and was tempted to leave it). I know that the difference those shiny artifacts have made on my inner life is roughly *zero*. I am still looking for the father's blessing, for the approval I never got, that came far too late and was way too little. A few months ago, I received an email from Jonathan Lethem in response to a piece I'd written on Philip K. Dick and autism. I printed up the email and put it on the wall over my desk. I can see it now. It starts with the words "something really special." Lethem is an established author whose books have been optioned as movies by David Lynch and David Cronenberg; he might as well be my own frustrated dream made flesh. (He also toys with the idea of being on the autism spectrum.) Receiving his blessing, the unequivocal praise of his emails (there was more than one), provided the validation I was desperately seeking. When an author who's universally recognized as being a significant literary figure recognizes me as a peer, does that mean I am getting close to universal recognition? Or am I doomed to being a writer's writer, recognized by his peers but not by the general public, at least not while alive (like John Fante, say)? Then of course there's the possibility—impossible for my mind not to play with, like picking at a scab—that The Lethem might be able to open crucial doors for me, to usher me from obscurity to prominence—by writing a foreword to this book, for example. Or an afterword. Or an interlude. How about a signed footnote?

A little after making contact with Lethem, I found this quote from him online:

> I felt I ought to thrive on my fate as an outsider. Being a paperback writer was meant to be part of that. I really, genuinely wanted to be published in shabby pocket-sized editions and be neglected—and then discovered and vindicated when I was fifty. To honor, by doing so, Charles Willeford and Philip K. Dick and Patricia Highsmith and Thomas Disch, these exiles within their own culture. I felt that was the only honorable path.

Apparently Lethem, unlike me, received his father's blessing when he needed it. He wasn't only okay with obscurity, he considered it *the only honorable path*. Naturally, because it was what he wanted, he didn't get it. So now we can both envy the greenness of the other's pasture.

Lethem's blessing can't really substitute for the father's blessing I never got. Lethem is only three years older than me, roughly the same as the difference between me and my older brother. My brother used to say that being an artist was "a license for obsession"; it was an obsession which eventually killed him, at the age of forty-eight. I will be forty-seven next year and, as I write these words, I feel my time running out. Either I kill this artistic obsession of mine or it kills me. Either I recognize and appreciate the honorability of obscurity—that this is the only path for me—and learn to love the darkness that defines whatever light I can pull out of me, or I am doomed to be eaten up by a chronic dissatisfaction which no amount of recognition—or tardy blessings—can ever satisfy. It doesn't matter how tightly you bolt the door after the horse has gone; the horse ain't coming back.

My horse has long gone. I am an exile in my own culture because that's what the prodigal son *is*: an exile. I *am* the horse that bolted, and with damn good reason. I wasn't made to be ridden.

Neigh.

*

I once had a chance to meet Polanski. It was in 1986 and I was nineteen. I had gone to Paris with my oldest friend, Adam. We grew up together and entered into shared movie-obsession in adolescence when we both discovered Clint Eastwood in the same moment, watching *Where Eagles Dare* in our separate homes and sharing our excitement afterwards. Polanski was performing in Stephen Berkoff's stage version of Kafka's *Metamorphosis*. Neither of us spoke French and we hardly understood a word of the play. Afterwards, we waited outside the stage door; my plan was to approach my childhood hero and shake his hand. I was nervous, and each time I saw someone come out of the stage door who looked vaguely like Polanski, I joked "There he is!" as a way to alleviate my fear. Eventually Polanski did come out but I failed to notice him. Only once he was getting into a vehicle did I realize who it was.

"Why didn't you say anything?" I said to Adam.

"You said you'd seen him," he said.

Of course I had. I'd said "There he is!" when Polanski came out, just as I had every time a *non*-Polanski appeared. My friend had simply assumed I'd changed my mind about approaching him.

It was my very own Hollywood fairy tale.

Part Two

Hollywood Glamor Magic

Impossible Objects

Chronic City *and Jonathan Lethem's Post-Fiction*

"Don't rupture another's illusion unless you're positive the alternative you offer is more worthwhile than that from which you're wrenching them."
—Jonathan Lethem, *Chronic City*

Over Christmas, having written the first half of this book, I read Jonathan Lethem's *Chronic City*. I took notes while reading. These are them.

Dreams for Sale (first thoughts, at page 96, chapters 1-5, Dec 23rd 2013)

Jonathan Lethem takes an active role in reshaping the culture that shaped him, not just by being a culture-maker (leading literary figure) but a culture-*un*maker. His aim is to turn the elements of his own cultural conditioning into the raw material of a mystery, a departure point into a *post-fictional reality*. Post-fiction is a stage/state in which the distinction between fiction and non-fiction is recognized as arbitrary and irrelevant, because impossible. As products of popular culture, like fish in the sea dissecting water, we can't identify ourselves as separate from it — we are defined by the fiction we write.

Is Lethem familiar with synchromysticism? A somewhat misguided attempt to apply Jung and Pauli's synchronicity to popular culture and trace patterns of meaning that are supposed to correspond to deeper/higher/occult realities. Synchromysticism falls flat because, instead of using collective culture as a way to uncover one's individual patterns and conditioning, it reverses the telescope and projects personal cultural preferences onto a supposed "mystic" cosmic reality, out there. The mistake is in supposing that external "mystical" reality is any more objectively "real" than internal fantasy and/or pop culture, when both are products of the same dissociative mechanism.

Lethem's is a refreshing voice in the field because of his apparent ignorance of/ indifference to "occult" symbolism, conspiracy theories, etc. He keeps the conspiracy local, and finds occult meanings where they are at least potentially of some practical use: not in the supposed "world at large" but in our own fantasy lives: the stories we tell ourselves to keep us in the dark.

*

Scott Fitzgerald: "The movies have stolen our dreams; of all betrayals this is the worst."

David Byrne: "Stealing all our dreams, dreams for sale, they sell 'em back to you."

Popular culture conditions us long before so-called high culture—religious, political, aesthetic ideologies—can get its hooks into us. Hence this is the primary program running our hard drives; the stories we dismiss as childish fantasies are the ones we secretly believe, at the deeper levels of being. Like the Matrix siphoning off our unconscious fantasy life and rearranging it into a semi-coherent narrative then feeding it back to us as "reality," the essence of the pop culture life is *our own essence*. The challenge (and what Lethem is attempting, if I read him right) is to extract the essence from the crust it's been encased in and take it *pure*. The stuff of dreams. Awakening means seeing reality as a dream and recognizing dreams as the original stuff of reality. It means returning to the source and ousting the pretender that peddles second grade product, the "corporations" (ideologies) that have turned water, oxygen, and dreams into commodities to control us.

Ideology is tyranny.

*

It's been a while since I saw it but I think *The Bourne Identity* might be decoded into a suitable illustration of the consciousness *coup* which Lethem's *Chronic City* is attempting. Through amnesia, Jason Bourne forgets his (false) identity, his social and political conditioning (ideology), but retains his core programming as a superspy, which is all he needs to survive. He uses his inside knowledge of the ideological control system that "created" him to infiltrate, subvert, and defy it, and ultimately to liberate himself from it. He can't actually destroy it (ideologies can never be destroyed, only returned to their unconscious constituents and made irrelevant, or better yet, retained as instructive reminders of the trap of taking fact for fiction and vice versa); but he can become such an inconvenience and a headache to it that it washes its hands of him. By becoming a thorn in the side of the lion-state, Bourne ensures his removal from the Matrix. The ideological body (culture) rejects him.

The child actor Insteadman in *Chronic City* is Jonathan Lethem's hostage-to-pop-culture, arrested-development self. Perkus Tooth is the jaded but world-wise adult who knows the nature of the Beast and who is vain (and jaded) enough to want to ride it. Both are drawn to save the other. As the child is father to the man, and the man can only become whole by fathering himself, each needs the special services of the other. Only by fully owning (up to) our unfinished childhood experience and completing it (tracing the pop cultural program back to its source) can we enter into adulthood, free from childhood illusions, to be Bourne again.

Home Away from Home (at page 186, chapters 6-10, Dec 24th)

Chronic City is a bit like *Foucault's Pendulum* without the occult symbolism and self-importance. That might sound like it doesn't leave much, and *Chronic City* is a strangely empty novel. It deliberately lacks momentum or suspense (so far). The space is there to be filled by the author's voice and sensibility, but these are equally vague, ephemeral, and diffuse. The action is lightly lethargic. What that leaves is the reader. *Chronic City* is a bit like a crossword puzzle waiting for its spaces to be filled; except it appears to be a puzzle with no right answer.

Lethem creates the sense that the real action of *Chronic City* (the world it takes place in, above and beyond the novel itself) is happening elsewhere. We are only glimpsing from the periphery the events that are determining these characters' fates. The characters don't seem to inhabit their lives. It's a novel of dissociation, neither fully here nor altogether there.

*

My initial reading (after five chapters) may have been premature projection and wishful reading on my part. It's hard to say for sure. The game Lethem plays with culture involves presenting it more or less "as is," then adding odd elements that don't belong in order to establish that this is not "our" world: it's a parallel culture in which astronauts write letters to abandoned partners, chocolate clouds descend on cities, and Marlon Brando (who may or may not be dead) delivers coded messages about the illusory nature of reality on *The Gnuppet Show*. Stuff like that.

The arresting images can easily be interpreted. The astronaut lover is the "lost object" signaling the protagonist's mother bondage. Brando, would-be savior of Manhattan, is the absent father, lost on his island eating ice cream (like a Polar bear starving to death on a block of ice). The chaldron is the transcendental object, signaling the existence of a higher dimension, that reality is indeed "elsewhere." But none of these interpretations are satisfactory. *Chronic City* isn't "that kind" of novel. Actually I don't know what to make of it at this point. And strangely, it doesn't seem to care much whether I understand it or not. It defies interpretation and even evaluation. Is it a good novel? Is it realistic? Ingenious? Poignant? Intriguing is probably the best word for it at this point. It describes a world of intrigue that's all the more so for being so banal.

The spiritual quest for higher meaning takes the form of a desperate bidding war on EBay. The devouring forces of the unconscious materialize as a runaway digging machine mistaken for an escaped tiger. Jonathan Lethem is an author in search of a story. He seems to write not in order to communicate meanings but in an attempt—part obsessive, part lethargic, always pleasantly dreamy—to locate meaning, somewhere, whether it's inside his own head or outside, in the culture which he has come to call, reluctantly and maybe a tad bitterly, home. A home *away* from home.

There's a tone of bewilderment that the author has found himself participating in such a dreamlike, two-dimensional arrangement; and not only participating but placed in a position of influence. Well? How did I *get* here? Lethem's determination not to be corrupted is like a small, murmured appeal between every line. It appears to take the form of a spiritual on-the-fenceness, a *"Neti neti"* approach to fiction, literature, and entertainment, "Not this, not that, don't be fooled by the reviews, this is not what it seems and neither am I."

Chronic City is not an important statement on anything, except perhaps on the author's inability-slash-refusal to take a firm position or make an important statement on *anything*. Except that. *Chronic City* depicts the author's mind wandering onto the page, seeking a place to settle, filling it, despite itself, with the author's surprise, bewilderment, and occasional delight at what comes out of him.

And you *may* ask yourself—*well*??

A Crisis of Authenticity (at page 294, chapters 11-18, Dec 25th)

The subject of *Chronic City* is revealed: as the "crisis of authenticity." A novel about emptiness, Lethem is striving to make it (himself?) empty enough to be filled, like a chaldron, which is a post-fictional Holy Grail (i.e., womb). He is hoping to see what the chaos looks like once he has withdrawn the wishes of his senses. An alternate title for it could be *Synesthesia*?

Nothing is contrived in *Chronic City*, yet nothing is arbitrary. Lethem-left-brain is a ruthless editor of the unbridled, shapeless explorations, exhortations, and exhumations of Lethem-right-brain. They make a pretty good team—understatement intended. But Lethem may be too "good" (too florid) a writer to be a great writer (yet). His loving, sensual relationship with language, and the respectful precision with which he approaches it (her?) seems unconsciously intended to prevent his prose from catching fire— his passions from consuming his "good sense." No wonder his breakthrough novel was about a Tourette's sufferer. Lethem's lack of wildness may be his greatest deficiency, placing his work dangerously close to twee. It's not that wildness is lacking; it's that it's not permitted expression. No wonder tigers roam hungrily beneath his sleepy city streets.

*

Insteadman is notable for his absence, or rather the absence of his "other": both his child-star self (which he has grown out of) and his female partner, who was shot into space and is slowly disappearing from the "ground" (feet) up. Insteadman is also "Unperson." He is one of the Permeables. The ghost of the writer whose presence serves to emphasize that Lethem, like every writer, is a ghost of himself.

The mayor, who has the only tangible chaldron in the novel, is described as "a gravitational sink hole, a place where other men's hopes had gone to die." The chaldron is absence as presence. It is Lethem's Ubik, a fictional reality so real to him he tattooed it on his arm.

It would seem my intuitional reading of the first chapters wasn't entirely random. At almost exactly the halfway point of the book (pages 228-9 out of 466), the ghost writer (Oona Laszlo) tosses out the possibility that they are all existing inside a virtual reality and that they may be nearing the end of existence. Lethem's characters get intimations, not only of their mortality but of their illusoriness, at the halfway point of their lives: a mid-novel crisis. Oona's logic is that, having created surrogate realities inside this one (one of the characters is engaged in a Second Life-type computer activity), they are causing too much of a power drain for their "simulators" — which would be Lethem. Perhaps he was expressing "fiction fatigue" at the halfway point of his creative undertaking?

Lethem manages to inject this now familiar scenario (that of a virtual world) with a surprising (or perhaps not, if the above is at all correct) degree of tension and energy. It's the most vital scene in the novel up to this point. Lethem has pooled his resources well. For a moment the book starts to make a new kind of sense (and stop making another kind). Later, Perkus Tooth refutes Oona's apocalyptic theory by suggesting that the program they are inside is built to conserve energy by only assembling itself wherever its inhabitants (simulants within the simulation) place their attention. Increasing the number of variables within the program, therefore, would not increase the amount of RAM needed to maintain its narrative flow. This could be read in any number of ways — including as a comment on Lethem's responsibility to the reader — and it may be a key not only to *Chronic City* but to the riddle of our existence (or should I say mine, since I don't know anyone else exists). We are only conscious of what we are conscious of. We don't perceive the gaps in the narrative flow, the failures of logic, because consciousness automatically stitches over the holes in the plot.

Holes. Spaces in between. To see them at all would mean the end of us. *Chronic City* is a novel about holes, but it itself is also a hole, like Noteless's memorial, waiting for us to fall (or dive) in. If we step closely enough to its edges, the vacuum at the center will take us.

*

There's an idea that I've been trying to formulate since I started reading this book. It's about culture and identity and how they both create each other and so can't be separated or known *by* each other. In Perkus Tooth's simulated reality scenario, it's attention that brings the false world into existence. Wherever our attention isn't, the world collapses into mere potentialities. It's a quantum model of existence, roughly. But the reverse is also the case. The world is not passive but interactive, even aggressively so as it vies for our attention in order to exist. And the world also shapes our attention: where we place it (our attention) determines to a degree the nature of it, and therefore where we are likely to place it in the next moment. This is the matrix of control, the conspiracy that is everywhere because it is nowhere. Attention.

There are no outside simulators. Logically, if the world that is shaping and directing our attention is also being created by it, then the simulants existing within the simulation can't be separated *from* it. It is all one information flow. Culture makes culture makers in order to perpetuate itself in new ways, and vice versa. As in *The Matrix*, the controlling element that has turned awareness, perception, attention into a closed system of endlessly repeating patterns or variables, a prison, a dead culture, is our own invention. It is not some outside agency with its own agenda (there *is* no outside, because nothing *can* be outside perception); it is only the product of our own ambition, delusion, and capacity for self-invention/self-extension—call it the ego or the false self, both the product and the producer of delusion. We may *think* that it's a living tiger hunting us mercilessly for its own pleasure or livelihood, but in "fact" (possibly) it's only a runaway piece of technology (knowledge) that has become dimly sentient by picking up the slack of our own numbed out insentience, our unconscious.

Maybe this explains why Lethem has his characters smoking pot the whole time? They are by choice languishing in the liminal state between fact and fiction, sleeping and waking, self-medicating, numbing out their senses and their awareness, opting for the symbiotic psychosis and dissociative trance state of plant dependency (mother bondage) in which the truth can stay pleasantly in the realm of fantasy, and all texts are ghost-texts. At least, that's the only explanation I can think of, because Lethem sure doesn't seem like a pothead to me.

And then there's the chaldron. A strange attractor of attention that transforms the observer through the act of observing. It is the clue we left to remind ourselves that the creation is happening every moment, in and through (and as) ourselves. In the spaces between where no one wants to go. That's the unwritten invitation which Lethem extends to the reader. If we create a vacuum in ourselves, in the fictional narrative which we stitch together in every moment, like the reader suspending disbelief to keep the novel going, if we allow the space to be there until, like a black hole, it takes everything into it, what will enter to fill that space?

Crucial Fiction (at page 384, chapters 19-21, Dec 26th)

Janice Turnbull the astronaut is the fiction within Lethem's post-fiction. She is the only kind of fiction that counts when the microchips are down: crucial fiction, a necessary delusion. She acts as a radiation shield to keep the cosmic rays of truth from permeating the protagonist's ghost-self and reducing it to something less than a memory: a *pseudo-memoir*.

Janice describes Chase Insteadman as the unseen object that keeps her living. Irony and (fearful) symmetry abound; she is really *his* lost object, the image of the mother/body which he keeps alive in his imagination, and which prevents him from fully living. She is a necessary fiction, but necessary to whom? Perkus discovers there is more than one kind of virtual reality, that he has (possibly) been living inside a manufactured narrative all along. (Of course he has: he's trapped inside Lethem's post-fiction!) His attachment to the mechanics of it are slight, however. The tiger makes his former life uninhabitable and leads him to find refuge in the arms of a three-legged dog, no doubt a symbol of something primal or primary in Lethem's own public-private dream narrative.

But Chase isn't so easily unplugged. His chaldron fantasy is central to the story, and in fact the story seems to hinge upon it (and his seeing through it). Chase's fantasy is Adam's dream: the original split between mother and child (astronaut and Earth), male and female. When Eve is taken out of Adam's side and then quickly strays, he is left forever incomplete. Out of his dream a world is born, but it's a fallen world: a story whose only sensible conclusion is apocalyptic.

What does that leave for Chase? Even the sacred pull of the chaldron turns out to be a red herring. There is literally no-thing that can ever replace the lost object because life is a movement not towards but *away* from original "oneness." The absence of God is the necessary acceptance for the embodiment of God — Jesus on the cross.

Does the word "God" even appear in *Chronic City*? If it does I didn't spot it. Lethem's world (the world of the literati) is post-postmodern; even godlessness is dead. It is just as if the Deity never existed. And not only "as if," either. In the magical innocence of his dreaming, it is as if nihilism has never occurred to Lethem. If a thing (divine/lost object) never existed, there's no need to negate it, or to lament its passing.

I suspect I am drawn to Lethem because, like my own late brother (a dandy like Perkus), he's my opposite number. Like my brother, Lethem stringently avoids any reference to spiritual or occult subjects, even though the range of his interest and the depth of his vision would seem to demand it. This makes it doubly conspicuous for its absence, a fitting status for "the occult." Lethem is aspiring to exactly the same pure perceptual experience as I am, but from the other side of the coin. We were both raised by irreligious artist-types, though in my case they were only artist-worshippers, not artist-doers. This may be a key difference.

At his best, Lethem aspires to communicate Spirit free from spirituality, probably the ultimate goal of language. Part of that aspiration seems to involve allowing his narrative to slip into irrelevancy. Freedom from false narratives doesn't mean finding the "true" narrative. It means embracing the chaos underneath the wishful linearity of prose/memory and locating the eternal moment. It is like presenting word without need or possibility of sentence. Where there is and never has been an object (because no subject), nothing was ever lost.

*

I am reluctant now to refer to Lethem's own mother, who was lost to him at the age of thirteen. But if that event is the heart (broken but still beating) of Lethem's personal narrative, then it is also what pumps life into all his fictions—what makes them truly crucial. And perhaps *Chronic City* is the first time he has allowed us (or himself?) to see that clearly, making it his first "mature" (fully honest) work? This is just a guess. Only Lethem can *know*.

Calling Down Tigers (at page 467, Novel's End, chapters 22-29, Dec 26th)

What Jonathan Lethem is looking for isn't readers. It's co-authors.

This could all be projection on my part. In fact, it *has* to be all projection. That's the *point*, of *Chronic City*, this essay, and everything in-between. The point is (if I've done my "job") there *isn't* anything in-between. This essay should fit effortlessly and perfectly into the hole at the heart of *Chronic City*, since that hole was meant only for me, its first and only witness/reader. Either that or I have misjudged the dimensions and fallen in at the deep end.

Towards the novel's tragic end, Perkus Tooth vacates his bowels of all that is not-him (inessential to his meaning), the cultural waste (apple of knowledge) which he has devoured, and becomes, for a moment, a dilapidated and dismal chaldron for archangelic forces. Is this Lethem's dream? But expunging the false self can prove fatal. Unplugging from the Matrix after a certain age is not recommended. To put it mildly.

The reason the word "God" doesn't appear in *Chronic City* (if it doesn't, I can't do a word search on a flesh and blood novel) is because Lethem has replaced it with the word "dog." The three-legged, scent-following Amy is Perkus's Higher (deeper/lower) Power that guides him back to the only reality there is: the body-moment. And the body-moment (in sympathy with the Doghead) is one long, eventually fatal hiccup. In this case, it is Perkus Tooth's attempt to vomit up the apple of knowledge, and rid himself of the original sin of projection.

Some die to be reborn; some simply die. Pure perceptual being is "the born identity."

Alternative title for the novel: *Impossible Objects*. Suggested title for sequel: *The Ruler of the Moon*.

*

Greatness lies in a willingness and an ability to be small. *Chronic City* is a great novel exactly in proportion to its willingness and ability to be a small one.

On page 449, Chase Insteadman settles on the terms of his defeat: "Daring to attempt to absolutely sort *fake* from *real* was a folly that would call down tigers ..." And what of it? The tiger is perhaps the one intrusion of pure beauty into the chronic fogginess of fakery of these characters' lives. Is this Lethem's advice to his protagonist or vice versa, their advice to him? Or is it his warning to the reader, not to attempt the *hubris* of sorting the seeds of Lethem's fiction from Lethem's life because one is a necessary outgrowth of, and defense against, the other? To separate the fake from the real is impossible, and yet (therefore?) it is the only task worth our time, as readers *or* writers in a post-fiction world. But the task isn't so much to distinguish the fake from the real but *internally from externally sourced values*. To what degree does our perception and response accurately reflect the interface between our inner and outer reality?

There is no real world or real self which can be separated from one another; only a real and final recognition of that truth, and a disappearing into it.

I have read *Chronic City* (in the five days leading up to and including Christmas, today is the day after) less as a follower of Lethem's work than as a correspondent and hopeful collaborator. I am one of the lucky few who has Perkus Tooth's eye and ear. Whatever the gulf in our literary status, I know we serve a common Mistress. Reading *Chronic City* while simultaneously writing this exegesis (as it turned out to be), knowing that I would send it to Lethem when it was done, and that he would almost certainly receive it, has allowed me to bring a quality of attention to the work which I never would have otherwise. My experience, and the book itself, can only have been enlivened by that attention, in the process becoming something *else*. No book is completed—or even exists—until it's read. Writer and reader are one because they are none. There is only the transmission and reception, which are also one.

When I read *Chronic City* I was looking for confirmation of kindredness, and this response is my affirmation of the affinity which I found. For me, *Chronic City* reads like a book-length letter from a long-lost brother, one who may or may not exist "out there," in the literary stratosphere where I visualize him floating. Our communication *appears* to have been created for the whole world; but secretly, I know it is only for us.

That real and fake are inextricably intertwined was my dandy brother's life-philosophy, a belief-negating belief which he literally died defending, as the means to protect a secret which he became a slave to. To recognize the fake is to identify what is real. And once the real has been seen, what is fake can never be *un*seen; paradoxically, it ceases to exist at all.

At the end of *Chronic City*, having sacrificed the apparent innocent, Lethem gives his protagonist an easy way out, and the reader too. This is perhaps due less to Lethem's faintheartedness than his compassion. He appears to know that the quest for the real is only for the very few, and that even they (or especially they) must be staunchly discouraged from ever embarking. Perkus's Parsifal-like innocence did not protect him—probably because it wasn't innocence but something else, a withdrawal from full embodiment through faintness of heart.

What killed my own brother was apparently the same thing that kills Perkus. The night before his death (of a heroin overdose), my brother saw a stage performance of his (ghost-written!) memoir, a fiction mounted on the memorial pit of his life. He did not like what he saw. His authentic fakeness couldn't withstand the touch of culture and commodification, and the unintentional parody he had spawned, like the picture of Dorian Gray, proved too much for him. It's the fake that reveals the truth, the fiction that discloses a life.

The secret exposes itself.

The Movie Nomad

Getting Lost at the Movies with Pauline Kael

"Like those cynical heroes who were idealists before they discovered that the world was more rotten than they had been led to expect, we're just about all of us displaced persons, 'a long way from home.' When we feel defeated, when we imagine we could now perhaps settle for home and what it represents, that home no longer exists. But there are movie houses."
—Pauline Kael, "Trash, Art, and the Movies"

In one review of *The Blood Poets*, I was accused (it wasn't a friendly criticism) of writing a book not only of cinephilia but with an even more narrow focus, *Kaelophilia*. It's true that the first volume was dedicated to Kael, and that, when she read it, she wrote me in Guatemala saying the book read like a long letter to her. She asked if there was a second volume, and then added simply, with characteristic bluntness, "I want it."

Of course I gave it to her.

*

Kael was arguably the most influential film writer of her day (i.e., *ever*). She may even have been the most powerful female figure in American movies. But that's beside the point. The point is that I have been in love with her writing in a way I can't say the same about that of any other writer. Reading Kael for me was almost better than watching movies. It provided the excitement of a fully immersive imaginative ("movie") experience with the intellectual stimulation of "great" literature. Why did I put "great" in quotes like that? Because I don't really believe that assigning greatness to works can be done without implicitly, sneakily, asserting one's own greatness, or at least ability to recognize it. I could paraphrase Greil Marcus (on Lester Bangs) and say that to understand Pauline Kael you have to recognize that the greatest American writer of the period might write only movie reviews. That's the kind of faintly pretentious statement which impresses people, or at least challenges them to argue with it. If I say that Pauline Kael is, or was, my own favorite writer from that period, however, no one's likely to be especially impressed or challenged. But really—what's the difference?

The Subject of This Piece

"Jake Horsley seems to arrive from out of nowhere, yet here he is—an almost fully-developed and only slightly stoned sensibility. This hothead fantasist offers the excitement of a wild, paranoid style. He lives in the movies, explodes them from the inside, and shares his fevered trance with us. But he doesn't lose his analytic good sense. He's not just a hothead, he's a hardhead, too. Maybe he could use more humor, but couldn't we all? (Intelligent movie criticism is being swamped in seriousness.) He's a marvelous critic. Tackling a new movie, he'll hang in there until he's balanced and sound. It's always a surprise."
—Pauline Kael, 2001

I got myself a copy of *Kiss Kiss Bang Bang* this Christmas. It arrived miraculously on Christmas Eve, although I'd only ordered it the week before; as a result I actually had a present to open the next day, even if only from myself. A couple of weeks earlier I had brought my Kael collection (from *I Lost it at the Movies* to *Taking it All In*, not counting *Going Steady*) over from England, and somehow *Kiss Kiss Bang Bang* wasn't among them. I wanted to re-read the books in sequence while working on this book, so I'd found a copy online and ordered it. On Christmas Day, I opened my present to myself and read a brief opening essay called "The Creative Business." Even though I must have read this book between a half and a full dozen times, I didn't remember this particular piece. I was so impressed by it that I read parts out loud to my wife, and found myself almost choking up at certain points. It wasn't so much the subject matter (which had to do with how Hollywood players reframe the idea of "creativity" to justify their own commercialism and contempt for art, and how they see themselves as victims of the system even while they to use it to their advantage). What moved me, I think, was a more visceral response to the depth, intensity, passion and precision of Kael's insights. The acuity of her intelligence was so penetrating that it made me want to cry.

Maybe it *was* to do with the subject matter at that—Kael's mini-essay cuts to the masochistic, self-hating core of a certain kind of exploitative American attitude—but I think it had more to do with how Kael put *all of herself* into her writing, how she didn't hold anything back and allowed a full psychic merging between herself and the reader. Her writing offers the sort of intimacy which we are *all* longing to experience, however we can get it, and it's that same desire for intimacy which draws people to art—and sex, drugs, and religion—in the first place. I realized that reading Kael had given me an experience that very nearly *was* sexual. Maybe this is why Kael injected sexual innuendo into her titles? And maybe it's why she left it out at roughly the same time the *oomph* went out of her writing—around 1983 with *The State of the Art*? Curiously enough, that was also around the time I discovered Kael. Thirty years later I have read her books countless times. It was re-reading Kael's oeuvre in Spain, in 1997, that inspired me to write *The Blood Poets*, hence the dedication: "To P.K., for taking me deeper into movies, and making me reel." Kael's response was to give me the blurb which I still refer to when emailing agents and publishers, a fragment of which appeared on the cover of *Matrix Warrior*: "Jake Horsley seems to arrive from out of nowhere, yet here he is!" (exclamation point added). As I'm summing all of this up for the reader, I realize that the strange insinuation is that Pauline Kael "midwifed" me into existence as a writer. I think it's more than just an insinuation.

*

I spoke to Kael once on the telephone, in early 2001, the year she died. I was staying at a cheap motel off of Hollywood Boulevard, having managed to sneak into the US across the Canadian border. I'd had business cards with "Movie Shaman" printed up and was doing the rounds with copies of *The Blood Poets* (dropping it off at David Lynch's house, with Brian DePalma's agent, and so on) and my Sam Peckinpah script (*Bring Me the Head of Sam Peckinpah*, as it was called at the time), which I delivered to Johnny Depp's house, having got his address from an artist in San Francisco. I was in the full swing of attempting to turn my Hollywood dream into reality.

Kael had given me her number through Charles Taylor (a critic who reviewed *The Blood Poets* at Salon), and I called her up to ask if she knew any movie people in LA. The irony of it! In fact, while during her heyday Kael may have been the most feared woman in Hollywood (before Warren Beatty cut her down to size, as the legend has it), she probably didn't have too many friends there, or even allies. In any event, we had a friendly conversation that lasted probably around fifteen minutes, though all I can remember is talking about Brian DePalma's recent movies, *Snake Eyes* and *Mission to Mars*. Looking back, it seems like one of life's great missed opportunities. Later, at my mother's suggestion (she was also a Kaelophile), I sent red roses to Pauline's home in Great Barrington, and I heard from Taylor that she appreciated the gesture. I was too in awe of her at the time to consider the possibility that my admiration might mean as much to her as hers did to me.

The only reason I am writing this piece now—as far as I can

tell—is because it gives me the feeling of being connected to Kael, in the same way that reading her does only more so. So why is it so important or meaningful for me to feel connected to Kael? That's the real subject of this piece.

More Than a Critic

"In many ways the perceptions and the observations are more important than the judgments. We read critics for the perceptions, for what they tell us that we didn't fully grasp when we saw the work. The judgments we can usually make for ourselves."
   —Pauline Kael, 1989

When Pauline Kael first joined the *New Yorker*, she was accused of treading dirt onto its pages with her "cowboy boots." Her style was anti-intellectual intellectualism: visceral, impulsive, sensual, bawdy, playful, punchy. Woody Allen accused her of being a great critic except for one thing: judgment. It's easy to find evidence to support that view. (I could count the ways, but why bother—it's all taste vs. taste anyway.) The problem people had with Kael, I think, had less to do with her occasionally dubious judgments than with how persuasively she could argue them. One of the things that impressed me the most about her reviews (and which I aspired to with *The Blood Poets*) was that she could change my mind about a movie (usually by making me see why a movie I liked was bad, rarely if ever the other way around). It's not just that she was a brilliant writer that got people's backs up, or even that she was an infuriatingly opinionated one. It's that her passion was so intense and nakedly expressed that it was infectious. It was impossible to resist her view except by opposing it. The only way not to love her, in other words, was to hate her. A bit like a mother.

The angry denunciations of her and her work (people are still arguing about her to this day) are probably an indication of just how seriously we take movies, or more precisely, how seriously we take our feelings about them. Kael possessed—or was possessed by—a far greater talent than most of the people whose work she wrote about. Her attention, her intense involvement with movies, demanded reciprocity, from the filmmakers, from readers, from movies themselves. She didn't just raise the bar, she changed the nature of the game. Naturally, people wanted to disqualify her from the field, and to the extent that her own power and influence went to her head, Kael appears to have played into the opposition's hands and skewed her own game. This was most openly symbolized—or enacted—by her taking Warren Beatty's "bait" in 1979 and going to Hollywood to try her skills as a producer. Adam tempted Eve, and in the end, Kael not only lost it at the movies, she seems to have wound up jilted and abandoned.

What I wonder now is, was it built into the relationship from the start?

*

Kael's take-no-prisoners style of criticism was sometimes called cruel and unnecessarily cutting. There are accounts in Simon Kellow's (disappointing) biography that suggest that her bite was not only lethal but vicious, and not necessarily reserved for the deserving; her famous acidic wit, some claimed, evidenced vitriol running though her veins in place of blood. It's impossible to separate the genuine complaints from those of angry, wounded egos (whose complaints are also valid, in their way); it's almost equally difficult to tell when Kael is applying her laser scalpel to save a life and when she's getting carried away by her own surgical virtuosity.

After writing the first draft of this piece (which poured out in under an hour), I found myself wondering: beneath all her brilliance and passion, was Kael really a cruel and vicious person? Had I let myself be duped by her intelligence and sophistication? I don't believe this is true (though there may be truth *in* it), but it occurred to me that my fear was an exact match for a similar dilemma I'd had with my wife. Most married men probably encounter the same fear at one time or another (Did I marry a heartless bitch?). I can't speak for them but, for me, this fear goes all the way back to my mother, who was neither brilliant nor sophisticated (unlike my wife), but was an artistically impressionable, deeply wounded soul with an unfortunate capacity for cruelty. (An odd detail. While I was watching a rare Kael interview on YouTube a couple of years back, at the time I was reading Brian Kellow's biography, I realized that Kael bore a striking resemblance to my wife, down to the hooked eagle nose. Love takes unexpected forms.) No doubt all this has something to do with why it seems so important for me to feel connected to Kael. And maybe also with just how difficult writing this piece, finding the proper form for it, is proving to be.

Re-reading Kael (maybe for the last time?) while working on this piece, I found myself bouncing back and forth between disappointment—the feeling that she's really not *that* great, after all—to relief that her writing still had the power to affect me as it once did. It's as if I am emerging from under the wing of her influence, at long last, and seeing her clear of all the projections and adolescent fantasy-needs which she both stirred and met in me, arriving at a more sober and balanced view. Inevitably, there's a feeling of loss involved.

*

Kael really did have erratic judgment, but only for a film critic. Her faulty judgments only seem so bad because they came with such fierce conviction and carried such weight behind them. As a moviegoer, her judgment was no worse or better, nor stranger, than anyone else's.

Determining what has true value—what's "good" and what's "bad"—is the critic's job, stated baldly. It's also everyone's task in life, and developing that faculty begins in infancy, when it depends on receiving the right sort of validation from the outside. Mother Kael validated my voice (and my judgment) as a film critic (I was "marvelous" and "balanced and sound"); to some degree, that voice served me well. It helped me to connect to my own mother (who loved my books), and even to my father (no mean feat); it even allowed me to pierce the indifference of the world "out there" (the book was well-reviewed at Salon, through Kael's connections). But that was about as far as it went. When I re-read parts of *The Blood Poets* now, fifteen years later, I cringe at the unruliness and self-indulgence of much of the writing, the faintly pretentious gushiness, and I'm amazed Kael liked it as much as she did. But maybe I shouldn't be. Since I learned much of this "reckless excess" from her, it's perhaps no surprise that I got to be the beneficiary of it, too.

Finding *a* voice isn't the same as finding one's true voice. The truth is I never really wanted to "be" a film critic at all. It was all just a ruse, because I didn't want to limit my expression to such a narrow venue. And now I don't even know exactly *what* sort of writer I want to "be." One thing that occurred to me while I was writing this piece was that, if Kael was an intellectual author— the very best kind—I'm really not. I'm closer to Jonathan Lethem—an intuitive-emotional type. When I read that short opening piece in *Kiss Kiss Bang Bang* this Christmas, it had the opposite effect to back in 1997, when I was inspired to write my own version of Kael. This time I felt discouraged. I thought, "I can't ever write anything that good, so why bother?" The answer is that I am trying to write something else altogether.

*

Judgment—who has it? What counts isn't how "right" a critic is but how honest they are. How close does their judgment get to being an authentic expression of their experience, how embodied is that expression, and how true and real is their voice? There's no such thing as impeccable taste—what would it be measured against? A critic risks falling into the trap of *being* a critic when he or she offers subjective experience as objective judgment. Why did Kael begin to use "you" in place of "I" more and more in her reviews? Wasn't she telling the reader what they were *supposed* to be experiencing while distancing herself from her experiences by replacing the subjective "I" with the more authoritative "you"? And yet, without taking an authoritative position at least *some* of the time, a writer can be accused of writing only about themselves, and of not deserving the title of critic at all. Not that it's such a great title to have, but there's a function for critics, just as there's a function for critical faculties. A good critic is both honest *and* discerning, which includes being honest about their lack of discernment by maintaining a fully subjective voice even when casting judgment. A good critic helps readers (which would include the artists being critiqued) to develop their own capacity for critical judgment.

That's what Kael, at her best, did for me. She offered an example of what a *relatively* authentic voice sounds like. That's why her work stands up as it does; not because she was a great critic, but because she was one of the very few American writers from *any* period with her own, unique *voice*. The degree to which Kael validated my own voice by endorsing *The Blood Poets* is a measure, perhaps, of both my own authenticity and the lack of it. After all, part of why she approved my writing, I suspect, was that it so skillfully and lovingly emulated her own. To this day, I still detect her voice in what I write, and I still enjoy finding it there.

Kael and I are what is known as psychically enmeshed. Writing this present piece seems to be a way for me to pull apart the threads of that enmeshment, one strand at a time, and bring about the end of our affair.

What Pauline Lost at the Movies

Interviewer: "When I'm at the movies, I feel like I'm swept up, lost."

Kael: "I feel as if I'm found."

Some of Kael's early pieces are actually transcripts from her radio broadcasts. The transcripts *read* like fully structured essays, but at the same time, they have the loose, conversational style which she eventually became famous for. There's a very obvious difference between written and spoken word pieces. When we speak, we do it with the total body and express far more than mere words can. Since there's no time for composing our sentences and the only editing happens in our heads *before* we speak, we have much less control over what we communicate. Kael's special gift (and what she gave to the reader, and to the field of film criticism) was that she wrote like she spoke, with immediacy, honesty, spontaneity, frankness, and a lack of preciousness, free of the dilly-dallying and mincing that bogs down so much literary and critical writing. Yet how she could speak! She used words like a master jazz improviser following some interior music that only she could hear. And this *was* the way she spoke: in her interviews she often displayed the same magical eloquence.

When Kael writes in her prime—when, in the memorable phrase of Sherlock Holmes, "the game is afoot!"—her surprise, delight, discomfort and bewilderment is apparent as fresh insights bubble forth from her insides and pour out her pen. I recognize this because I am starting to experience it in my own writing: things that aren't "thought out" just appear on the page or screen; they *feel* true, right, and so I put all of myself behind them and hope for the best. Most of the time (lately at least), they do turn out to make a strange kind of sense; they allow for more coherent and rational discoveries that confirm the rightness of the intuition. But in the moment which the insights spring forth, like Athena born fully grown, they are as unexpected as they are improbable. That amazement is apparent in Kael's writing, at its best, and it's probably the surest proof that a writer is transmitting something above, below, and beyond their conscious awareness or intentions.

Kael acknowledged this in her last piece for *The New Yorker*, "The Movie Lover" (March 21st 1994), when she said, "I don't fully know what I think until I've said it. The reader is in on my thought processes." What communicates in such a literary "reveal" is far more (but also less) than the insights or the imagery being described: it's the delight of a writer recognizing his or her own unconscious processes, and the reader gets to be *right there*, in that moment of truth. There's really no literary substitute for that (and it really is like sex).

The danger of this, the trap, is when a writer gets so good at setting up these little epiphanies that she starts to think that she is doing them herself. It then becomes possible to *simulate* the experience and to assume the guise—the pose and the prose—of "authority," independently of being a genuine mouthpiece for Truth. When a writer gets "hooked" (the title of one of Kael's later books) on the high of being an authority, they can end up performing an unconscious subterfuge, mistaking the external *form* of inspired writing for the internal *content*. They can learn to fake their epiphanies.

My guess is this has to do with a writer's gaze becoming overly focused on the outside, on the readers, the reviews, the movies being critiqued, and losing touch with the inner discoveries occurring—or trying to occur—via the process of writing itself. Regardless of the subject, writing is primarily about *bringing unconscious material into consciousness*; without that primary goal being allowed to dictate the rules of engagement, it becomes an empty mastery of words. And what fills that emptiness is a different sort of unconscious material, the kind a writer won't—or *can't*—become conscious of, even once it's out here—even if others invariably will.

*

What happened with Kael's writing, I think, was this. Kael began writing about her experience of life, using movies as the focal point, like a sounding board to bounce her impassioned insights off. Writing about movies was a way to discover what was going on, not in the world out there, but *in her;* in a way, movies were the least of it. This searching intensity runs through her best books, *I Lost it At the Movies, Kiss Kiss Bang Bang,* "Trash, Art, and the Movies" from *Going Steady,* and *Deeper into Movies,* from the period between 1954 and 1972. By the end of *Deeper Into Movies,* and continuing with *Reeling* and *When the Lights Go Down* (1972-78), it was as if the movies had begun to respond to Kael's loving, searing gaze—and her *touch.* They began to *reciprocate,* to meet and match her expectations, to prove themselves worthy of the attention she was giving them; and so the movies came of age, through an act of love.

The turning point for this would have been 1967—the year I was born—when Kael's review of *Bonnie and Clyde* helped turn around critical opinion about the movie. Later, Peter Biskind credited the movie (and by association, somewhat exaggeratedly, Kael's review) with kick-starting "the New Hollywood," i.e., the period of intense creativity that fired Kael's passion in the early to mid-70s. What makes Kael's love affair with the art form so compelling is that it was *reciprocal:* it was an *active,* not a passive affair. If *I Lost it at the Movies, Kiss Kiss Bang Bang,* and *Going Steady* described the deflowering and courtship phases, *Deeper into Movies* and the following two books recount the full consummation and first, crucial years of marriage. They map the period when the power of Kael's projections became all-consuming and potentially lethal, and when the inevitable disillusionment began to set in (whether it was noticed or not). Kael's writing over this phase became increasingly focused on the movies themselves—because they *demanded* it. But at the same time something was lost in the process; the proof for me is that I enjoy her earlier books more, even though the movies she writes about are much less interesting to me. In those first few books, it hardly mattered what movie Kael was writing about, she usually found a way to dig *deep* into the ground (the social context) from which the movies emerged. The later books—even the astonishing middle period that mapped the rise and fall of the new Hollywood—didn't do this so much, they stayed focused on the virtues or failings of the specific movies. And because of this narrowing of focus, I think Kael's writing also revealed less of her *internal* experience.

In the courtship and even the early consummation period of a love affair, the tension and excitement is especially intense because the hunt is still on and the desire to understand—to bridge the gulf between oneself and the other—is overpowering. But eventually the price of putting all our attention on the other person leads to losing our sense of our own individuality. And then, inevitably, tragically, the bubble bursts.

Kael's trip to Hollywood at Warren Beatty's invitation (or seduction?) clearly marked the end of Kael's love affair with movies. It marked the time, as in any marriage, when the partners are faced with a choice. They can let go of their illusions and expectations and move *past* the projections, into the deep discomfort of adult intimacy, complete with all its life traumas, rage and disappointments; or they can agree to keep to a comfortably superficial and civil relationship, "for the sake of the children," etc. etc. (The other option is separation.) Even as "the New Hollywood" was ending, Kael did what many couples do, she tried the geographical cure and moved to Los Angeles. Like couples who try spicing up the marriage by bringing in sex games, she tried to take her "movie love" to a new level, not a deeper one but a more exotic and exciting one. Marriage *is* a kind of war, and Kael's mistake, I think (if there was one), was that she let the "enemy" dictate the terms and choose the battleground for her.

"Why Are Movies So Bad? Or The Numbers," the opening essay in *Taking It All In*, is the summation of everything Kael learned during her stint in Hollywood. (The other fruit was that she helped green-light David Lynch's *Elephant Man*, no small feat.) "Why Are Movies So Bad?" sees Kael still near the top of her game as a writer, but in retrospect it's also her swan song, the dying war cry of "General Kael," the High Priestess of Movies. After that, I think Kael's pieces (with some exceptions) became progressively more impersonal and less impassioned, revealing or surprising, less *vital* in both senses of the word, until, by the time of *State of the Art*, she had lost not only her innocence but her edge. The movies had disillusioned her, and by the time she realized it, she had already given them the best years of her life.

This kind of disillusionment either spells a new kind of freedom or it spells defeat; there probably isn't much ground in-between. Kael's last books seemed to acknowledge this, not only in their lackluster content but in the titles, *Hooked* and *Movie Love*. Considering the quality of most of the movies she was hooked on, her titles conveyed less a sense of passion than one of resignation and muted despair. For me, they invoke the image of a foolishly faithful lover, trapped in a listless relationship, with nothing left to keep her there but rationalizations.

Roses & Thorns, Good Points & Bad Points

"Kael's chief weakness is her lack of affinity or understanding for the more 'spiritual' dimensions of movies (we'll leave life out of it), a common enough failing for the 'intellectual.'"
—Jake Horsley, *The Blood Poets*

It seems as though every in-depth psychological exploration of a writer I have done ends up being some sort of cautionary tale. The lesson of all my mentors or role models seem to be, "Beware of what you wish for: there but for the grace of God go you." This doesn't seem fair to the subject, but then, we invariably wind up resenting our influences—at least until we have sorted the good from the bad seeds. Which brings me to "the Paulettes." Kael's heyday—the prime of her power and influence—began around 1967, with the release of her *Bonnie and Clyde* review. According to most of the accounts I've found, Kael was done with romance by this point, and devoted to her daughter, Gina. (Gina was born in 1948, and some people have speculated that Kael's attachment to her was smothering, controlling, even "imprisoning.") Kael lived on Central Park West during this period and hosted parties for her chosen circle of associates, most of whom were male. These associates eventually became known as "the Paulettes," an obviously derogatory term.

"The Paulettes" (the males ones) included Paul Schrader, Michael Sragow, David Denby, James Wolcott, Roger Ebert, David Edelstein, Joe Morgenstern, Terrence Rafferty, Ray Sawhill, Charles Taylor, and Allen Barra. Kael first met many of them when they were still undergraduates or graduate students, when they reached out to her with their first efforts at film criticism. She took them into her circle, invited them to sit with her at screenings and to attend her *soirees*. She also advised them and helped advance their careers. Or so the story goes. This isn't a biographical piece and I'm not about to conduct my own interviews to verify any of this information, so all this should be taken as hearsay. The fact that it has become the "narrative" around Kael doesn't mean it's accurate, but it *does* mean that it's become the narrative. Certainly some of the "Paulettes"—most vocally David Denby, in his piece for *The New Yorker*, "My Life as a Paulette," but others too—complained that, at a certain point, Kael turned on them, treated them coldly, rudely disparaged their writing, or simply cut off all dealings with them. Charles Taylor has suggested that Kael was merely being brutally honest with her protégés and that some of them took it badly; others have implied that she was a jealous and possessive den mother (or sorceress) venting unconscious abandonment issues. Probably it was a combination of both, with plenty of other factors also at play.

Some "Paulettes" have said that they eventually felt the need to break away from Kael (to leave the nest) under their own power, that they felt stifled or dominated by her. Certainly, more than one of these intense "affairs" did end in a severing of all ties between Kael and her acolyte. There's plenty of evidence of this "syndrome" even in the testimonials of (male) writers who *didn't* know Kael personally, but who seem to have gone from fawning adulation to scathing condemnation. The amount of hostility directed at Kael on the Internet isn't particularly surprising, but it even shows up in some of the reviews and retrospectives that appeared in 2011, with the release of Kellow's biography and *The Age of Movies* (a huge collection of Kael's most memorable essays). Kael's legacy is a complicated one, and it seems to include a disproportionate amount of anger and resentment.

By the time Kael discovered me (2000) it was too late for her to do much to help my career, besides which, I was on my own shaman-bender/trajectory and interested in a very different kind of discipleship (not to Morgan La Faye but to Merlin). So I escaped the fate of becoming one of Kael's "Paulettes" by about ten years. But even if we *had* connected ten years earlier (about the time I gave up an inheritance and went to North Africa to disappear into my own *cinema verité* tragicomedy), I doubt I'd have met the necessary criteria. Maybe that was one of the things she liked about me (my prose, I mean), that, even as I was doing my best imitation of Kaelspeak, I was openly defying her jurisdiction over my judgments. My love letter contained barbs, as well as roses.

*

David Denby is one "Paulette" whose break with Kael was acrimonious, and in his *New Yorker* recollections (October 20th 2003), he referred to the Kael circle as a "cult that never admitted its existence, a circle that never discussed its exclusions."

[F]or many of us, her tossed out judgments on movies and books, and particularly, the remarks aimed at us, kindly or razor-edged, were accepted as a pure expression of spirit—an authentic, spontaneous creation. People sought her praise so energetically because there was little chance that she would ever give it out of politeness. And when it arrived it was enthralling. Literally so—some people became addicted to it and belonged to her forever.

James Wolcott also wrote a critical piece for *Vanity Fair* about his apprenticeship with Kael, but by the time of his book, *Lucking Out*, he seemed to have gotten over it. My guess is that, as is often the case with "cults," it was up to the individual members how much they submitted to "groupthink." In the above-cited piece, Denby presents a curious paradox:

She never pretended that she was objective or above the fray, and she refused to place her opinions on the table as just another view. She insisted that she was right about everything, and you would be right, too, someday, if you worked like hell and stayed loose ... It wasn't discipline but freedom of the most flagrant kind that Pauline demanded, license, with quick penalties (her scorn, followed by group ridicule) for a mistake.

Every tight-knit group has the potential to become cultish; but it also presents an opportunity for its members to find their own freedom by breaking *from* it. (I speak from personal experience.) How much a group's visible leader is aware of this potential—and how much they may subtly encourage such "breakaways" — is notoriously hard to say. But if there's one thing Kael's whole literary style and personality seemed to have been opposed to, it's slavish devotion.

*

In her appraisal of my writing, Kael followed the words "slightly stoned" with "almost fully formed sensibility." If stoned suggests being "out of it," or disembodied, "almost fully formed" suggests the opposite: a fetus coming to term. I wonder now if this was perhaps a nod to the fact that my "sensibility" as a film critic was significantly formed through *her* influence? As she was to the other "Paulettes," Kael was my psychic/literary *mother*, and a male child must always break loose from his mother in the end. Either that, or remain a momma's boy.

Developing a literary style—an identity or "voice" as a writer—is like finding a city to live in: there are good points and bad points. Growing up with my mother, I experienced the shared gaze of movie watching, the symbiosis of having our eyes focused on a common *object*. Reading Kael as an adolescent combined that shared gaze with an even deeper symbiosis—one of shared *thought*. (The act of reading entails *thinking the writer's thoughts as if they were one's own*.)

My experience of having my opinions about movies subtly altered by Kael's lucid critiques was probably only the tip of the iceberg. The degree to which she influenced me at an unconscious level is, by definition, unknown, but it's probably that much more profound precisely *because* it was unconscious. It's doubtful if I would have developed such an enduring passion for (obsession with) movies if I hadn't read Kael when I did. She licensed that obsession, blessing my relationship with movies—

my self-engineered movie autism—even as I entered all the way *into* it. And, like a possessive mother, she infected me with an impossibly high standard for intimacy and engagement. Movies *were* like sex for me; they may have even seemed better than sex, or at least safer. They offered the excitement, the *thrill*, and the immersion, without the messiness and discomfort of exposure, the dreaded aftermath. The only catch was they weren't "real."

It's perhaps no wonder that people found it so upsetting when Kael's judgment was "off" (i.e., didn't agree with their own). Her prose invites such intimacy that disagreement can feel like a brutal awakening, like hearing one's lover moaning someone else's name in mid-*conjuctio*. The spell is broken so violently that it's experienced as a betrayal—the primal split reoccurring.

*

In Brian Kellow's biography, he quotes a eulogy given at Kael's memorial service by her daughter, Gina:

> Pauline's greatest weakness, her failure as a person, became her great strength, her liberation as a writer and critic. She truly believed that what she did was for everyone's good, and that because she meant well, she had no negative effects. She refused any consideration of that possibility and she denied any motivations or personal needs ... This lack of intro-spection, self-awareness, restraint or hesitation gave Pauline supreme freedom to speak up, to speak her mind, to find her honest voice. She turned her lack of self-awareness into a triumph.

Isn't lack of self-awareness another way of saying that Kael lacked understanding for "the spiritual dimensions of things"? It's an odd equation to make, in any case, between a lack of introspection and "an honest voice." (Gina seems to be equating insensitivity with fearlessness.) My experience is exactly the reverse. And if writing doesn't allow for a deepening of self-awareness, what's it good for? With her strange choice of words, Gina seems to have been implying—consciously or not, but certainly discreetly—the opposite of what she said: that Kael's "liberation" as a writer couldn't be separated from her liberation as a human being, in ever-deepening relation to other human beings, and that both could only continue for as long as there was a deepening of *self*-awareness. Is there such a thing as a great writer—or a great critic—who lacks introspection? I don't see how, and I'm reasonably sure Kael would have agreed, at least at one time.

But then, I only really knew her through her writings, which were, as she acknowledged, "*her* story."

Lost in the Dark

"What is getting older if it isn't learning more ways that you're vulnerable?"
—Pauline Kael, 1989 review of *Casualties of War*

Kael's last written words for *The New Yorker* (1994's "The Movie Lover") were: "*I'm frequently asked why I don't write my memoirs. I think I have.*" In the acknowledgments to *Deeper into Movies*, Kael wrote, "I would feel a fake if I dedicated a book to anyone, because I know I write because I love trying to figure out what I feel and what I think about what I feel, and why." Another way of saying this is that Kael wrote to figure out why she wrote—which may be the only honest reason for writing *anything*.

Kael was notorious for never going back on any of her judgments about a movie and for never seeing a movie twice. The latter claim is demonstrably false, since Kael admits to seeing *McCabe and Mrs. Miller* a second time (to make sure it was as good as she thought it was) and having seen *Taxi Driver* without the musical score (at a private screening) and then later with. That she never changed her mind about a movie seems to be accurate, however; or if she did, she never admitted it. Kael scorned "saphead objectivity" in a critic, but she also seemed to believe—talked and wrote as if—her judgment was the only correct one. As Gina said at a memorial tribute to her mother, "Her inflexibility pleased her. She was right—and that was it." Changing her mind about a movie would be tantamount to admitting she'd been wrong, which would mean acknowledging she could be wrong again. To a large extent the urgency, immediacy, and power of her critical voice *depended* on the absolute certainty—the inflexibility—of her present judgment.

There's a paradox here, because, as already mentioned, Kael's *style* of writing was one of self-discovery: she didn't know *what* she thought and felt about a movie until she wrote it down. Yet once she *had* written it down, that was it. It was as if she wrote herself into being and both the writing and the being were set in stone thereafter. To change her perspective, even a little bit, would have meant undoing the past—to deconstruct and undermine her "memoirs" would have been akin to revealing them as the products of a lie.

For Kael to change her mind she would have had to *rewrite* her past. The fact that she refused to edit or alter her old reviews in any way because she wanted them to accurately represent her original impressions is reasonable and right; but that she felt the need to continue to hold those views and to defend her original impressions is something else altogether. It implies that she was confined to—imprisoned by—a false identity built from words and phrases, opinions and judgments. Ironically, this present work is an attempt to address a similar dilemma in my own life. I'm attempting to reevaluate past experiences by revisiting old writings and deconstructing them, to find out what's underneath them and reach a truer, more authentic (because more *present*) voice—even if it means revoking all previous statements (even the most recent) until there's nothing left—like an onion having its layers peeled away, one by one.

This present chapter on Kael has proven to be one of the hardest things I've ever written, and I think it shows. My feelings, my opinions, about the subject are changing, both subtly and drastically, through the process of writing them down. My words and sentences keep undoing themselves; by this point I don't know *what* my opinion of Kael is. I can't have a clear, coherent, precise perspective on her because she's too deeply entangled with my own psychic formation, my development as a writer. It feels unsafe, forbidden, to admit that I might have been wrong about her or that I may have been deceived or negatively influenced by her writing in some way. And yet I know this is unavoidably the case, because it's true of *everything* in my past. None of it is what it seems and to a degree it's *all* a lie and I am wrong about everything. It's all forged memoirs, bricks in the prison house of a false memory syndrome. Screen memories.

Confronting the original sin of projected imagery—the psychic mother lode—is like pulling the main plug-in to the Matrix; it's the microchip that holds the whole circuit board together. Facing off with the movie dominatrix—General Kael, the high priestess of trash and art, my fairy godmother of phantasy—feels a lot like putting my soul in peril.

My guess (and it's only a guess) is that this was also the peril of Pauline, a peril which she faced on a daily basis and which she used writing—among other things—to rescue herself from. But like I say, it's only a guess.

*

Every artist is attempting the same thing: to discover and express what's inside them that's unique and to *individuate* from the collective that spawned them. The undisclosed goal of the individuation process is to become a "star," not in the movie sense of being adored by the masses, but in the sense of becoming an individual source of light, complete unto oneself, a "creator."

The creative process, when it's fully succumbed and committed to (committed to *by* succumbing to?), when it's seen *through* to the end, isn't a process of creation but one of discovery. And it's discovery through destruction, like mining for gold. How could an individual soul ever be created? Yet for the soul to be discovered it must be expressed, and that's a paradox that requires creativity to grasp because how can something be expressed before it's discovered? The desire to bust open the hypocrisy of all our false narratives and half-baked beliefs, theories, judgments, and opinions, is what drives the creative process. The subject of every critical study is always and finally the author himself. Or herself.

Pauline Kael was an artist before she was a critic. Because her artistry went into criticism, she may have eventually undermined her creative process, that of breaking down her own resistances and making the unconscious conscious, let the chips fall where they must, judgment be damned. Or maybe not. Film criticism only *seems* less creative than fiction writing (or filmmaking) because it's less obviously *imaginative*—because it doesn't conjure images from the unconscious but refers to already conjured ones. But whatever the genre, every sentence tells a story.

Imagination isn't only necessary to express one's unconscious life but also to discover what's in there to be expressed. It requires imagination to even recognize that creative potential is there to *be* expressed. Kael recognized potential in filmmakers, sometimes far beyond their own capacity to recognize it (or at least to discover and express it). I think, now, that she also fell short of recognizing and of owning her own potential. Her frustration and disappointment with film artists and their work was perhaps at least partly an unconscious expression of her frustration with herself. On the other hand, her delight when that inner light *did* come through in others fired her own creative expression as an artist-critic, causing her writing, for a brief while, to *shine*.

Like an infant star flashing its tiny light across endless darkness, seeking a home that no longer existed, Kael signaled furiously for a response, *any* response. The intensity of that signal fueled my own determination to shine, to express all of me at whatever the cost, to signal *back* to a fellow traveler. I responded to Kael not just because we shared a passion for movies (movies were the least of it), but because we were lost in the same darkness.

Lost *and* found.

Kael Kael Bang Bang

The Kael-Eastwood Feud & the Lie of the Western Hero

"All of us have probably had the feeling of being divided between what we got from our mother and what we got from our father, and no doubt some of us feel that we've gone through life trying to please each of them and never fully succeeding because we have always been torn between them."

—Pauline Kael, *When the Lights Go Down* (review of James Toback's *Fingers*)

Movies are heavily cut with fantasy, and when that fantasy spills over into the lives of the people who make them (or make a living writing about them), it becomes difficult to separate fantasy from reality. Above and beyond the movies themselves, the deeper meanings I'm seeking (by performing this examination of Kael's influence on my development) are to be found in the lives of the filmmakers and writers *behind* the movies; not by gazing at the wizardry on the screen but by studying the movements of the people behind the curtain. Wherever Kael "is," now that the lights have gone down on her life, these are the "morality plays" I'm drawn ever deeper into, to find out what's really there—both outside and inside of me.

Saint Clint Vs. General Kael

"A lot of people thought [Pauline] was really turned on by Clint Eastwood. He was the big, macho, alpha male, and Pauline just loved beating up on him. And I think there were reasons *why* she loved beating up on him."

—Ray Sawhill, to Brian Kellow

Kael's reviews of *Dirty Harry, Magnum Force,* and *The Enforcer* appear in *Deeper Into Movies, Reeling,* and *When the Lights Go Down,* respectively, all of which I read at roughly the same time (and maybe even before) I first saw those movies. All I really I knew was that Eastwood had responded publically to Kael's description of *Dirty Harry* as "fascism medievalism" (in "Saint Cop") by insisting that it didn't bother him because he knew she was "full of shit." But however little I knew of the ongoing feud between them at that time, it definitely made an impression on me. I adored Eastwood and I admired Kael, and I knew Kael despised Eastwood. It was a bit like being raised by parents who badmouth each other any chance they get and act out their animosity in front of the children. It leads to divided loyalties.

A couple of years ago, reading a small book by Paul Nelson, *Conversations with Clint Eastwood,* I found out how deep the animosity between them went. Oddly enough, Nelson was a friend of Jonathan Lethem, and Lethem provides an introduction to the book (I'd never heard of Lethem when I read it, so I didn't pay special attention to it). At one point in the book, Eastwood and Nelson are bitching about Kael and Eastwood says,

> She's really suckered them into thinking she knows something. That's what's so funny. It becomes *a kind of a joke.* Just making a lot of outrageous statements not having any bearing on anything, but you're doing them because you've found that that's the avenue to get attention. That's exactly what the secret to Kael is: she's found a way to get attention. [Emphasis added; I noticed also the way Eastwood changed pronouns, from "she" to "you," as if having an imaginary dialogue with his Nemesis.]

That's Clint's version in a nutshell. And while it may seem improbable to anyone who has seriously followed Kael's work, it's true enough that she got *Eastwood's* attention, and maybe that's what Clint is implying. If so, there may be something in that, too. Symmetrically enough, when Kael was asked about Eastwood's steadily growing reputation in a 1994 *New Yorker* interview (three years after she retired), she saw it as a "delicious joke—further proof that there's no such thing as objective judgment in the arts." What does it mean when two movie powerhouses try to publicly reduce each other to a joke? Turning someone into a joke is a way to strip them of their power, to reduce them to a buffoon. It's an offensive-defensive strategy, probably sparked by a fear of being powerless oneself: something in the other presents an inexplicable threat, and must be *reduced* by whatever means necessary.

In a footnote in the Nelson book, there's a quote from Sondra Locke's autobiography which states that, after Kael's review of *The Enforcer*, Eastwood asked a psychiatrist to do an analysis of Kael based on her reviews of his movies. According to Locke, Eastwood claimed that the psychiatrist's conclusion was that Kael was sexually attracted to Eastwood. According to Locke, Eastwood also claimed Kael had called him up to apologize to him for her reviews, but that he later admitted he'd made the story up!

Earmarks of an obsession? If it sounds from Locke's account more like Eastwood was inexplicably attracted to Kael, it pays to remember that such dangerous attractions (as seen in *Play Misty for Me* and *The Beguiled*, two Clint movies which Kael declined to review, or even mention) usually go *both ways*. The anecdote certainly betrays Eastwood's own bias: apparently any woman who was trying to get (his) attention could only want to be fucked by him. This plays out in an overt—and overtly macho—form in *High Plains Drifter*, Clint's first film as a director after the woman-fearing fantasy of *Misty*. A character played by Marianne Hill insults Eastwood's Stranger on the street, insinuating that he's less than a man in what is a very obvious "come on." His response: "If you want to get acquainted, *why don't you just say so?"* He then drags her off to the barn and gives her what she "really wants."

*

In fact, Kael's appreciation of Eastwood's physical attributes *was* evident from the very start, in the notorious *Dirty Harry* review which ignited the feud. In the second paragraph of "Saint Cop," Kael describes "soft-spoken Clint Eastwood—six feet four of lean, tough saint, blue-eyed and shaggy-haired, with a rugged, creased, careworn face that occasionally breaks into a mischief-filled Shirley MacLaine grin." (This loving description is made all the more curious by the comparison to MacLaine: Warren Beatty's sister! What would Freud make of all this?)

A few weeks before her *Dirty Harry* review, in "Notes on New Actors, New Movies," Kael acknowledged her susceptibility to the kind of *"male fascism* that makes an actor like Robert Redford or Jack Nicholson dangerous and hence attractive" (emphasis added). Apparently Clint's shrink was onto something, but if so, it didn't do much to assuage Eastwood's righteous indignation. In a 1996 "authorized biography" (read: hagiography) of Clint Eastwood, Richard Schickel claimed that Kael's review of *Dirty Harry* continued to haunt Eastwood throughout his career. Eastwood even asked Schickel if he'd happened to see an interview with Kael in which she said that one of her regrets about retirement was that she no longer had a forum in which to criticize Eastwood. "Can you imagine that kind of bigotry?" was Eastwood's question to Schickel.

Kael *was* unusually relentless in her disdain for Eastwood. Besides *Dirty Harry*, she conspicuously reviewed only his worst films, staying away from ones which—I would guess—she wouldn't have been able to excoriate to quite the same degree (*Coogan's Bluff, The Beguiled, Thunderbolt and Lightfoot, The Outlaw Josey Wales, Escape from Alcatraz,* or *Bronco Billy*). It's also undeniable that Eastwood's performance in *A Fistful of Dollars* *was* a kind of breakthrough, and that fifty years later it still stands up as a matchless piece of stylized acting and as the birth of one of the most enduring characters in movie history. Kael had kind words to say about almost every major male star of the period—not just Beatty, Redford and Newman but James Caan, Steve McQueen, Lee Marvin, Burt Reynolds, even *Charles Bronson* (who she compares to Christ) and *Ryan O'Neal!* Yet Eastwood was nothing but a "tall, cold cod"? Admittedly, she didn't lose any love on John Wayne, but even so there does appear to be something besides simple faulty judgment at play here.

Even if Kael was insincere in her disdain for Eastwood (she seemed to view baiting him as a kind of sport—or maybe schoolyard flirting?), bigotry is still a strong word for him to use to describe it. (Eastwood seems to view himself as a creed to be followed.) When he made the remark, in 1996, Eastwood was a fully established film legend with all the critical endorsements (and Oscars) that anyone could ever wish for, surely more than enough for him to feel secure in his legendary status? So a more pertinent question for him to have asked might have been: why did he still *care* so much?

*

As is invariably the case with rabbit holes, the deeper I went into this "movie," the darker it got. While I was searching the Internet for clues, I found the following passage:

> There's a scene in the final *Dirty Harry* movie, *The Dead Pool* [1988], in which a female film critic is brutally slain. Clint was thinking of Pauline Kael, his harshest critic ... The critic in this film is made up to resemble Kael as she appeared during this film's release as an in-joke.

I downloaded the movie—it's the worst of the *Dirty Harry* series, all-but unwatchable—and watched the scene. The middle-aged, large-nosed, dark-haired, and diminutive film critic Molly Fisher is writing at her desk in a night gown when she hears a sound. She gets up and closes the sliding doors. A masked killer grabs her from behind and holds a knife at her throat. "Do you ever notice how time seems to slow down at night?" he says. "Just like in my films—*a dream world.*"

In Kael's review of *Magnum Force*, "Killing Time," she referred to Eastwood as "the hero of a totally nihilistic dream world." And there's more. The masked killer in *The Dead Pool* is pretending to be (or deluded into believing he is) *a film director whose violent fantasies Fisher has panned in her reviews.* Fisher pleads with him by mentioning her weak heart. "A critic with a heart," says the killer, "that's a laugh." He then drags her over to the couch and throws her down, as if to rape her. He wants to know if she likes his films but she doesn't know who he is. "What kind of a film critic are you?" he snaps, then lists several films for her so she can identify him. "What do you think of my films?" he demands. "Give me your honest opinion." "I like them," Fisher says weakly. The killer calls her a liar and thrusts the knife towards her. The film cuts to the next scene; it's daylight and Harry arrives with his token oriental partner. The oriental makes a joke about the murder by giving it points out of ten, as if rating a movie. Dream worlds within dream worlds.

Did Kael know about Clint's little "in-joke"? Hollywood is a small town—or a small state of mind—so chances are she did. It was as if he was sending her a personalized message wrapped inside his tawdry little movie. (Ironically, and if nothing else, it would be a way of all-but compelling her to watch it!) This darkly occult anecdote echoes, rather grimly, my own simulated adolescent revenge fantasies involving movie scenes of violence against women. It also makes a pretty strong case for a Freudian analysis of Eastwood's Kael-obsession. Now that I think about it, what was the famously prosaic, anti-analytic Eastwood doing in therapy anyway? In a showdown between Dirty Harry and Dr. Freud, who's going to walk away with his armor intact?

"Sometimes, doc, a gun is just a gun!" (*Blam!!*)

Mother-Father Issues

"I want what I do to move along by hidden themes."
—Pauline Kael

Returning to Kael's own possible father-fixation on Saint Clint: apparently Eastwood not only missed the subtler allusions she made in 1972, but also the above-quoted 1994 interview, in which Kael made probably her first and last concession, both to Eastwood's acting *and* his sex appeal:

> I did think Eastwood's performance in *In the Line of Fire* was one of the best he's ever given, perhaps the best. But when he was fun in his early movies it wasn't because of his acting skill, and now that he has a little skill he's lost the spaghetti sexiness that made him fun. He's all sinews. He has become a favorite of intellectuals just when he's losing his mass audience. It has to be a consolation prize.

Kael calling Eastwood "fun" is a very far cry from her more-quoted descriptions of Eastwood as a "cold cod." In light of her more famous eviscerations, this is a perhaps striking case of dishonesty in her writing. If Kael really found Eastwood sexy and fun, why didn't she say so? Why did she imply the reverse? And, on the other side of the spaghetti stand-off, in light of their decades-long feud, why wasn't Kael's admission that she *enjoyed* Eastwood's "spaghetti sexiness" received by him as the olive branch it clearly was? Was it because it only rubbed salt in the wound? Wasn't it just like a woman to admit she *had* found him sexy all those years ago, now it was too late for him to do anything about it?

At the risk of getting overly Freudian about it, the picture all this paints is of an all-powerful male icon reduced to an angry, petulant child by the continued disapproval/rejection of a mother/anima figure immune to his charms. On the other side of the rift, there's a hugely influential female critic showing a seemingly disproportionate hostility towards a soft-spoken, saintly, masculine hero/father/animus figure. Mom, meet Dad. These sorts of unconscious psychodramas (even when as impersonal and long distance as this) are invariably symmetrically arranged. If Kael somehow unwittingly acted as a receptacle for Eastwood's mother issues, then Eastwood would have inevitably been a close match for Kael's unresolved "father stuff."

*

In his movie roles, Eastwood is pretty much indifferent to female charms (there are a few exceptions, but he mostly regrets it). In his public life, he was as contemptuous of Kael as she was of him in hers—though who started the playground bickering remains unclear, even after all these years. Also, Eastwood's career wasn't in any way *damaged* by her attacks; it may even, as Schickel suggests, have been boosted by them. It's likely that this— evidence of her powerlessness as a critic—would have rankled on Kael, even as her derision of Eastwood's acting skills and her suggestion that he was an unwitting dupe for Nixonite agendas would have wounded *his* pride. (Actually, Eastwood *was* buddying up to Nixon at this time, and eventually he did go into politics, though strictly local.) Apparently they were triggering each other's *power issues*—and power issues for grown-ups invariably come down to "sex," though also, at a more superficial level, money, status, and *influence*.

Kael was an anti-moral moralist; she despised message

movies and famously wrote, "If there is any test that can be applied to movies, it's that the good ones never make you feel virtuous." Yet there *were* movies that incited her wrath and moral indignation, and Eastwood's were most frequently in the line of her fire. I find it especially suggestive that, in her closing remarks in "Saint Cop," she describes a scene which she supposedly witnessed while leaving the theater: a little girl telling her father, "That was a *good* picture." Kael doesn't include the father's response (I'd love to know what it was); she merely offers it up as an implicit, dire warning that this "almost perfect piece of propaganda for para-legal police power" (a rare case of Kael alliterating for impact) had achieved its aim and colonized the consciousness of an innocent.

If the little girl was a point of identification (a stand-in) for Kael, both as a daughter *and* a mother, then perhaps such parental concern was preeminent in her disdain for Eastwood's pictures, and fueled her conviction that his saintly killers were unsuitable as ideals for the young, male *or* female? There are all kinds of nuance to this. *I* was using Eastwood as a role model, and I couldn't have helped but pick up on Kael's disapproval of my choice. At the same time, even her indignation is strangely ambivalent: Kael betrayed her attraction to Eastwood not only implicitly in "Saint Cop," but also explicitly in perhaps the last words she said publically about him. Separate the threads of ambivalence and what's revealed is something like Kael's *disappointment* with a strong male figure who proved unworthy of her hopes or expectations. Paging Dr. Freud.

It's telling also that Kael allegedly stopped having serious romantic relationships around the time she began reviewing films at *The New Yorker*. But that's a can of worms I will only tap lightly.

*

Unlike Clint's movie characters, Kael (born and raised in the West) never wore cowboy boots—even if she was accused of doing so because of her writing style. As if to compensate for her diminutive size and soft high voice, her prose had a noticeably masculine flavor: bawdy, sexual, frank, aggressive, and (unlike Eastwood, well-known for his laconic, instinctive, *anti*-intellectual personality) intellectually super-potent. Kael's independence and freethinking nature would also have been what made her both a threat and a challenge to movie studs like Eastwood and Beatty, for whom, *one imagines*, women were to be treated like horses...?

As an adolescent, I was obviously aware of being heavily influenced by Eastwood: I *chose* him as a powerful male figure to emulate. What I *wasn't* aware of was that Kael was an equally essential role model for me at the time. In fact, Kael had a much more profound influence on me because she was a writer, and writing, not acting, was what I ended up dedicating my professional life to.

For a male child, a strong mother figure is an unconscious influence that tends to far outweigh the more conscious influence of the "father." In my own experience, this is a fairly common situation for male children, and the open conflict between these public figures, with hindsight, *was* very much like seeing my parents going at it (something I grew up with but have no conscious memory of). I even tried to reconcile them (or at least to square the conflict of loyalty in myself) with *The Blood Poets*. The book was dedicated to Kael but gave special mention to Eastwood, "*el hombre sin nombre*," in the acknowledgments. I was aware that Kael might read this, and hoped it might soften the edge of her animosity towards Clint. I was careful to incorporate her point of view into my appraisal of Eastwood, as well as expressing my own, hoping to "Trojan Horse" my way past her defenses. I never had any illusions about Clint reading the book, which was also a match for my actual parents: I had close relations with my mother throughout her life but barely connected to my father at all (though he did read the book).

It seems logical to deduce from all of this that, without Mother Kael whispering in my ear, I would have been considerably more vulnerable to the influence of Father Clint. It was also probably inevitable that Kael won out. My love of Clint wasn't enough to override my allegiance to her judgments, but Kael's view of Clint certainly influenced mine. Reading her critical attacks on the *Dirty Harry* films at the same time I was seeing the movies for the first time would inevitably have leavened my responses to them. It didn't stop me loving the movies, but it can't possibly *not* have increased my awareness about their more questionable social and political implications — and about Eastwood's suitability as a role model. At a *conscious* level I didn't care; and yet here I am, thirty years later, still trying to figure out the degree to which Hollywood's glorification of violence has negatively impacted my psychological development. And I have become increasingly indifferent to Clint's more recent movie offerings, some of which are depressingly "conscientious" — as if to make up for past sins.

*

When Eastwood made *Unforgiven* in 1992, the film elevated him from a mere movie star icon to a *film artist* legend. *Unforgiven* was superficially presented, and received, as a kind of *apologia* for Clint's previous track record of violence-avocation. And while it's true he hasn't done anything overtly pro-violence since that film (even *Gran Torino* had him martyr himself), it's questionable just how convincing a case against violence *Unforgiven* really made. The film is *vocally* against violence — courtesy of Eastwood's self-castigating, philosophical musings in the film — but scratch the celluloid and underneath lurks the same Western myth of "man with violent past coming to the aid of helpless villagers" (in this case prostitutes), using violence to save the community. As I wrote in 1999, "*Unforgiven* is more complicated than deep—its complexity comes not from a conscious ambiguity so much as a kind of schizophrenia that exists between its intentions and its methods." Presumably this schizophrenia—or dividedness—exists in Eastwood himself.

If with *Unforgiven* Eastwood was genuinely trying to make a new start, somehow he couldn't quite do it, and he was rewarded (like a politician) for his intentions rather than the results. (He came closer to succeeding with *Gran Torino*, which forgoes the violent revenge climax by having the character triumph by sacrificing himself.) The fact he even *tried* to come clean, however, is reason to wonder if Kael's protests didn't get through to him at some level. Maybe at least *part* of the reason Eastwood was so "haunted" by her calling him a fascist medievalist was that, deep down, he knew she was right? Kael got his attention, and she held it as long as it took for the penny to finally drop. Not all women were only looking to get fucked. Maybe *this* accounts for his continued anger and disappointment when Kael didn't receive William Munny's attempt at "repentance" and continued to badmouth him, even post-*Unforgiven*? (Except for the bit about his sexiness.)

Unforgiven indeed.

Dream Worlds

"Movies—a tawdry corrupt art for a tawdry corrupt world—fit the way we feel ... Movies are our cheap and easy expression, the sullen art of displaced persons."

—Pauline Kael, "Trash, Art, and the Movies"

So why was Clint so sorely in need of forgiveness, and what was it about Kael that was so badly scarred that she could not forgive? In *Kiss Kiss Bang Bang* ("Saddle Sore"), Kael writes,

My father went to a Western just about every night of his life that I remember. He didn't care if it was a good one or a bad one or if he'd seen it before. *He said it didn't matter ...* The Old West was a dream landscape with simple masculine values; the code of the old Western heroes probably wouldn't have much to say to audiences today. But the old stars, battling through stories that have lost their ritual meaning, are part of a new ritual that does have meaning. There's nothing dreamy about it: these men have made themselves movie stars — which impresses audiences all over the world. *The fact that they can draw audiences to a genre as empty as the contemporary Western is proof of their power.* Writers and painters now act out their fantasies by becoming the superstars of their own movies (and of the mass media) ... When it makes money, it's not just their fantasy. *The heroes nobody believes in — except as movies stars — are the result of a corrupted art form* [Emphasis added].

This was written in August of 1967. The three Leone-Eastwood Spaghetti Westerns were released in the US between in January, May, and December of that year, so *at that precise time,* Eastwood was in the middle of becoming internationally famous. Kael was writing not about Eastwood but about John Wayne, Robert Mitchum, and Kirk Douglas — the *old* Western stars who took her father away from her, into the empty fantasy space of the movie theater. A point which Kael doesn't make, but which I think is implicit in her account, is that her father chose to withdraw into Western fantasy rather than spend time *with his family.* "He said it didn't matter." The implication (for me at least, maybe I'm just cynical) was that it didn't matter as long as it got him out of the house.

There's further evidence for this reading — albeit circumstantial — in her review of *Hud,* in which she mentions her father several times. She describes "my father and older brothers charging over dirt roads ... in Studebakers," apparently a man-only activity to which she wasn't invited. A few pages later she recounts a memory of her father,

> taking me along when he visited a local widow: I played in the new barn that was being constructed by workmen who seemed to take their orders from my father. At six or seven, I was very proud of my father for being the protector of widows.

She then admits that he was "adulterous," comparing him to Paul Newman's Hud, adding that he was "opposed to government interference" but "in no sense a social predator." He was "generous and kind" she says, and "democratic." She leaves out any indication of how she felt when her child's dream-view of her father as a "protector" was shattered by the adult realization of his adultery. And despite her kind words about him, the three incidents recounted all have a single theme: her own exclusion, as a little girl, from her father's life.

Kael's father was a Polish, Jewish immigrant living in the West, running his own farm and in charge of Mexican workers. Probably another reason, consciously or not, he went to see a Western every night was because he was trying to learn about his new homeland, trying to figure out the proper "form," and John Wayne movies would have offered a kind of fantasy schooling on how to pass as an American. But whatever it was that pulled him or pushed him out of the home and into the movie theater—that *displaced* him—this dream landscape of cowboys, Studebakers, and adultery apparently took Kael's father from her. Behind the dream was something not at all dreamy: the crass opportunism not just of philandering husbands but of movie stars *exploiting the corrupted art form which created them*. Heroes of a totally nihilistic dream world.

No wonder Kael was so dedicated to saving the art form from

corruption. And no wonder she felt such hostility towards a star like Eastwood—except there *were* no others like Eastwood; not for Kael. He was her *bête noir*. He embodied that corruption the way the filmmakers tried to make Hud the embodiment of small-town evil—a cheap stunt which Kael rightly called them out on. So why Eastwood, then, and not Wayne or the old time stars? The obvious answer is that Eastwood was on the ascent where Wayne was on the downward curve. Kael was after the biggest game in town.

Eastwood would go on to direct his own Western fantasies and to seize the Western crown from Wayne. Wayne himself was allegedly so disturbed by *High Plains Drifter* that he wrote Eastwood a letter, complaining that "the real West" was nothing like this, that it was full of good people (like Kael's father?) who pulled together to tame the wilderness! Wayne would have been fully aware at that time (1972/3) that he had already been super-seded and that his time in the sun was done, the proof being a shabby little *Dirty Harry* imitation he made the following year, *McQ*. Kael—with a characteristic mix of heartiness and heart-lessness—blasted it to smithereens. Eastwood, by his own account, never replied to Wayne's letter.

In a very curious side note, Wayne died of cancer a few years later, cancer which allegedly he contracted as a result of witnessing an atomic detonation while playing Genghis Khan(!) in *The Conqueror*, in 1955, for producer Howard Hughes. The name of the atom bomb, bizarrely, was "Dirty Harry." Were the makers of *Dirty Harry* slyly referencing this incident in their film? Was it a conscious (or semi-conscious) message to Wayne that the same system which had given him life was now taking it away? The Western king is dead. Wayne's last film, in 1976, was *The Shootist*; it was about a gunfighter dying of cancer, and it was directed by *Dirty Harry*'s Don Siegel.

*

In her writing at least, Kael clearly disliked Westerns, not just the bad ones but the classics too. The only ones I can think of which she unequivocally praised were Peckinpah's *Ride the High Country* and Robert Altman's *McCabe and Mrs. Miller* (really an anti-western; apparently she also loved *Red River*, however). In *Going Steady*, she dismissed *The Good the Bad and the Ugly* in a couple of paragraphs, as if beneath her to even write about it. But in 1973, in "Killing Time," she took a more nuanced stance. Spaghetti Westerns, she wrote,

> stripped the Western form of its cultural burden of morality. They discarded its civility along with its hypocrisy. In a sense they liberated the form: what the Western hero stood for was left out, and what he embodied (strength and gun power) was retained.

"In the figure of Clint Eastwood," she added, "the Western morality play and the myth of the Westerner were split." Kael linked the idea of a "liberation from morality" (and how she hated pious movies!) to the "fascist medievalism" of the Clint Eastwood-style anti-hero which came about when the Western myth was transposed to the modern urban milieu, via the police actioner. In her view, the liberation of the Western form, weirdly and in some tangly, spaghetti-like, roundabout way, led to the creation of "a nihilistic dream world." Apparently Kael herself was divided: as much as she loathed the hypocritical sentimentality of the Wayne Westerns, it was still preferable to Eastwood's nihilism.

Her view makes a certain sense if we consider that American values are all tied up with the *imaginary (corrupt) vision* of the West, and that nihilism is the absence of all values. (Fundamentally, nihilism relates to *the absence of the father*, God, i.e., that which bestows true value.) The values which Western movies and movie stars exploited for shallow gain were the same values that made such exploitation possible. The illusion is that these values were ever real to begin with. The Wild West was not won by heroes but by opportunists: by conmen, robber barons, murderers, rapists, and thieves. The mystery is, how were entire generations of Americans tricked into feeling nostalgia for a time that never was? Movies can take some of the blame for that, but by no means all of it.

*

Nihilism is also the word Kael used (in *When the Lights Go Down*, "Notes on the Nihilist Poetry of Sam Peckinpah") to describe another filmmaker who attempted to liberate the Western form from the cultural burden of Hollywood/American morality (= hypocrisy). In her own words, Sam Peckinpah was, of all contemporary American directors at that time, the one Kael felt "closest to." (She meant it in personal terms—they were friends—but also I think in terms of responding to his work.) Though she didn't review the film (due to her writing only six-months a year at *The New Yorker*), she called Peckinpah's *The Wild Bunch* "a beautiful, self-destroying machine"; while she was once again crowing about how the genre was dead, she wrote that "the new wine of *The Wild Bunch* explodes the bottle" of the Western.

There's something here that I can't quite get at but that I can clearly see bubbling under the surface. It has to do with how Kael was looking for a movie hero (filmmaker/star) to "liberate" her from her "cultural burdens" by exploding the American fantasy (dream world) of the Western hero. This would have to do with her own father projections, and it would go all the way back to her father's "abandoning" her to escape into Studebakers, widows' arms, and the fantasy world of Western movies. You think? It all adds up, even if it also all seems somehow... fantastic. As fantastic as an atom bomb called Dirty Harry killing Genghis Khan/John Wayne...?

When Peckinpah made *Straw Dogs*, released a few weeks after *Dirty Harry*, Kael referred to the film in almost identical terms to those she used on *Dirty Harry*, calling it "a fascist work of art." Peckinpah's response (in *Playboy*) was that, much as he liked Kael, she was "full of shit" —exactly the same words Eastwood used. Whether this was a phrase Kael's father employed, it was almost certainly one she favored. (Peckinpah also used a more colorful phrase: Kael was "cracking walnuts with her ass" — presumably Sam's imaginative way of calling her a ballbreaker.)

To bring it all into an even more incestuous perspective, Peckinpah and Eastwood —the two "male fascists" on whom Kael had set her sights—were slated to work together at *exactly that time*, with *Jeremiah Johnson*. The film was eventually made by Sydney Pollack and Robert Redford, from a script by *Magnum Force*-writer John Milius, and of course Kael slammed it. It was a Western, after all.

*

From adolescence to adulthood, Eastwood was my favorite actor and the person I most desperately wanted to *be* like. Despite superficial resemblances (height, leanness, a heavy brow), it wasn't a comparison anyone was likely to make (even if my school friend did). Yet curiously, Pauline Kael used the word "stoned" in reference both to myself and Clint. In "Killing Time" she called Eastwood "the first truly stoned hero in the history of movies"; twenty-five years later, in her generous response to *The Blood Poets*, she referred to my sensibility as "only slightly stoned." Naturally this led to the question of exactly what Kael meant by "stoned."

One obvious meaning is "out of it," out of touch with reality, dissociated. This fits with Kael's description of Eastwood as being somehow disembodied. ("There's an odd disparity between his deliberate, rather graceful physical movements and his practically timbreless voice. Only his hands seem fully alive.") Kael saw Eastwood as lost in a narcotized, "nihilistic [Godless] dream world" of his own creation—a kind of movie trance state. Eastwood may even have acknowledged this, in an oblique way, when in *Unforgiven* William Munny admits that the only reason he was so dangerous was because he'd been half drunk the whole time: his "stoned" state slowed down his movements and allowed him to keep his cool, while the other guy panicked and fired off shots blind.

Kael was probably the only movie critic to equate Clint's coolness with being stoned or dissociated. Eastwood's movie characters are usually associated with autonomy (even to the point of rebelliousness), individualism, uncompromising integrity, and ruthlessness. His public persona is also associated with these qualities, as well as with phenomenal worldly success and high social status (and latterly, artistic integrity). All of these are *superficially* masculine qualities. Yet throughout his career— up to and including his breakthrough "artistic" film *Unforgiven*—violence, and the implicit or explicit glorification of male brutality—had been *the predominant ingredient*. This was Kael's main "truck" with Clint.

If, as Slavoj Žižek and others have argued, violence is a show not of strength but of weakness, then maybe something similar can be asked about Eastwood's *apparent* creative independence and achievements as a film artist? How much has his stonedness, say, allowed him to be used as a *celebrity-tool* for parapolitical agendas (propagating violence), and how much has that contributed to his success as an actor and a filmmaker? If Eastwood's output implicitly reveals a *lack* of authentic autonomy (masculinity), was it this, and the "truly stoned" quality that signaled it, which Kael was reacting so violently against?

Her rejection of Eastwood as a suitable role model for the young would have been fired not only by this awareness but, less consciously, by her own experience of being let down and deceived (and perhaps worse) by such a man. Was this (and not just Eastwood) what Kael was implicitly, and of course indirectly, warning me against? My sense (based on direct experience) of this stoned, disembodied state has to do with a child remaining immersed in the mother's psyche/body, in the absence of a father (God) to "fish him out," to draw him into a fully embodied, autonomous state of being. Admittedly this might seem a bit of a stretch (no pun intended), but maybe Kael (like many independent women) was especially on the lookout for, and on guard against, this sort of "stonedness" or lack of embodiment (mother bondage) with all the men in her life? Kael's own apparent masculinity (her writer's voice, those cowboy boots) would have been partly her way of "fathering" herself. It would have been a way of compensating for a lack (or an excess) of such maleness in her upbringing, but also an unconscious expression of her *need* for embodied, *unstoned* men. Like all unconscious behavior, however, it would have often had the opposite effect, that of attracting emasculated males—like the Paulettes. Eastwood *seemed* to have all the desired qualities, both in his film roles and in his life, of a *manly* (fully embodied) sort of man. Maybe that was what Kael saw in him at first—his "spaghetti sexiness." If so, she quickly changed her view of him, and with such ferocity that there was almost certainly something personal—some feeling of betrayal or at least disappointment— behind it.

This doesn't mean Kael's view of Eastwood wasn't correct; only that it was fueled by unresolved emotions and irrationally argued, deceptively "loaded" with unconscious charge. This would also account for the degree of anger, hostility, and violence which she unwittingly—I could say *naively*—provoked, not just in Eastwood but in so many other men (including ones who never met her). Kael's identification of the *corruption of the art form* centered on the movie star as a Western hero; her implication was that it wasn't just that playing Western heroes made an actor a movie star, but that, by playing the Western hero, movie stars *kept the (false) Western ideal alive.* It was a two-way trade and it was 100% illicit. It was a lie, because *the idea of the Western hero is completely at odds with the idea of a movie star.*

The Western ideal is that of an independent man, unshackled or burdened by the constraints of civilization, unsocialized. The movie stars who played these heroes were men of culture whose status—*livelihood*—required them to be shackled to, and in service of, the social system. They were like kept horses, trained and saddled to be ridden, and they were as saddle sore as the cowboys they played. It was the sneaky sleight of hand of capitalism in Hollywood microcosm: the movie ideals of masculinity and independence, by being falsely associated with social status, wealth, and influence, were part of the implacable machinery which "civilized" the West, and by which the "heroes" (including Kael's father) were emasculated, tamed, "broken in." The ideal of the free man was central to the ideology that enslaved all men.

*

If much of this seems presumptuous, so it should! I am joining all sorts of dots based on very little intimate knowledge of Kael's private life or psychology, based only on having read her reviews so many times and so closely that I feel as if I *do* know her, intimately. This may be a misconception, but if so it's a misconception Kael herself encouraged. Her statement that her film reviews were also her memoirs can be read two ways. It could indicate that Kael went so deeply into movies that she revealed everything worth knowing about herself. Or it could suggest that she kept such a tight lid on her private, inner life, and lived so much for and *through* movies, that there wasn't much else *to* know about her outside of her critical responses. In a way the two statements are the same, but I think both are inaccurate. (This is why I found Kellow's biography so disappointing. Kellow took Kael at her word, and even then, he didn't dig up many bones from the official burial ground of her "memoirs.")

My own view is more like this: following in her father's wandering footsteps, movies were Kael's "dream landscape." Like so many of us, she buffered herself from the tawdry corruption of the real world by escaping into movies. As she grew older, she opposed the tawdriness of the movies themselves by approaching them critically, *as a writer*, hoping to somehow redeem them through her passion, her *attention*. If the movies captured her father's attention—with their phony Western ideal of manhood which they dangled, like a carrot before a horse—so deeply that he went missing from her life, she would give the movies *that same level of attention*. It was the same attention she had wanted—*needed*—as a child but hadn't received. Simply put, movies had to somehow be made worthy of having stolen her father's attention from her. Redeem the movies and she could redeem her father, and, by extension, herself.

By writing about movies in the way she did, Kael imbued the act of moviegoing with an almost religious (definitely sexual) depth and meaning. By adding her own energy and attention to the light-stuff of phantasy, by attempting to rescue them from the tawdry corruption of men like Wayne and Eastwood—the "cowboy killers" she both scorned and unconsciously emulated—and by looking to people like Peckinpah and Beatty as "rescuers," she gave movies a third and fourth dimension. By adding the images taken from her own dream or interior life, she did temporarily redeem the landscape, and reclaimed her dreams into the bargain.

Even as I write this, I feel sure I am right. There's a reason I feel sure. It takes a displaced, hothead movie fantasist to catch another.

Peddlers of Astonishment

Tales to Astonish & Nostalgia for the Present

There's a quote from F. Scott Fitzgerald which I've been using for years but which I've never been able to locate the source of. "The movies have stolen our dreams. Of all betrayals, this is the worst." It sounds good but what does it *mean*? Who betrayed whom, and why and how did it happen?

Childhood is the period of transition between being culture-free and culture-immersed, to being empty of external images to filled to saturation point with them. Childhood is also an endless capacity for astonishment, in which everything seems new because everything *is* new. Until it gets old. A personal example. I started collecting Marvel comic books at around the age of six. That's around the same time my (semi-) linear memories begin. Is there a connection? If identity is bestowed on us by culture, then pre-culture, did an "I" even exist? What kind of world was I living in? What kind was I escaping from? I don't remember so I can only deduce. My deduction is that when I was growing up my reality was hostile and unsafe and there was nowhere I could escape to except fantasy. Comic books, and later movies, provided an external source for fantasy, they were the raw material I used to build my Fortress of Solitude and furnish it with "marvels." Over time, that fortress became a prison.

The objects and inhabitants of my inner space became fixed outside of me. As objectively "real" characters on page and movie screen, they were immune to the influence of my imagination, yet they were fueled and given substance *by* it. They became the guardians of my inner galaxy, my prison keepers. I was possessed by the spirits of Winnie the Pooh, Piglet, Spiderman, the Thing and the Silver Surfer, then later by Elvis Presley, Clint Eastwood, Bud Cort, Woody Allen, David Bowie.

My inner guardians protected me but at a price: like Rapunzel in her tower, I could never leave the Phantom Zone. I became a hostage to the outer images I'd invited into my inner space.

The proof of this wild hypothesis? You are reading it. Thirty, forty years later, I am still writing about these same characters. Here's looking at you, kid.

*

The comic book writer Alan Moore got flack recently for calling superhero fans "emotionally subnormal." Chris Claremont (the writer of *The Uncanny X-Men* in the 80s) said more or less the same thing: "Rarely will you find among fans, comic or SF, a magnificent physical specimen of humanity. Because if you're that good mentally or physically, you don't need the fantasy—the reality is good enough."

Who are these people for whom reality is good enough, I wonder? If they exist, they're definitely not artists. Don't Moore and Claremont make a *living* at escaping into fantasy?! Talk about ingrates! Moore's point was that superheroes were originally written for kids and adolescents but that now those kids were in their forties and fifties (like me) and still infatuated with the same formulae of tawdry little empowerment fantasies. "I think it's a rather alarming sign," Moore said, "if we've got audiences of adults going to see the *Avengers* movie and delighting in concepts and characters meant to entertain the 12-year-old boys of the 1950s." (Actually the Avengers were created in 1962.)

When I watch the spanking new Hollywood versions of the Marvel heroes I grew up on, I experience a mixture of nostalgic excitement—the echo of past astonishments—with queasy distaste. I know that these movies are hugely expensive corporate products tied into all kinds of merchandising, that they are exploiting the dreams of new generations of kids while being almost wholly divorced from the original surge of inspiration that created those characters and stories back in the 60s. And I know that, because many of these movies are filled with military hardware and (openly or implicitly) backed by the US government and armed forces, they are part of a much larger "fantasy": that of propaganda for a crumbling capitalist system. This gives the violence and destruction a very different flavor. The 2013 bloated obscenity *Man of Steel* was like *Triumph of the Will* for the smartphone generation—except that *Triumph of the Will* was reputedly a work of art and *Man of Steel* was unrecyclable garbage, the toxic waste of a sickening empire.

The dream has been stolen and the dreamer betrayed. This played out in the real world too, when the DC Corporation left Superman's creators, Jerry Siegel and Joe Shuster, out in the cold. The intellectual property of "Superman" belongs to the corporation not to the creators. (The same thing happened to Jack Kirby at Marvel, and a host of other artists and writers.) The way a relationship ends shows the potential that was there from the beginning. However long it takes for the rot to sink in, the seeds of corruption must have been present at the start.

*

The problem with living in a world of fantasy is that it's lonely. The problem with living in the real world is that it's overpopulated and extremely difficult to get other people to agree with you or to get things to turn out the way you want. (Hence the need for fantasy.) The best of both worlds is to create your own fantasy-reality (like Moore and Claremont) and get people to come in and populate it. The catch with this is that then you will be obliged to hang out with "emotionally subnormal" people who desperately need the relief of *your* fantasy. This is probably why Moore and Claremont are so nonplussed with the state of their (former) fans—they don't like what the cultural mirror is reflecting back at them.

If we need fantasy to survive, why are we so sure it's bad for us? Isn't turning fantasy into reality the basis for just about *every-thing* we do? Where's the line between reality and fantasy? How would we know it if we found it?

The French philosopher Jean Braudrillard (I've never read him, though I tried once) quipped (if French philosophers quip, I don't know), "Disneyland is presented as imaginary in order to make us believe that the rest is real," when in fact America "belongs to the hyperreal order and to the order of simulation." In the same way, movies serve to help people forget that their *existence* is a movie, a waking dream state that's externally, as well as internally, generated.

How so? Images from the past play endlessly on the interior screens of our minds and keep us voluntarily lost inside the pseudo-narrative of our lives. The goal was to get so swept up in the movie narrative that we'd forget all our troubles, forget ourselves so completely that we'd forget we were even *watching* a movie or that we'd ever agreed to suspend disbelief, and start to believe that *this was life*. We paid our money and we made our choice.

When the French artist, writer, and filmmaker Jean Cocteau asked Sergei Diaghilev (an art critic and ballet impresario) what he could do for him in the realm of the theatre, Diaghilev's reply was: "Astonish me." That's art's function: to astonish, to spellbind us. When the fantasy astonishes us so deeply that it trumps reality, we get what we always wanted: relief from a Disneyland reality that isn't, that *shouldn't* be, good enough for anyone. And when you strip all the fancy adornments and rationalizations away, isn't that what everyone wants, the relief of being utterly and truly astonished by life?

*

Back to the personal. I remember when I was about eight, the cupboard in my playroom where my comic collection was stored, inside cardboard boxes in numerical order. I found images from those comic book covers on the Internet recently (*The Mighty World of Marvel, Spider-Man Comics Weekly*), and while I was looking at them it felt like it pierced all the way to the core of my being. I'm not even sure if "felt" is the right word for it; it was more like an invocation, a metaphysical tremor, a wobble in reality, an echo from another time when fantasy images seemed more real to me than reality does now. I can remember, dimly, what it felt like to be *that* raw, *that* open, *that* susceptible to astonishment.

Yet those tales that astonished me weren't the real source of my astonishment. In a sense, they were what stole it from me. By causing me to fixate on fantastic images, on marvels outside of my direct experience, they made ordinary life seem, well, *ordinary*. I associate those images and stories with astonishment now, not because they were so astonishing but because they captured the endless capacity for astonishment which I possessed then, and *fixed* it, like a butterfly in amber. Now I don't remember the astonishment, I only remember the tales.

When I was eight or nine I started to write and draw my own comic books, mostly using Marvel characters. Later I began to write scripts and imagined the movies I would make with my favorite actors. Those were the not-so-humble beginnings of my artistic aspirations, aspirations that continue to this day. As a reader and moviegoer, I want to be astonished; as a writer, etc., I want to astonish others and get the credit for it. It seems harmless enough—even natural. Who *doesn't* feel that way sometimes?

But now that I am trying to write about what drives me to write, to get at what's underneath all the fancy rationalizations and intellectualizations and bust open my own fantasy narrative, my writing is starting to dry up and I can barely form sentences the way I want to. My writing is slowly transmogrifying into an

apology for writing—how dourly English!—and yet, ridicu-
lously, if I didn't feel the need to apologize, there'd be nothing to
apologize for. So maybe amends is what I'm shooting for.

Creating products (like this one) out of one's inner life via
arrested-adolescence superhero fantasies of "the will to power,"
or whatever, and then using them to impress others (starting with
"mom" or "dad")—maybe *this* is where the *original* betrayal
occurs? Is this how, and when, the exploitation first begins, with
the exploitation of oneself? The day I let pop culture infiltrate me
and swore allegiance to it, I became a carrier for it, in lifetime's
service to it. Anything for an identity, anything to be a
"somebody." What does it benefit a child if he gives up his
internal kingdom to gain a mighty world of marvels?

I'm talking about pop culture but it applies to all kinds. It
begins with pop culture because that's what grabs us as kids, and
I do mean *grabs*. Culture is a bacterium that lives off an organism
and transforms it. It can be benevolent or malignant or a bit of
both. It can even move between benign and malign, depending
on the nature of the host organism or the relationship between
the two. What it can never be is integral to the system it lives off.

Who doesn't want to be astonished? Astonishment is the most
precious commodity there is. Without it, nothing amounts to
much, but with it, wonder of wonders, even the smallest offering
becomes enough. We are drawn to art—both as recipients and
creators—as a way to get free of the bogus tales of the past, still
playing endlessly out on our interior movie screens, to return to
that raw, open feeling of being in the present. Ironically, because
that in-the-moment living experience, that innocence, is lost in
the distant past, when we try to recapture it we are trying to
bring the past into the present and we end up getting lost in the
past. It's like we are seeking to feel nostalgia for the present.

That's how the cultural bug of fantasy gets transmitted, from
host to host and sea to shining sea; that's how the whims of the
fathers and mothers are passed down to the sons and daughters.

When we adopt the mistaken belief that we need extraordinary things to feel astonishment, we lose our capacity to be astonished by ordinary things. We seek to make our lives extraordinary, to become artists, visionaries, superstars. We look for ever-more tales to astonish.

The especially gifted become peddlers of astonishment.

Sympathy for the Damned

Weird Scenes from a Movie Underworld

"There is no decent place to stand in a massacre."
—Leonard Cohen, "The Captain"

In *Kiss Kiss Bang Bang*, Kael describes an encounter with the screenwriter Sydney Buchman, who wrote a film about a pedophile called *The Mark*. The pedophile in *The Mark* is a pedophile in thought but not deed, wracked by guilt at his illicit desire. Kael reviewed the film on its release, and Buchman wanted to know what she'd had against it. He assured her that he'd only been trying to get people to feel sympathy for "the mentally ill." Kael asked Buchman what sort of compassion was needed when the central character was innocent of any wrongdoing. Buchman admitted that the case the film was based on was of an actual child rapist, but that, if he'd told the truth, he "couldn't get people to feel compassion for him." "I didn't want to tell him that that was almost a definition of the artist's task," Kael wrote, "so I just let it drop."

A definition of the artist's task.

Why do children like fairy tales in which gruesome things happen to the characters? The simplest answer is that scenes of horror in a fantasy framework provide a way to safely re-enact forgotten or suppressed experiences of a different—less fantastic—sort, mundane horrors that are unresolved in a child's (or adolescent's or adult's) psyche, thereby providing catharsis.

What does this have to do with the artist's task being to help others feel compassion for a child rapist? My own primary goal as writer is very close, if not identical, to Kael's definition. My guess is that one of the main reasons I feel this way is because of a need to understand my own, more aberrant appetites as an adolescent. The need to invoke compassion in readers for seemingly "beyond the pale" characters reflects a less conscious appeal for compassion for myself. I want to make sure I am not beyond the pale.

There was a movie I saw shortly after I turned twenty that changed my life. It was called *Blue Velvet* and it was about a young man's attempt to solve a local mystery that turned into a rite of passage. Central to Jeffrey's rite of passage was a discovery of his own capacity for, and attraction to, darkness and sexual deviance. The film's villain, Frank Booth, played by Dennis Hopper, is a terrifying but also a heartrending figure, a tragic villain. What struck me most about the film was that it invoked compassion for this monstrous character. However aberrant he was, he was not beyond the pale. He was all-too-human.

I remember as an adolescent smoking my first cigarette behind my father's house, being physically aroused by the act simply because it was a taboo. I think I was drawn to extreme movie violence for the same reason: because it was forbidden. When I was growing up there was a great furor around "video nasties"; by following this latent interest, I quickly gained an acute, and unwelcome, awareness of my own capacity for darkness. Like Jeffrey, I was seeking sensation, but beneath that was a deeper urge, the urge to understand what it was in me that was seeking sensation. I was a detective hunting a deviant, only to discover that the deviant was myself. I was an artist exploring madness and aberration, only to discover that the madness, and the aberration, was my own.

A (Family) Snapshot from Hell: The Texas Chainsaw Massacre

"Whatever makes a soldier sad will make a killer smile."
—Leonard Cohen, "The Captain"

I think I first saw *The Texas Chainsaw Massacre* at a rerun cinema on Charing Cross Road, London, long since closed. Back in the early 80s, the film was playing at that particular movie theater for years. It was part of the urban landscape which I was exploring, as I took my first few tentative steps away from troubled home life, into the darkly alluring world of adulthood. Originally, it was comic books that inspired me to make daytime pilgrimages to the Big City. Later, movies provided the lure, the impetus, to venture into those strange, potentially hostile lands. But down those mean streets a boy had to go who was not himself mean.

Some fifteen years later, I wrote about the film in *The Blood Poets*. By that time I considered it a work of art. Here's what I wrote:

> In the film's first really shocking scene, Leatherface, having already bludgeoned one of the male characters to death, grabs the dead boy's girlfriend and, as she flails wildly about in his arms, impales her on a meat hook. He leaves her helplessly thrashing while, before her unbelieving eyes, he carves up her boyfriend with a chainsaw. We get a genuine sense here of just what must be going through the character's mind in her last moments—the absolute horror of being so abruptly and ruthlessly dragged from her pleasant, everyday oblivion, into a world of madness, pain, and dismemberment.

That's a pretty good summary of the whole movie, and of the entire horror genre. *Texas Chainsaw Massacre* is as well-known as it is for a *reason*: it's probably the most baldly horrific horror movie ever made. I find this passage striking because it communicates something basic about the kind of experience horror movies offer (and that I was so avidly seeking), and yet so rarely deliver. How often does a horror movie take us all the way *into* the experience and put us squarely in the position of the victim? With *Massacre* the experience goes beyond compassion—I didn't feel *sorry* for the victim, I experienced her pain and horror. This isn't what a horror movie is *expected* to do. A horror movie is supposed to entertain us not traumatize us. This is what made *Massacre* more than just a horror movie, for me, and why I found it appropriate to call it a work of art. The emotional intensity and realness of it is what I associate with art, not exploitation.

We in the audience are never given any more reason for this than she is, and we are left with little choice but to identify either with the victim, and find ourselves hanging from a meat hook, or to side with the "victor," and wield the chainsaw. The third alternative is total detachment, a luxury the film doesn't allow us. It's not a pleasant choice to have to make, and *Texas Chainsaw Massacre* is by no means a film for everyone—it's strictly for those who feel compelled to confront the darker parts of their psyches, whether for pleasure or for the more complex, cathartic business of understanding, and maybe purging, their own evil.

Not a film for everyone. Yet *Massacre* was a massive hit, and certainly not with the "art" crowd. From reports I've read, audiences sometimes cheered the action, so evidently they were anything but traumatized by it. What were my responses? They varied. I found the film horrifying and deeply disturbing when I first saw it. Later, on at least one occasion, I found the brutality of it arousing—which in a way was even more disturbing. In the first case, I was identifying with the victims, feeling their horror, powerlessness, and pain as my own; in the second, I identified with the tormentors and experienced what, presumably, they would have experienced: the sexually-charged rush of *power*. There is a third possibility, which I think depends on allowing for a fusion of the first two, and it's here that the real horror is found.

In a murderous scenario such as forms the basic context/structure of the slasher movie, there are only two possible points of identification—that of the murderer and the victim. Given such a choice, most people will, understandably, choose the point of view of the killer ... In a murderous society, there are only two possible roles to assume. The passive witness is of course a third option, appropriately enough to the couch potato generation; but one must ask—just how "passive" can a witness be in a massacre? At the profoundest level—that of perception—we are all active participants. In which case, the question remains, basically, kill or be killed. Fight or flight. Passivity, then, equates not with the position of the witness, but the victim.

The luxury which moviegoing offers *is* the luxury of passive witness. Movies allowed me to see, up-close and personal, every imaginable horror without ever being physically threatened. Movies gave me a decent place to stand (or sit) in a massacre. Previously, historically, this position was reserved for emperors and kings. Therefore, the passive position of witness becomes a position of supreme *power*.

The film gives us a *huis clos*, a no way out situation, precisely because it leaves us with no solace, no refuge—it is either kill or be killed. [The director Tobe] Hooper ensures that his killers are such a foul and degenerate bunch that there can be no pleasure or relief in siding with them [or, only the most deeply unsettling kind of pleasure]. They are all-too-real, and we get to feel instead the insanity, the alienation, even the pathos, of such abject creatures whose only pleasure is to give pain. *Texas Chainsaw Massacre* is one of the very few horror films that suggests that the real horror is not in the point of view of the victim, but that of the killer.

This was really the cornerstone of my philosophy, and how a post-adolescent interest in low-budget horror movies and video nasties naturally led to a more adult passion for Dostoyevsky and depth psychology. While the victims in *Massacre* aren't especially well-drawn or memorable as characters, they are made real to us, most of all by the depth of their suffering. The more real the victims are (even if only because of how realistically their victimization is depicted), the more human, conversely, their tormentors are made to seem. I don't know, but my guess is that this is because there's no clear dividing line between the psychopath and his or her victim, that the act of victimization—even when devoid of any obvious complicity—in some strange fashion binds the two together. This may even be what the psychopath is seeking, and what his victim is unconsciously seeking, too (or rather, seeking liberation from an *inner* bondage caused by a past experience of victimization). Whatever the case—and this is highly sensitive subject matter—I think that the killer in a work of fiction can only be as real to us *as* a killer as his victims are allowed to be, and vice versa. If we take this to a more "moral" level, true compassion for the victim becomes dependent on equal compassion for the perpetrator, and vice versa. Compassion is like an artist's sympathy for his or her creations: it cannot be selective.

Leatherface is one of the most utterly deranged and yet eerily touching psychopaths in American cinema. There is a scene in which we see him alone, having just slaughtered another intruder and shoved a half-dead victim back into the refrigerator. He moves about the house, distressed and at a loss, as if waiting for somebody to tell him what to do. He sits by the window and stares into space, thinking God only knows what, running his tongue over misshapen teeth. The poignancy and the horror of this moment is as intense as anything in the film, because for a second, this monstrous killer becomes childlike, a deadly innocent behemoth, wholly unaware of the evil of his actions. In this moment he becomes lost, confused and all-too-human. Leatherface may in fact be the most wretchedly human of all movie monsters (more so even than *Blue Velvet's* Frank Booth) because Leatherface *is* monstrous, obviously. There's nothing much else *to* him — he's like an impersonal force of madness and destruction. But at the same time, he's a pathetically *sad* figure. The fact that he wears a mask and we never get to see his face, to *identify* him, I think accounts above all for this strangely pathetic quality.

This isn't the case with Jason in the *Friday the 13th* films or Michael Myers in *Halloween*, however, characters who are not made more but *less* human for wearing a mask. Yet with Leatherface, the mask somehow humanizes him. We don't generally feel hatred or disgust for a grizzly bear or killer shark that devours "innocent" victims in a movie, or for the Creature from the Black Lagoon, King Kong, or Frankenstein's monster. The fact that they are less than human gives them a kind of innocence. Innocence is a childlike quality, and it is hard to see a child as anything but a victim. In fact the common theme to many of these movie monsters is that they *are* innocent because they are only doing what their nature (even if it's aberrant) compels them to do. Often it's due to them being taken out of their natural environment (like King Kong) or their having it invaded, which is the case in *Massacre*. Sometimes, as with Frankenstein's monster, it's due to their being *misunderstood*. As horror movie-goers, we naturally and easily identify with these less-than-human characters, even when their only expression is one of violent and destructive rage. Perhaps that's precisely *why* we identify with them? They appeal to something primal in us — and something infantile. Leatherface (like King Kong or Frankenstein, other monsters from the Id) is like a great big, monstrous infant.

The film peaks quite late, in an electrifyingly ghastly scene in which Sally (Marilyn Burns) is invited to dinner with the family. She is tied to a chair made with human arms (her hands strapped to the severed hands on the chair) and put at the head of the table with a plate of (presumably human) sausages and potatoes before her. She is prodded and pulled and mocked and gloated over by the two demented "kids," while Pop looks on and alternately chuckles and berates his children for torturing "the poor girl." Eventually Sally passes out from sheer terror, and when she wakes it takes a few seconds for her to realize where she is. The elements of this waking nightmare come back into focus one by one, and she begins screaming again ... As she screams, Junior and Leatherface join in with gleeful, derisive hoots and shrieks, and the film becomes one prolonged howl of anguish and delight; in the words of Edgar Allan Poe: "utterly anomalous and inhuman ... such as might have arisen only out of hell, conjointly from the throats of the damned in their agony and of the demons that exult in the damnation." The scene is perhaps the single most excruciating and traumatic piece of Surrealist art to ever appear in a horror film. It's a snapshot from Hell.

It is also no coincidence that the scene is a grotesque parody of *family life*. The whole film is that too. It depicts a world in which there is no easy way to separate the tormented from the tormentors, because both are part of the same lineage. As in all good horror movies, the horror is not in what is strange to us, but what is *familiar*.

Totem and Taboo: The Video Nasty

"Then you live with it."
—The Stranger, *High Plains Drifter*

Dinner time was the only time I spent with my family as a teenager. It was something to get through as quickly as possible before withdrawing back into my private world, on the top floor of the house. In my last years at home (from fifteen to seventeen), I was living in the attic with my own entertainment center (TV and VHS video recorder), and I had an intercom system linking me to the kitchen to let me know when meals were served. Besides school and going drinking and smoking at weekends, I stayed up in my attic pretty much the whole time (like the monstrous child of fairy tales). We were among the first people in the area to get a video recorder and of course it went straight into my den. It wasn't long before I figured out how to put two video recorders together and started pirating my favorite movies and building my own private collection. The reality I was withdrawing from—home life, and school—inevitably shaped and colored the fantasy world—my attic of solitude—which I was escaping into. Like the town of Lago in *High Plains Drifter* (one of the first movies I owned, *The Texas Chainsaw Massacre* was another), it was painted blood-red (figuratively speaking).

Pirating (or stealing) movies on tape was like bringing trophies of my hunting excursions back into my lair. By surrounding myself with these "sacred" objects, I was arranging the elements of my worldly persona—like a tribal chief who hangs shrunken heads, scalps, and other proofs of his "kills," outside his hut, to signal his prowess and fierceness to potential enemies. (My mother hardly ever came up into my attic lair.)

In *The Blood Poets*, I wrote, "As an adolescent, my interest in ordinary pornography was fairly minor compared to my fascination for violence." Actually I don't think I even saw anything that would pass for porn nowadays until I was in my twenties (though I may be forgetting). The grim irony of this is that I considered myself "above" ordinary pornography in some way. Unlike most teenagers, these days at least, I wasn't experiencing sex firsthand either. The two things are obviously connected, since they are both related to my teenage predilection for watching scenes of sexualized violence. As I wrote in 1999, this was a predilection which

I thoroughly indulged for several years (most "formative" years at that—between the ages of sixteen and twenty, roughly). [During this time] a film was of interest to me simply and wholly because it looked to contain scenes of explicit violence. I suppose any gore would do, but especially attractive was violence against women. This was not a taste I had to invent or develop for myself. Back then, browsing through a video shop's horror section meant gazing at endless images of large-breasted women being terrorized or brutalized by monsters or madmen. The images (rarely if ever actual stills from the movie) were designed to arouse sexual interest, and they often had little or nothing to do with the film itself—a fact I learned to my chagrin by sitting through a vast quantity of boring and inept trash horror movies, waiting for scenes that never came. The sensation-stimulation effect of violence in these films (if there was any) was intended basically to be sexual in nature. The attraction of the video nasty was little more than an extension and a perversion of the taboo-appeal of hardcore pornography.

It is a strange and troubling experience to nurture a vice and not be able to share one's thoughts and feelings about it with others, not even to know if there *are* others like oneself. Now of course I know there are (even if I still haven't talked to them); but back then I didn't have the wherewithal to do the math and deduce this, from the evidence at hand. Obviously there *was* an unacknowledged appetite for such fare, an appetite which the hysteria around "video nasties" was acknowledging. But as far as I know it never addressed the central question—psychologically sensitive as it is—that young people were using images of graphic violence for sexual arousal. Since then, the pornography of violence has not only been acknowledged, it has gone mainstream. Examples of "torture porn" have been endorsed, even produced, by highly respected "film artists" like Quentin Tarantino. The queasy but crucial question as to whether people who watch these films (or people who make them) masturbate to the graphic depictions of violence, again so far as I know, remains unaddressed. Which means (since it's unavoidable that some people *do*) there's no discussion as to *why*. From *Blood Poets*:

> We are, after all, only watching a movie, and if it is acknowledged (as I think it's only wise to do) that the sadistic impulse is shared by everyone, at some level, then the viewer may feel "entitled" (or permitted), for the duration of the movie, to indulge feelings he would normally be horrified to admit to.

Or maybe not, these days. It may be too simplistic to say that "the sadistic impulse is shared by everyone"; even if it's true, how could I have known that when most people wouldn't admit it, sometimes not even to themselves? Talking about taboo experiences is notoriously fraught because we don't *know* what other people's experience *is* and no one wants to risk admitting too much for fear of being condemned. Either the reader empathizes with my indulging sadistic tendencies (enjoying sexualized violence) or s/he doesn't. Either you recognize a valid need to discuss these subjects, or you don't. But I don't see any way to talk about movies *without* talking about the seductive appeal of violence. To do so would mean drawing a line where no line exists, a line of "good taste." Apparently there *is* a connection between the basic appeal of movies (their fantasy-dissociative-escapist qualities) and the ways in which they tap into and exploit our violent, destructive, and sadistic urges. If nothing else, maybe it's this: since movies are manifestly "all just make-believe," they allow us—both moviegoers and filmmakers—to explore and express desires that we wouldn't otherwise feel safe admitting to. The temptation to indulge those desires—to exploit and be exploited—is unavoidable, and it's here that art and exploitation share common ground, and why the one can so easily and unexpectedly lead to the other.

A hardcore porno movie or a video nasty is designed and packaged (if not actually made) to exploit a particular demand, and so create a market. Without the demand, there would be no market; but it's also safe to say that, without the product, there'd be no market either. With the video nasty, children and teenagers became aware of a "new taboo," and, like sex, drugs, and rock 'n' roll, these films became part of growing up. Violence—simulated but extreme—became as much a part of adolescent rites of passage as sex. [Totem and taboo.] I don't think that any single movie—or even a whole genre of movies—can even begin to bear responsibility for this changing appetite. I think it goes a lot deeper than that. In many ways violence—specifically murder—was *the last taboo*.

This is an almost Biblical statement. If the original sin was sex, then the first fruit of it, Cain, was violence. If the first taboo was sex, the last taboo is not murder but murder *as a sexual act*.

An exploitation film that arouses pleasure by showing scenes of violence or torture may not actually be harmful; it may, on the contrary, serve to alert a person to his darker, more buried tendencies. Such tendencies, unacknowledged, might come out in less vicarious ways that *are* harmful to others. If, by watching and even enjoying scenes of violence, a person, shocked and troubled by his own reactions, discovering a side of himself he never knew existed, becomes more sensitized *to* it, his actual behavior may become more compassionate. He may feel the need to *atone* for the urges awoken in him. The only real remedy for "evil" is not denial but awareness.

There are a lot of assumptions here. Obviously I was writing about myself in the third person to distance myself from the subject matter and make it less uncomfortable for the reader. Certainly, my early immersion in sexualized violence alerted me to my own darker proclivities (how could it not?); but as for it making me more compassionate, that's harder to say. I had more *sympathy* for characters seen by most people as beyond the pale, people like Hitler or Frank Booth. But that doesn't mean I felt compassion for *myself*, which is where real compassion begins. I now think that enjoying scenes of violence was a way to exploit my own trauma and direct my rage (against mother, father, brother, sister) *inward*, where it could do no harm—except to myself. Like all pornography, it was a way to arouse myself and to numb myself at the same time, to numb myself *by* arousing myself.

*

When I was growing up, the closest I got to a real snuff movie was a cheap little exploitation movie called *Snuff*. It had nothing to do with the subject but it had a ten-minute segment stuck on at the end, a clumsily staged scene of a supposed film director tricking an actress into staying on after shooting a soft core sex scene and then killing her brutally on camera. There was never any question as to the veracity of the footage (it was obviously faked), and the fact I found it arousing wasn't compromised by any queasy doubts about it being real. This may not be the case with young people today. I know someone who grew up in the 90s who had access to unsupervised internet use as a teenager; around the age of thirteen he was introduced by a friend to a website that featured "graphic real-life violence and sexual depravity of every variety." Certainly, if I'd had the same sorts of opportunities growing up I would have taken them, and probably be in considerably worse shape today. As it was, all I had was video nasties, and even they were in the process of being banned just as I was getting interested.

The first time I watched a movie on video cassette, I was at my father's house. He got a video recorder before just about anyone in the area (since he was rich), even though he didn't care about movies and probably never learned to use it. (I probably suggested he get it.) I would stay the weekend at my father's house a couple of times a month, and as soon as he got the video recorder I rented a pair of movies from a shop called Video 2000, and took them to his house. I waited for my father and his wife to retire, then, consumed by the kind of fevered anticipation that probably only teenagers feel, I began to watch them.

The first movie was *The Exterminator*—a now-forgotten, shabby little 1980 revenge fantasy which I found uninteresting even then. The next movie was at the top of my "movies to see" list, Sam Peckinpah's *Straw Dogs*. Why did I want to see it so badly? I think at a conscious level it was more to do with it being notorious for its violence, but I don't suppose it hurt that the poster for the movie was a close-up of Susan George's breasts with a smaller image of Dustin Hoffman between them, pointing a shotgun towards the viewer. I also knew that the film contained a graphic depiction of Susan George's rape. In her review of the film, "Peckinpah's Obsession" (in *Deeper into Movies*), Kael described the rape scene in *Straw Dogs* as "one of the few truly erotic sequences on film." I don't know if I read that review *before* I saw the film or after, but I do know that I found the sequence erotic, and that I did what any other fourteen-year-old kid would have done, alone with the material. Looking back on it, that night set the precedent: the first time I saw a movie alone on video cassette, I masturbated to a rape scene. After that, movie simulations of rape became my dish of choice. What's surprising is to realize that it was sanctioned and approved by "movie parents," Peckinpah and Pauline.

The fact this happened in my father's house is probably significant too. What better place to take my first, shaky steps towards adult sexuality—though of course my father was not present to oversee the "initiation" (he was more likely in a drunken slumber, in the room above me).

Now It's Dark: *Blue Velvet*, Frank Booth, & Infant Sexuality

"I don't know if you're a detective or a pervert."
Sandy to Jeffrey, *Blue Velvet*

I left home at seventeen and went to live with my sister in London. At eighteen, once I came into my family inheritance, my sister and I bought a house together. On my twentieth birthday, in 1987, I moved to New York to pursue my dream of becoming a filmmaker. I didn't do much "pursuing," however. I was reading Dostoyevsky's *Crime and Punishment* at the time and working on a script about a serial killer called Ed. (Ed kills for no conscious reason, not even pleasure, simply because he can, and because it's his only way to feel *real*.) Within three days of arriving in New York, I had rented a tiny bedsit on 3rd street, between 3rd and 2nd Avenues, bought a TV and video recorder, joined the video club at Tower Records on Broadway and 4th Street, scored some pot, and settled in.

It was the first time I'd ever lived alone. I didn't know a soul, I was there with nothing but a private fortune and a half-baked plan to become a filmmaker. It was as if I believed, by putting myself in the right place at the right time, things would happen. What happened, predictably enough, was that I transposed my routine to a new locale: I went out drinking every other night, stayed home watching movies and smoking pot the nights in between. I developed a liking for cocaine. I cried myself to sleep with disturbing frequency. The essential elements of adulthood, for all I knew, were money, alcohol, drugs, and movies. Movies were as essential as any of the others, because without the dream, the future vision, which they represented, I would have rapidly become aware of how lost I was. I was trying to find a way into the world by becoming *of* it, with no ticket to enter besides a half-finished script about a sensitive serial killer. Whether I was asleep and dreaming, stoned awake and watching movies, or out drinking with barflies, I was lost in a nihilistic dream world.

In those days, watching four movies in a single night (while smoking as many joints) was part of the routine. I don't remember much of what I did twenty-five years ago, but I'm pretty sure that the first movie marathon I enjoyed after getting set up in New York included *The Texas Chainsaw Massacre Part Two* and *Blue Velvet*. I hope I had the good sense to save *Blue Velvet* for last, because I remember how badly *Massacre 2* sucked, and how profoundly I was affected by *Blue Velvet*. Over the next few years, it became *the* film for me. The first question I asked people on meeting them was if they had seen it. If they had, and hadn't liked it, the conversation ended right there. As Jonathan Lethem wrote about *Fear of Music*, my identification with Lynch's movie was so intense that, if you'd replaced my head with a copy of the movie poster, I'd have considered it adequate representation. So what was it about the film that got so deep under my skin?

*

From *The Blood Poets*:

> The plot of *Blue Velvet* unfolds lazily, at its own pace and rhythm, following a logic both internal and occult—hidden—

each event leading smoothly and directly to the next. Yet there's no apparent momentum to this "plot," other than that applied by the characters themselves, no *deus ex machina*, because everything that happens is a result of Jeffrey's own motions, his investigations. And as Jeffrey himself is motivated by curiosity (that most pure and universal, but deadly, of motives), the film itself seems not so much to advance as to unfold, to reveal itself gradually to the searching intensity of our (and Jeffrey's) gaze. Every scene in the film is absolutely essential and integral to the whole. An indication of how this works is the superb manner in which Lynch creates and conveys the "child's eye view" of the film, an eye that perceives everything as strange and wonderful, terrible and mysterious, as an opportunity for knowledge and experience. As Michael Atkinson wrote: "[E]very frame of the film pulsates with appalled innocence, with the shock of a child trying to come to grips with the adult cosmos."

Jeffrey's journey was my own journey. I knew that intuitively from the very first time I saw the film; but only now are the particulars starting to become clear to me.

The first thing that happens in *Blue Velvet* is the collapse of Jeffrey's father. The film's action all develops, then, from *the removal of the father from a position of uprightness or authority*. He is struck down by unexplained forces while watering the garden (attending to "Mother" nature). The imagery of the spurting hose is overtly sexual; less so, but still suggestive, is the small dog snapping wildly at the water spray. Then comes the close-up of the beetles: the chthonic underworld of the psyche, the repressed but irrepressible forces of the unconscious. After which, the film proper begins. The essence of *Blue Velvet* is not simply that nothing is what it seems but, specifically, that the shiny, smooth surface of life always conceals (but also reveals) a dark, daemonic under layer, and that, once this hidden aspect of reality is seen, the nature of the visible surface is forever transformed. The "dark side" can never be unseen, but nor would we want it to be. Without the underlying depths, the surface is only a façade; with them, it becomes substantial, real, authentic. The rite of passage is not from innocence to corruption but from childhood to adulthood.

The film's antagonist, Frank, mirrors its protagonist, Jeffrey, precisely, because Frank is *an arrested infant*. He is what happens when the child grows into physical manhood without developing internally, a monster far more disturbing than anything Frankenstein (or ordinary horror fiction) could ever create. The horror of *Blue Velvet*—as well as the wonder, the two go hand in hand—is that of childhood, brought kicking and screaming into adult awareness. Essentially, Jeffrey's quest is the quest to discover the nature of the strange forces that struck his father down, to prevent those same forces from doing the same to him and stripping him of his manhood. Essentially, it's the quest of every man whose father "fell down."

[Re: the scene in Dorothy's apartment when Jeffrey witnesses Dorothy undressing from inside the closet and then watches Frank's assault on her.] Lynch has finally got us where he wants us, just as Jeffrey has finally made it where he needed to be. The film has arrived at its basic, central motif and meaning: the mysterious, deadly mix between fantasy and voyeurism, in which the witness, at the terrifying point of realizing his actual role as *participant*, is dragged inexorably out of dream and into reality. From innocence to experience.

Isn't this is the appeal and the problem of movies in a nutshell? They invite us to indulge in fantasy from a safe position, but they also forbid active engagement. It is (mercifully) impossible to have Jeffrey's experience at a movie, to be dragged out of the closet and into the scene we are witnessing. If it weren't for that safety guarantee, I would never have felt safe enough to allow my fantasies to become conscious. Movies awaken the id and the libido, but they don't provide either opportunity or instruction to know what to *do* with that released energy. The same might be said for the role of the mother with her infant: the mother awakens the infant's desire, but, after a certain point, she can neither satisfy it nor direct it. The child must turn to the father for this guidance.

The actual set-up in *Blue Velvet* is so basic, so simple, so archetypal, that it's funny, because it's a straightforward literalization (and liberation) of the male fantasy syndrome: to gaze, while simultaneously hidden from sight, upon a desirable [but forbidden] female [i.e., the mother] in a state of undress. Subsequently, following Jeffrey's brief excursion into participation/reality—and his ensuing return to the closet—he will enact an even more primal (or Freudian) fantasy situation, when he gets to watch the most forbidden act of all, the act of copulation. What he witnesses is a perverse, terrifying caricature of the sex act, however, which Kael called "a sick-joke version of the primal scene, as this curious child watches his parents do some very weird things ... He has been pulled—with no kicking or screaming—into the inferno of corrupt adult sexuality."

Now I would ask, is there any other kind? (Kael apparently gave up sexual relationships—if not sex—in her fifties.) On the other hand, the sort of sex Frank has with Dorothy is corrupt, but is it really adult? Frank's first words to Dorothy are a furious injunction to call him "Daddy." (Quite ironic for me, since my own father refused to answer to anything but "Nick.") Once the sex ritual begins, he calls her "Mommy" and himself "baby." The corruptness of their coupling is not because it's adult but because it's *infantile*. Frank's libido has been wounded by early trauma and remained "stuck" at the infant stage of development (it has become genitally organized, in the Freudian jargon). For the infant sexually imprinted by the mother—bonded to her image—sexual desire is inherently forbidden, and the ordinary sex act is impossible because it is *unsafe*. The infant fears that the mother will devour him, the father will kill him, or both.

Voyeurism is the first safe alternative; after that there are the weird ritual enactments such as Jeffrey witnesses between Frank and Dorothy, and such as he later performs with Dorothy once Frank, the father, has left the scene. Why did *Blue Velvet* mean so much to me that it was practically all I could talk about for several years? Because it laid out in precise, symbolic terms the nature of the trauma—the beetles in the grass—that lurked and festered under and inside my obsession for movies. It answered and explained my need to be a voyeur and my predisposition for "darkness," my getting lost, like Frank and Jeffrey (and Lynch), in a dream world of sexualized violence and "romantic" obsession. And because it was *art*, it also showed the way out of that dream. (I think...?)

Frank represents, in no uncertain terms, the first, terrible surge of energy of Jeffrey's newly awakened id, his libido ... Frank is the runaway libido with a vengeance, our very worst nightmares of the (male) sexual animal run amok. Frank is a true soul in torment—a sufferer of both mundane (all-too-human) and cosmic proportions. He is so excruciatingly aware of his own degeneracy that he can't even bear to be looked at; all he can do is wallow in it. He wields his madness as both a shield and a sword to attack and defend himself in the battleground of his hellish existence. Frank knows nothing of pleasure—he is racked by pain, rage, contempt, sorrow, and above all impotence ... His agony and despair is all metaphysical: he's at another level, but it's a level *below*— one few people have the imagination or the courage to admit is there. Frank is there to remind us, and if he represents Jeffrey's (and our) demons, it's only because, as one of the damned, he is driven by demons all his own.

The above description reminds me now of my father. My father was quite like Frank (highly sexed, a hedonistic and non-reflective personality), yet at the same time completely *unlike* him, someone who, in my experience at least, lacked the imagination or courage to own up to his demons. The dedication to the volume of *The Blood Poets* in which the 1999 essay on *Blue Velvet* first appeared reads: "For Freddy [Krueger] and Frank and the legions of lesser demons: Your time is nigh at hand. And to the Father, for courage beyond the call of duty."

I numbered my father among the demons.

*

"Frank to me, is a guy Americans know very well. I'm sure most everybody growing up has met someone like Frank. They might not have shook his hand and gone out for a drink with him, but all you've got to do is exchange eye contact with someone like that and you know that you've met him … Frank is totally in love. He just doesn't know how to show it. He may have gotten into some strange things, but he's still motivated by positive things."
—David Lynch

From *The Blood Poets*:

In interviews, Lynch insisted that *Blue Velvet* is a love story, as much between Dorothy and Frank as between Jeffrey and Sandy. [This gives some indication of the sort of background Lynch comes from.] Frank sees and feels and knows things that most people only ever dream of. That's what makes him nightmarish: he's a messenger from the same place our deepest fears arise from. He's the realization of Jeffrey's awakening id—its first manifestation—and Jeffrey is "responsible" for Frank just as surely as if he had materialized him out of thin air with the force and perversity of his own will.

Which is exactly what Lynch did, with the help of Dennis Hopper (who claimed to *be* Frank). Frank is Jeffrey's own dark potential. This is how he could end up if he ignores the "lessons" which Frank, the id-monster, brings to him. In place of the fallen or absent father, the demon-father emerges. The demon-father is the shadow of the fallen father but also *the thing that caused him to fall*. What the father doesn't bring forth from within him destroys him, but never in a way he can recognize. Jeffrey survives Frank because both of them recognize the affinity, the sameness, between them ("You're like me"): that they have sprung from the same "home" (womb), born from the same psychological complex or *traumata*. They are twins in trauma. Frank is there to help Jeffrey in the absence of an actual father, to help him avoid the same fate which dragged Frank down to Hell (unconsciousness).

[In the film's centerpiece] Jeffrey—dimly but acutely—realizes his complicity, his affinity, with the demon Frank, and recognizes that Frank is his "familiar."... Frank's nightmare and Jeffrey's dream collide and merge until they are inseparable. Jeffrey knows it; Frank knows it; and *we* know it. There's one psyche, split into warring fragments. It's only once Jeffrey has possessed Dorothy completely and succumbed to her desperate, pathetic demands that he hit her, that he steps all the way into the role of "Daddy" [the shadow father]. As soon he strikes Dorothy, Jeffrey feels the surge of energy—primal delight and vicious power—that joins him to Frank and to every other male "beast" who ever lived. Jeffrey completes his initiation into the mysteries, not merely of love but, its twin horns of power, sex and violence. By awakening the monster within, Jeffrey becomes a man.

An interesting thesis this, because it precisely echoes Peckinpah's with *Straw Dogs*. Although the movies could hardly be more different, two basic ideas can be found in both works: 1) a woman likes to be sexually dominated and even brutalized; and 2) entering into manhood requires a violent initiation. *Blue Velvet* combines the two ideas into a single scene, however (which is perhaps a key difference), because Jeffrey's sexual initiation includes hitting Dorothy. (Jeffrey also strikes Frank immediately after.) Also, Jeffrey's initiation culminates with his severe beating (and possibly rape) at the hands of Frank.

In my own childhood-to-adulthood journey through a pop cultural underworld, in search of an identity as a man and in the absence of a father to guide me through those first, crucial and potentially fatal explorations of sexual desire, there seems to be a progression. In seeking a face to the id as it stirred into awareness, I went from the innocent animals of Winnie the Pooh to comic book images of the Hulk and the Thing, to Leatherface, before finally arriving at Frank Booth. As it became progressively more human, paradoxically, the face of my id became also more corrupt—or simply more *real*. (Though even Frank, like Leatherface, wears a mask—an oxygen mask through which he inhales his unnamed drug.) Recognizing the libido—owning it— is the *sine qua non* of coming of age; in my case, that involved recognizing the condition it was in.

A male whose libido has been hijacked and crippled by the possessing mother and the absent or abusive father—what choice does he have but to express his sexuality through violence? Becoming potent with a strong, liberated woman is not possible, because the experience of his own powerlessness is too great; the threat of being devoured paralyzes him and makes him impotent. Rape, or some sort of enactment of it, is the only way *through* that paralysis for him. Even to speak of this is *verboten*, and in today's world such a man is well and truly *screwed*, so much so that he's lucky if he ever gets to *fuck* with even a fraction of his manhood. Frank certainly didn't. The verdict on Jeffrey is still out. Maybe Lynch can provide a sequel—*Jeffrey and Sandy, Twenty Years On?*—that's if he's not too busy transcending.

*

Lynch's *Blue Velvet* succeeds where pretty much every other movie that attempts to explore sexual violence fails. (*Casualties of War* is another exception.) It shows the full horror of a damaged psyche without making it loathsome, supernatural, or incomprehensible, without placing it outside the bounds of compassion, without *damning* it. In the context of the Hollywood marketplace of mainstream filmmaking, that's practically an act of grace. By speaking so directly to my experience, the movie confirmed a necessary belief: that movies were worthy of the attention and devotion I had given them. They were worth dedicating my life to. Art was better than life, because art forgave, and art redeemed. Life just happened.

*

To explore the jungle isn't the same as trying to tame it. The inextricability (which isn't the same as equivalence) of sex and violence is as unavoidable as thorns are while picking blackberries. If you don't want the pricks, don't pick (go to the supermarket).

We want so badly to believe that sex is good and violence is bad that it's no wonder that movies, rating laws, and religion work so hard to convince us of the opposite. All I know for sure is that I am drawn to both, in different ways and for (somewhat) different reasons, but always with the same end: *to find out what*

I am made of. Their appeal is that they offer us the *organic* experience, a chance to see what we are on the inside as it comes *out* and shows itself, in all its messy, visceral *realness*. Sexual shame and horror are closer than we think. If movies are a disembodied (and dissociating) medium, it makes sense that we look to them to remind us, as frequently and furiously as they can, of our physicality. Children love fairy tales that are gruesome and gory, probably for the same reason.

*

Returning to Kael's definition of the artist's task and her frustration with Buchman's movie. Easy compassion is for the suffering that wants to act but doesn't; it makes us feel virtuous and superior in our open-mindedness by reassuring us that we are above such urges ourselves. Real compassion is something else. It means sharing in the suffering, and in the passion, that desires *and* acts and that is damned for it. It means tasting of both sin and damnation. Being an artist means being willing to think the unthinkable. Art recognizes no barriers, of decency or anything else. And because it doesn't judge us for our failings (unlike family members), and turns no one away from its doors, it provides a home for the displaced.

A spiritual guide (Dave Oshana) once told me I was only as damned as I feel. The only one who can condemn us or forgive us is ourselves. Self-rejection is a sin (aberrational behavior) and the original sin is self-rejection. They go hand in hand. Maybe it's a coincidence that seeing *Blue Velvet* in 1987 more or less coincided with the decision (at the age of twenty) to stop using scenes of sexual violence for auto-erotic stimulation? Maybe, but I sincerely doubt it.

Where the sickness is, seek the cure.

Black Magic Realism

*Ironic Detachment, the Naiveté of Cynicism, & New
Levels of Depravity in* **The Counselor**

In early February, 2014, I watched *The Counselor*, the 2013 movie directed by Ridley Scott from a script by Cormac McCarthy. I almost didn't watch the film; the reviews I'd seen were so scathing that they'd created a repellent aura around it; I'd expected a gaudy piece of self-indulgent, decadent filmmaking. Watching it with my wife, I kept waiting for it to fall apart and dissolve into pointless violence or disjointed surrealist hijinks, but instead what I saw was some of the most fiercely original writing ever put on the movie screen. It occurred to me that, in a way, the critical reception of the film actually confirmed its meanings. The world most critics and audience members are living in is a very different world to the world portrayed by *The Counselor*. As a vision of evil, *The Counselor* is completely persuasive. Its depiction of soullessness as eerily sumptuous, even sickly erotic, of moral incoherence as the driving force behind civilization, is almost Lovecraftian. With its relentless, seductive insistence on horror as the soul of the plot, it could be the first postmodern horror film, and in some ways, the film affected me as deeply as anything I'd seen since *Blue Velvet*. What was a lot less clear to me was *why*.

One time, I saw *Blue Velvet* at a midnight showing in New York, and I was both surprised and disturbed to hear the audience laughing throughout the film—including at some of the most horrific parts. It was my first real taste of how people distance themselves from disturbing material by viewing it ironically, through the lens of a kind of assumed aloofness or sophistication. I was positive Lynch hadn't meant his movie to be seen that way, but at the same time, he may have unconsciously allowed for (if not catered to) that kind of ironic distance—especially in light of his later work such as *Twin Peaks* and *Wild at Heart*.

Ironic detachment is the way most "sophisticated" people keep from being overwhelmed by existential horror and moral revulsion as the facts of life unfold around them. Ironic detachment is made easy by certain kinds of movies and TV shows (*Breaking Bad* was all ironic detachment), because they allow us to feel like we're being exposed to life's brutal, bleak realities (violence, corruption, drug addiction, disease, poverty, insanity, moral collapse) without ever having to bear the brunt of those realities ourselves. This creates a "seen-it-all" superiority and cynicism that's at the same time pathetically naïve, because it magically locates all the horror outside of our own direct experience, on the other side of a movie, TV, or smartphone screen. The entertained, meanwhile, enjoy the luxurious detachment of the consumer lifestyle that's been assembled for them, by and through and as a result of all that corruption being miraculously recycled as "entertainment" (though really, as instruction and ideology).

Audience members and critics may have actively resented *The Counselor* because it required them to *think*, at least in ways they weren't accustomed to thinking and that made them uncomfortable. They may have had difficulty getting to grips with a movie that was really *about* something but that didn't tell them how to feel about it. *The Counselor* doesn't have the built-in mechanism of films like *American Beauty*, *Unforgiven*, or *Up in the Air* that give a nod and a wink to viewers and encourage them to congratulate themselves for their sensitivity and intelligence in embracing "difficult" or "radical" subject matter. These films prop up the culture that spawns them while subtly (or not-so-subtly) promoting the dominant values even as they *appear* to subvert them. *The Counselor* breaks the rules of engagement between viewer and viewed, not only by ignoring the narrative conventions (a heist movie without a heist, a "hero" who is no more than a witness to the consequences of his own poor judgment), but because it doesn't offer the satisfaction of a resolution. The protagonist doesn't rescue the girl and he doesn't go on a mad killing spree to avenge her. He's swallowed up by grief and implodes in a dirty hotel room—pretty much exactly as we all would.

The horrors which the film piles up don't lead to catharsis, and catharsis is the unwritten promise of every Hollywood action movie (and even of Hollywood "issue" movies) ever made. The film builds the internal tension to bursting point without ever providing release, emotional or otherwise. It left me with a knot in the gut that nothing could get rid of except amnesia or suppression (or writing about it). I saw it twice in one week, and both times I felt somehow unclean, and faintly nauseous, by the time it was over.

The Counselor isn't about murder, it's about annihilation, existential erasure. The problems it presents aren't just social or political problems; they aren't even exclusively human ones. They are metaphysical problems, and as such all equally unsolvable from an ordinary, human perspective. There is no God separate from Satan, no evil one to blame and no hero-savior to save us. There is no retribution that doesn't smite the "innocent" along with the guilty, because no one is innocent in this world. There are no bystanders and no decent place to stand in a massacre, because to see is to participate, and to participate is to be compromised, to be complicit. *The Counselor* breaks the contract between movie and moviegoer, the contract that promises that, no matter what we see on the screen, and no matter how it makes us feel, we will not be implicated and will be allowed to leave the theater as spotless as when we entered. *The Counselor* is like an *anti*-Catholic confession ritual: I came out stained by the newly gained awareness of my own hypocrisy.

American Heart of Darkness

"When gods were more human, men were more divine."
—Cormac McCarthy, *The Counselor* script

One thing that struck me about all the reviews of *The Counselor*, negative and (occasionally) positive, was that none of them referred to the real-world events which the film used for its storyline. I did some online research and found a whole lot of substance—dark background—to back up McCarthy's bleak vision. In "The Disappeared and Mexico's New Dirty War," (November 21, 2013, at NACLA.ORG), Peter Watt wrote that it was "becoming increasingly difficult for Mexican officials to pretend that the massive number of murders and enforced disappearances is not part of a deliberate government strategy." Attributing the disappearances to drug cartels, as well as the idea that the Mexican and the US government are waging a war on organized crime, Watts insisted, was "a pervasive but totally false myth."

This didn't come as a surprise to me, but I knew it was something most people—at least most *Americans*—preferred not to know. The drug wars in Mexico are pretty much common knowledge to Americans, but they're probably mostly seen as evidence of how backward, brutal, and barbaric life is in Mexico, not of the consequences of US interference. And yet the motivation for the United States' (and the European Union's) presence in Latin America isn't really any different than that of the Spanish, Portuguese, British, French and Dutch colonialists before them: the plundering of natural resources and cheap labor. According to another online article (sourcewatch.org), this is "compounded these days by neo-colonial extraction of forcibly contrived 'debt.'" I didn't fully understand the mechanics of it, but I got the general gist. One of the things *The Counselor* shows, implicitly, simply by dealing with this subject matter, is that the

Mexican drug cartels—the barbarian hordes depicted in the film—aren't a threat to the stability of the US but *part of the machinery of capitalism that sustains it.* In *To Die in Mexico: Dispatches from Inside the Drug War,* John Gibler wrote:

> In 2008, drug money saved the major global banks from collapse and thus, stretching just a bit, saved capitalism from a devastating internal crisis when the speculative capital markets imploded. Drug money—truckloads of cash, actual physical money—would appear to be one of capitalism's global savings accounts.

Adding some substance to this bold—though again not really surprising—claim, in "How Drug Profits saved Capitalism" (which I couldn't find online, only quotes from it at a website, counterpunch.org), James Petras wrote:

> While the Pentagon arms the Mexican government and the US Drug Enforcement Agency enforces the "military solution," the biggest US banks receive, launder and transfer hundreds of billions of dollars to the drug lords' accounts, who then buy modern arms, pay private armies of assassins and corrupt untold numbers of political and law enforcement officials on both sides of the border. Drug profits, in the most basic sense, are secured through the ability of the cartels to launder and transfer billions of dollars through the US banking system. The scale and scope of the US banking-drug cartel alliance surpasses any other economic activity of the US private banking system. According to US Justice Department records, one bank alone laundered $378.3 billion dollars between May 1, 2004 and May 31, 2007 (*The Guardian,* May 11, 2011). *Every major bank in the US has served as an active financial partner of the murderous drug cartels.* [emphasis added]

Probably critics ignored this material for a number of reasons. Firstly, *The Counselor* wasn't the kind of socially conscious movie that obliged audiences to think deeply about its subject matter. It wasn't *Schindler's List, Gandhi,* or *Philadelphia,* and it almost dared viewers to take it seriously at that level. Secondly, more importantly, these weren't social issues that most critics, especially not American critics, were willing to look at. Even if they were, the publications they wrote for probably wouldn't allow it.

While I was working on this piece, I went with my wife to see *American Hustle.* Before the film started, there were three previews. The first was for *Heaven Is For Real,* the second for the new Jack Ryan movie, *Shadow Recruit,* and the last for *Lone Survivor,* a supposed true story about "an elite unit of Navy SEALs who encounter an army of Taliban forces in the Afghanistan mountains during a raid in 2005." The first movie was a blatant work of Christian propaganda about how good people (including a soldier) go to Heaven; the second was yet one more glamorization of CIA skullduggery; the third spoke for itself. What struck me about the trailers was just how brazen the propaganda aspect of Hollywood moviemaking has become. There wasn't even a token attempt to disguise it. Ideology has replaced entertainment.

Diamonds Are Forever

"The beheadings, the mutilations—that's just business. You've got to keep up appearances. It's not like there's some smoldering rage at the bottom of it."

—Westray, *The Counselor*

The counselor believes he can have dealings with the "crime world" in order to get what he wants from it and bring it back into *his* world. His choice to become *of* that second world—to succumb to its temptations—is so catastrophic for him because it happens before he has entered all the way *into* it. He has no idea of what he is agreeing to become part of. Awakening to reality for the counselor means awakening into a nightmare, the nightmare of his own complicity. The counselor's sins are legion, but the folly of buying the diamond for his fiancé Laura (Penelope Cruz) is first among them. In his exchange with the Sephardic diamond dealer (Bruno Gantz), the counselor receives his first piece of advice. He's told that the diamond trade is "a cynical business—we seek only imperfections" (a perfect diamond would be pure light). If I read McCarthy's strange, pulp-archetypal narrative right, diamonds are stand-ins for souls, placing the sage old (Jewish) diamond dealer in the role of Satan, who looks not for merit but for imperfection: to tempt us and snag our souls. *The Counselor* works on at least two levels: that of an action fantasy crime drama and that of a religious, mythic narrative about temptation and damnation.

As played by Michael Fassbender, the counselor is slick, smug, shallow, but basically a sympathetic character. Without the emotional intensity—the suffering—which Fassbender brings to the role, the movie would be weightless, its horror nothing but titillation. The counselor is a player, but no more than most of us would secretly (or not so secretly) like to be. He thinks he's in love but really he is after his "glory." He thinks he can fraternize with criminals and killers and reap the benefits without being one of them himself. He's both cynical and naïve— his cynicism *is* his naiveté, and vice versa. He has no idea of the forces at play, both within and without, in his psyche and in the world. The irony of the title is that the counselor never counsels anyone but is constantly asking for and receiving advice from others, and then ignoring it. In fact the counselor receives three warnings before he takes the step that will bring about his ruin. The diamond dealer shows him "a cautionary stone" and talks about how the brevity of our lives in no way diminishes us—in retrospect a foreshadowing of Laura's death. Reiner (Javier

Bardem) also warns the counselor ("You won't see it coming at all"). Lastly, Westray (Brad Pitt), the counsellor's mysterious business associate, cautions him about drug deals gone bad, and then describes "Scot's law": "*an instrument in which one person stands in as surety for another.*" "It sounds a bit primitive," the counselor replies. He has no idea.

The counselor is the negotiator between worlds who winds up crossing a line which he didn't know was there, becoming hostage to the deal he only *thought* he was making. In fact, he *was* the deal, his "soul" the desired merchandise that's "purloined" and purchased—by means of Laura, the "surety"—property which a creditor can claim in case the client defaults on their obligation. Laura is treated as the counselor's property because that is how *he* treats her, as a precious object to be secured. When the counselor finds out from Westray that the deal has gone terribly wrong and that he is a marked man—even when Westray warns him, "It's not that you're going down, it's what you are taking with you"—the counselor's attempts to protect Laura are almost unbelievably careless (when he calls her, he tells her to go home). Yet because the counselor is the only character who recognizes the depth of his folly and becomes fully cognizant of his "damnation," he's also the only one in the film with even a thimbleful's chance of being redeemed.

*

An unusual quality of *The Counselor* is how it opts to tell rather than show the most shocking elements of its narrative and yet is all the more disturbing for it. When Westray warns the counselor not to imagine there is anything these people aren't capable of, it's the emphasis on this fact (which echoes John Huston's famous speech from *Chinatown*), rather than any visible examples of it, that's the real horror. The way Pitt plays these scenes confirms something I have long suspected, deep down, and which the film plays up: we *want* to believe the worst about human depravity. The idea of people acting without any moral compass or checks or bounds is weirdly attractive *because* it is so horrifying, but also, it's horrifying because it's attractive. It's the allure of taboo. In a world where everything is permitted, the only possible defense is to tell ourselves that none of it is true, that *nothing* is. That's ironic detachment. The characters in *The Counselor* all have it, but few of them survive it.

The Mexican cartels traffic not only in drugs and money but in human flesh, specifically the flesh of young women and girls (preferably virgins), though in the end, any flesh will do. The ritual beheadings which are turned into snuff movies aren't just for the amusement of the elite: they feed the engine that maintains the empire, giving spiritual evil a power *base* in the world. And they appeal to the basest instincts in us all.

*

"The extinction of all reality is a concept no resignation can encompass."
—Jefe, *The Counselor*

There are lesser characters in *The Counselor* who don't seem to be subject to the rule of this nightmare circus slaughter world, but who, like demigods, enforce the rules. The diamond dealer is one: his role is to tempt and instruct the counsellor, to tempt him *by* instructing him and vice versa. He seems like a kindly old man at first, but by the end of the movie he has started to look more like a demonic keeper of souls. If the diamond dealer is Satan, then even more unexpectedly, Jefe, the cartel member played by Rubén Blades, appears to be in the role of God (the Catholic God, who is the Jewish God in disguise). Jefe quotes the poet Arturo Machado to the counselor over the telephone and tells it like it is; he's the bearer of neither good nor bad news but simply the cold, stark facts. (Truth may not have a temperature, but it can freeze your soul and burn your heart out.) Jefe (it means "boss") is the character (besides Malkina) most overtly identified with the creeping evil of the film, and yet he is also by far the wisest and most likeable character, an almost paternal presence. His sympathetic demeanor may befit such high levels of power—in McCarthy's dream reality—since true power can afford to appear "soft." Jefe is beyond social norms of "good and evil"; he is merely an instrument of divine justice. Gently, almost tenderly, he presides over the counselor's awakening.

As Jefe patiently explains it to him, the counselor's fatal mistake is that he "continue[s] to deny the reality of the world [he is] in." He *is* the world he has created. The counselor is a victim of "moral hazard" but also its perpetrator. Moral hazard arises when an individual or institution doesn't take the full conse-quences of their actions and so has a tendency to act less carefully than they would otherwise, leaving others to face the conse-quences. Laura pays the price of the counselor's actions because she knows almost nothing about them; the counselor likewise is acting out of ignorance and soon discovers that he's just a useful tool, or simply a handy victim, for those with more knowledge than him. At the same time he's succumbed to the dangers of proximity contamination or conditional corruption. He's associated for so long with criminals, been offered so many temptations, crooked deals, and easy gains—and been complicit with helping criminals to continue with their activities—that he doesn't even *see* the line until it's just a faint smudge in the distance behind him.

The City of Lost Women & the Hollywood Dream Factory

"With grief the normal rules of transaction do not apply. Grief transcends value, yet you cannot buy anything with grief,

because grief is worthless."
—Jefe, *The Counselor*

Although I lived in Mexico for several years (in 1989, and later in 2004), and although I'd heard about the ongoing drug wars in the North, I wasn't familiar with the finer details until I looked into it after seeing *The Counselor*. I soon found out that the film in no way exaggerates the horrors occurring. Ciudad Juárez, where the film's deadly drug cartel is located, has been known in Mexico since the early 1990s as "the capital of murdered women." According to a 2011 article in *The New Statesman*, "Mexico's Disappeared Women," many locals believe the killings were "a form of blood sport for the city's elite," and/or related to satanic cults, snuff films and organ theft. An accurate number of victims was said to be impossible to gauge, and inevitably, the number of women reported missing was far higher than that of confirmed dead (bodies found). Some of the most powerful companies in the US have installed factories in Chihuahua (the state Juárez is in), including Ford, General Electric, General Motors, RCA and Chrysler, and these factories are known as *maquiladoras*. Creating "an abundance of jobs," the *maquiladoras* have attracted a steady stream of arrivals to Chihuahua, and to Juárez in particular, from all over Mexico and (presumably) also from Central and South America. A significant portion of this influx of hopeful workers are young women.

Not only are *maquiladoras* implicated in the city's broader problems, but often their own staff are victims of kidnapping and murder. The factories operate 24 hours a day. White buses move around the suburbs, collecting women for their long shifts. The lack of security on these routes has been blamed for many of the disappearances. The buses leave the women near their homes, not at or outside them. This obliges them to walk the unlit streets, where many are kidnapped. ["Mexico's

Disappeared Women," *The New Statesman*]

The picture this paints (to me) is of a tightly organized, long-term and large-scale agenda for the luring and abduction of women, in which US corporations, as well as local managers and government officials, are all implicated, at least indirectly. The locals blame the police and politicians, and to some extent probably the factory owners too, for what is happening. One woman whose daughter went missing insisted that the authorities "know where this problem is coming from and there are people who know the places where these girls are being tortured" (strip clubs and brothels found throughout Mexico). As depicted in the movie, the article reported photographs of missing women on storefronts, house walls and lampposts throughout the streets of Juárez, gangs of teenagers driving around, waiting for instructions for their next "hit" (and possibly abduction), for a fee of less than $20. The article describes the overall mood of the city's inhabitants as one of numbness and despair, a kind of nihilistic resignation to the forces of corruption that have overtaken their lives. *The Counselor* depicts this same world, locating it not only in Northern Mexico but on the other side of the border, in the land where an excess of opportunity leads straight to hell.

The counselor pursues his happiness by making deals with the Mexican drug cartel to secure his diamond and his girl, but he loses them both to the chthonic forces of chaos which he's invoked. He realizes that his life isn't worth living without that "glory"—the *anima* being his own soul—and so he follows both the girl and the diamond to Hell (Juárez). By this relatively selfless act, he surrenders to the inevitable consequences of his own thoughtlessness. Unlike Orpheus, he can't bargain with Hades; the Plutonian forces don't care about his suffering (though they share their wisdom with him). The counselor soon learns he can't ever bring Laura out, that he can't even trade places with her (though he is willing). All he can do is take up residence there, hopeless and alone, and submit to his fate, signified by a DVD brought to his room (by a child) which we can only presume contains a snuff movie of Laura's torture and murder, a jolly "*Hola!*" scrawled on it.

The film does offer a dim ray of hope, a possible way through the unremitting darkness that follows "the extinction of all reality." The diamond dealer assures the counselor that "At our noblest we announce to the darkness that we will not be diminished by the brevity of our lives." Jefe tells the counselor the story of the poet Arturo Machado, who only became a poet after his beloved died prematurely. "I'm not going to become a poet," the counselor replies grimly. Jefe assures him it wouldn't help him if he did, yet the point has been made. The reference to the despised, buried philosopher's stone which reveals the true nature of all human plans indicates there is a "treasure" to be found, but only once all hope and meaning—"all reality"—has been cruelly and irrevocably extinguished, forever.

In *The Matrix* (a movie-myth I spent several years identifying with and living by), Thomas Anderson's emergence from the dream he has been living inside is traumatic; he's told that they rarely take people out of the matrix after a certain age because their minds can't take it. Thomas gets off lightly: he only has to throw up. The protagonist of *The Counselor* isn't so lucky; in the film's centerpiece and strongest scene, he is given clear vision of the truth and what he sees devastates him (though also frees his soul). For me, these scenes come closer to showing the true price of awakening than just about any movie ever has before. *The Counselor*'s spiritual clout is in the absolute logic of the horror that befalls its protagonist. The meaningless depravity which he becomes prey to is *an exact response* to his own blind, greedy pursuit of personal happiness in a universe that does not tolerate blindness, that punishes it as ruthlessly as any imaginary avenging God ever punished "evildoers." It is religion beyond faith and beyond nihilism: *gnosis*.

If spiritual awakening, as Jed McKenna wrote, is the psychological equivalent of being skinned alive, then that's what the counselor gets. The counselor's world (which is also our world) is built on the blind exploitation of others for the sake of personal gratification, a world in which the human soul (*anima*) is harnessed to *maquiladoras* as fuel for the most depraved kind of desire. The price of unchecked greed is never-ending grief. The world of *The Counselor* might seem disproportionately bleak to a lot of people. One particularly obtuse critic I read complained that "The milk of human kindness does not flow through *The Counselor*'s veins, not even close." But *The Counselor* isn't about the milk of human kindness (not even close). It's about a soul-deep corruption reflected by social, political realities, by historical facts.

For a Hollywood movie to draw on real world atrocities—such as the abduction, probable rape and torture, and murder of young Mexican women, and the complicity of US government organizations and big business (really the whole of western civilization, including you and me) with those atrocities—*is* problematic. Quite apart from its philosophical accomplishments or its validity as social commentary or indictment, *The Counselor* is stylish, sensational, visceral entertainment. It cost millions of dollars to make and (though the film wasn't a success) presumably made millions for studio executives, its writer, director, and stars. By using the real-life miseries of Mexicans to inject their preposterously gripping witch-brew with a powerful sense of pathos and gravitas, it could be argued that the filmmakers were exploiting that misery. The people involved in making it, after all, belongs to the same capitalist elite *behind* the atrocities which the film so grippingly exposes. These are some of the same people involved in movies such as *Mr. and Mrs. Smith*, *Black Hawk Down*, *Hannibal*, *Skyfall*, *Knight and Day*, and *World War Z*. Certainly, it would be hard to see them as victims.

Scot's Law

"If you think you can live in this world and be no part of it, all I can say is you're wrong."
—Westray, *The Counselor*

Hard, but perhaps not impossible? Ridley Scott's brother, Tony Scott, allegedly committed suicide during the filming of *The Counsellor* (Ridley shut down the production for a week), and how could such an event not have influenced the film's tone? When he died, Tony Scott was in preproduction for *Top Gun 2*, a film about drones with Tom Cruise; he apparently didn't have brain cancer or any other terminal disease, as was widely reported at the time of his death as the main reason for his (alleged) suicide. Maybe *The Counselor* was Scott's dark commentary on Hollywood itself? While researching this chapter, I came across something at the filmmaker Alex Cox's blog about the Scott brothers that seemed to support this reading:

> [The Scotts] made commercials, and when they moved to the States became absorbed into the Pentagon's Hollywood cheer-leading machine. The bros created glossy, highly dynamic recruitment propaganda like *Top Gun* and *Black Hawk Down*, and—in the case of Tony—torture propaganda in the form of *Man on Fire*. So I wonder as to the contents of the various suicide notes Tony Scott left before jumping off that bridge. For a police force famous for leaking celebrity gossip, the LAPD has been close-mouthed about the matter. Perhaps the notes were merely tender messages to his family. Perhaps they were long screeds condemning the Hollywood studios for being a duplicitous, blacklisting mafia cartel. Or—and this is what I hope—perhaps they have been kept secret because they are a *mea culpa*: an apology for the years Scott wasted his

talents working for the Pentagon and the CIA, promoting torture and war. [Supporting his case for Tony Scott's involvement in US propaganda, Cox cites Tricia Jenkins' *CIA in Hollywood*, including a list of] actors, directors, writers, producers and studio execs who the author links to the CIA, usually found 1) visiting CIA headquarters to party with the spooks, 2) taking instructions from CIA, or 3) actively helping to encourage CIA recruitment. Tony Scott heads the list: Jenkins reports that CIA was particularly fond of his masterpiece *Top Gun*, "the single best recruiting tool the navy — and specifically naval aviation — ever had" and "was looking for a project that could help them do something similar."

Conditional corruption can be defined as follows: "individuals' unethicality does not depend on the simple calculations of cost-benefit analysis, but rather depends on the social norms implied by the dishonesty of others and also on the saliency of dishonesty." ("Contagion and Differentiation in Unethical Behavior.") Translation: people behave unethically not just because they want to get something for nothing but because it seems like *the normal thing to do*. It seems normal because it *is* normal. Outside of movies and documentaries, I don't have much personal experience of the world of lawyers and bankers, corporate criminals, CIA manipulations, drug cartels, or million dollar deals (Hollywood or otherwise). But it's probably a fair bet that, when the opportunity for moral lapses are rife — when they are even business-as-usual — the perceived risk of *not* succumbing and of getting left behind with the other "suckers" (which would include anyone more ethically-minded), or worse, becoming the victim of somebody *else's* crooked scam, may start to seem greater than the risks of giving in to corruption. If you're trained and conditioned to believe that success is the measure of self-worth, then moral considerations are eventually going to get sacrificed to "good business sense." Corruption tends to be incremental, and the nature of rot is that it obscures its own evidence, especially since one of the first things to go is a sense of smell. When we succumb to corruption, maybe we don't *see* it as corruption? Maybe we think we are just doing whatever it takes to secure our own "happiness"?

When they made their movie, McCarthy and Scott were no doubt aware of just how pressing moral hazard and conditional corruption has become over the past few years in the corporate world (which is *the world*). They wove these concerns into their infernal parable deftly enough for the movie to seem grounded in current events and real-world issues, while remaining true to its own surreal landscape of black magical realism. It's an impressive accomplishment, and it's too bad so few people— especially so few with the power and responsibility to draw others to the film, i.e. critics—were willing or able to recognize it. But then, probably very few people want to recognize the truth behind *The Counselor*'s elaborate fiction, since the rot being revealed is in their own basements and backyards, and the septic tank carries *everyone's* shit.

When the art form comes clean and puts the rankness right there on the screen, it may be time to leave the theater and not look back. Ironic detachment doesn't protect us from reality; it only gives us the *illusion* of being above it all. Naiveté and cynicism are synonymous in *The Counselor* because it's naïve— fatally naïve—to think we can gratify our own desires while ignoring the cost to others and still get away "clean." There's always a bigger predator out there that will find us eventually; and the bigger we get, the tastier we start to look. Cynicism sets us up for the axe-fall. Naiveté means we don't ever see it coming.

Crucified Hero

The Mythic Reinvention and Morbid Self-Destruction of a Dandy

"My father was a nihilist. But nihilism, if you like, is the beginning of faith anyway."
—Sebastian Horsley, 2002

What follows is a passage from *Paper Tiger*, a short book about my brother Sebastian which I wrote a few months before his untimely death. (In the end I decided to leave the passage out.)

Our father pooh-poohed everything; he was a hard-headed rationalist with a soft, sentimental center (i.e., a liberal). Our mother was the reverse: an irrational thinker with a tenuous grasp on "reality" (logic), but with a tough, ruthless core and a cruel streak. In terms of his religious belief, it might be argued that our father had to negate God, repeatedly throughout his life, as the only way to keep the terrifying possibility at bay. Since what we resist grows stronger, the idea of God became progressively stronger for each of his denials, a fact of which I am the living proof. Our father's denial of God drove me all the way to the opposite extreme, until an affirmation of invisible forces became the defining element behind everything I do. This placed my brother in the opposite position, unconsciously mirroring our father's stance of materialism, atheism, and nihilism—most especially with me, since I was the inverse of this inherited pattern. If actions speak louder than words, our father was actually closer to a true nihilist (despite his social conscience) than my brother would ever be.

My brother's nihilism is really a case of "the gentleman doth protest too much." He is a seething mass of contradictions. He despises religious faith yet he is an obsessive compulsive who performs endless rituals to maintain his peace of mind. He scorns all spiritual and occult ideas and insists that the universe is random chaos, yet adheres religiously to astrological principals. He is a virulent anti-Christian who chose to be crucified. He was thrown off the cross "by a God [he] didn't believe in," and wrote in his journal at the time that he had no doubt that he had been rejected for *hubris*. Soon after, however, he decided that a combination of poor craftsmanship and his own excess weight was really to blame, and, realizing that his fall from the cross only made the piece all the more of a show-stopper, continued with his self-promotional (*hubris*) campaign. After the crucifixion (during which he passed out), my brother told me, "If that was death, then there's nothing to worry about." It was an astonishing admission for a nihilist to make, but it was apparently just for me. Publicly, he continued to profess his anti-religious dogma: "I've had quite a few near death experiences and I can tell you for a fact there's nothing on the other side."

Further contradictions abound. My brother adores our mother (he has called her his prefect audience, and she has referred to him as her dream date); and yet in his [memoir, *Dandy in the Underworld*,] he turns her into a sort of caricature, a drunken disaster, vain and egocentric, just like him. This isn't actually *in*accurate: our mother does possess these characteristics, just not in the way he depicts them. For me his portrait of her is woefully inadequate and doesn't even pass for a convincing fiction, much less a real person. He puts his own words into her mouth and creates a Frankenstein's monster patchwork of a mother, designed to serve the ends of his own mythic reinvention, which is the true, unspoken intent behind his novel.

I finally read the whole book a few weeks ago, and it was as if I were re-experiencing something from my past that I hadn't been aware of until now. Here was my brother, creating his own particular version of events as a means to put himself squarely in the spotlight. And there was I, in the midst of this shameless self-aggrandizement, once again being reduced to a bit player, pushed out of the picture: shot, stabbed, slapped, and getting the wind kicked out of me. It was *déjà vu* all over again.

Although the book passed itself off as a factual account, what I read was closer to a parody populated by caricatures. Yet journalists who reviewed the book or interviewed my brother were reporting falsified incidents from my own past as if they were historical facts. My mother attempted suicide four times? I had no idea. (It was actually once.) My stepfather was an alcoholic? News to me. (I don't remember ever seeing him drunk.) And although my brother makes no bones about being "the classic unreliable narrator," this didn't prevent journalists from taking him at his word. If it makes a good story, print the legend. By the publisher's own admission, they didn't fact-check the book, only ran it by their lawyers to make sure there was nothing actionable.

It might be argued that any autobiography is limited by the subjective memory of its author: we can only ever report our own perceptions, so "What is truth?" But there's a difference between a subjective interpretation presented as such and a deliberate distortion presented as fact. What sort of impact does a willed distortion of facts (in the interests of creating "a good read") have upon those directly represented by such a false narrative, or even upon those (like myself) mostly left out, who were present for many of the events depicted, and who then get to be present to witness the effects of these distortions?

Great Expectations

"If someone were to set up a production in which Bette Davis was directed by Roman Polanski, it could not express to the full the pent-up violence and depravity of a single day in the life of my family. It was a foul octopus from whose tentacles I would never quite escape."

—*Dandy in the Underworld*

All of my early memories of my brother have to do with fire. When I was around five, he recruited me in a dastardly plan to set fire to our sister's old pram in the basement. It was next to the boiler and, as the story was told to me later, if our mother hadn't intervened the whole house (a mansion called High Hall) might have blown up. Around that same time, our gardener went crazy and tied up my brother's friend and tried to start a fire under him, as if having flashbacks of the Inquisition. A few years after that, in our next house, New Walk, my brother dressed up and painted his face like Gene Simmonds from Kiss, then breathed fire by inhaling fly spray. Around that same time, he was electrocuted and almost died while mowing the lawn (I was a witness). With such an early blueprint, it's amazing he lived as long as he did.

Another memory I have from that time (when I was between the ages of seven and nine) is of sitting on the stairs outside his bedroom on the top floor, listening to Kiss' "Great Expectations" through his closed door. The song was on the band's best album, *Destroyer*, which my brother listened to constantly back then. Whenever I heard this particular song starting, I would quietly position myself outside his bedroom to better listen. It stirred an unknown longing in me. Later, when we were both in our forties, my brother would never tire of reminding me that "Unhappiness is the gulf between our talent and our aspirations." If this is true, then it's a gulf which he eventually fell into, and it swallowed him whole. For my part, I am still unhappily aspiring to bridge it.

*

My brother was an artist most celebrated for his potentially (and in the end actually) self-destructive pursuits. In his early twenties, he went into business with Jimmy Boyle, a notorious ex-gangster from Glasgow. He went diving with great white sharks and painted the experience. He became a junky and a crack user, slept with "thousands" of prostitutes, and worked as a male escort. For his *coup de grace*, in 2000, the year I turned 33, he went to the Philippines to be crucified, filmed it, and did a series of (disappointing) paintings about it. My brother lived his life like someone laying the groundwork for a racy, sleazy, action-packed memoir. Later, *Dandy in the Underworld* was turned into a Soho stage production that premiered a few nights before his death of a heroin overdose, in June of 2010.

My relationship with my brother was never not-fraught. At the time of his death it had broken down completely (not for the first time) and we hadn't spoken in a year; I had been having fantasies about knocking his top hat off and punching him in the face. We were both completely dissimilar and eerily alike, like matter and anti-matter, drawn to one another and at the same time fiercely opposed. He was the nihilistic dandy hedonist, I was the spiritual shaman ascetic. Whenever we got together, it was to argue our way to agreement. I always loved to see him—even when I hated it.

My brother was my first and greatest influence. He was four years older than me and he was the first model I had of what growing up was supposed to look like. His favorite movie as an adolescent was *Jaws*, hence swimming with sharks as an adult. Sure enough, when I began making lists of my own favorite movies, *Jaws* was number one. His infatuation with Hammer horror movies also passed down to me, like a dark family heirloom. We read the same *Spiderman* comics and occasionally even drew them together. When I was fifteen or so, he gave me an old, vomit-stained copy of Talking Heads' *Fear of Music*, which eventually became my favorite album. He was one of the first punks and passed his old clothes down to me. Even before that there was my use of his coat and passport to get into my first X movie. In his early-twenties he started to dress all in black, wore shiny boots and a genuine leather Nazi great coat, which he later gave to me as well, at fifteen; I bought my own black boots to go with it.

Probably the central incident for me growing up with my brother is one I already described in *Paper Tiger*. It was at New Walk and I was eight or nine years old (the same period in which I was terrorizing gerbils and escaping into superhero fantasies of empowerment). It was past my bedtime but I was out on the landing, in my pajamas, listening to the adults downstairs having a dinner party, eavesdropping on one of the guests playing guitar and singing—more covert music listening. I had a small piece of blanket, called my "smelly," which was my comfort and which I held to my face and breathed into. My brother came down and saw me. He took my smelly and threw it over the bannister, to the hall below. I probably cursed him and went down the stairs to get it. When I reached the bottom of the stairs, my brother shouted out my name, asking what I was doing out of bed; his plan was to signal the adults and get me into trouble. I don't think it worked—either the adults didn't hear or they didn't care—but I was furious. As I came back up the stairs with my smelly, I cursed my brother like a sailor (swearing wasn't discouraged in our household); he swung out his leg and kicked me in the stomach, hard. I doubled up and started to cry. He went up to his room and I crawled into mine. The door to his room was visible from the floor below, I could see it open a crack and I could see him standing there, the light behind him. I shouted up that I hated him and that I was going to throw away everything he had ever given me. I ran through the items one by one so he would know I was serious (a clay representation of a giant severed thumb is the only thing I can remember—a symbol of my castration?). I could feel my brother's sadness and regret— just the fact he was standing there signaled it—though as far as I remember, he never apologized. I never did throw away those items.

Is this what Carlos Castaneda called "a sorcerer's blueprint"?

My brother took from me my comfort and exposed me in my childishness. I reacted with anger and asserted my adultness by cursing him. He asserted his greater strength through violence and reduced me to a helpless child. I swore to dispose of everything he had ever given me, but never followed through on my pledge. It's been over three years since he died and I am still trying to get free of his influence.

*

"I am forever poised between Savile Row and Death Row."
　—Sebastian Horsley

When I was around thirteen, my brother left home and moved to Edinburgh. A couple of years after that he went to art school in London (St. Martins), taking a flat just off King's Road, in Chelsea. (I stayed with him on my movie pilgrimages, as well as when I ran away from home once.) Later, he moved to Edinburgh and became involved, in more ways than one, with Jimmy Boyle. My brother met Boyle through our paternal grandfather, Alec Horsley, who had arranged for some of Boyle's sculptures to be exhibited in Hull. Alec had strong liberal values about reform, or so we were told, and he was definitely impressed by celebrities, which Boyle was at that time. My brother first met Boyle at Stevenson's College, where Boyle was doing a "Training For Freedom" course, working two days a week at the local community centre then returning to Saughton prison at night. Boyle was imprisoned for murder in 1967, the year I was born, and was released in 1982. Despite the viciousness of his crimes (an enforcer and debt collector for the Glasgow mafia, he was known as "Scotland's most violent man"), Boyle was given a reduced sentence, partly, or even mainly, due to his sculptures and his critically and commercially successful memoir, *Sense of Freedom*, which was turned into a BBC film. I'm not sure but my grandfather's support may have also been instrumental in reducing Boyle's sentence, since Alec was a well-respected, semi-public figure. A year after his release, in 1983, Boyle and his wife Sarah (a psychiatrist, and daughter of the aristocrat John Trevelyan, the former British film censor) opened The Gateway Exchange, a rehabilitation center in Edinburgh for alcoholics and drug addicts that encouraged creative expression. My brother and his then-girlfriend (eventually wife), Evlynn Smith also came aboard the project. "Within a month of its launch," Sebastian wrote, probably with the usual exaggeration, "the Gateway was full of murderers, junkies, lunatics and sexual deviants—I was well camouflaged." Elsewhere, he describes himself as Boyle's "servant":

> Boyle was an imposing person, with a self-confidence bestowed upon him by the violent edge that made others cower. When he gave commands there was nothing to do but obey. For me, he took the place of an absent parent. He knew just how to frighten and to be tender, a method of persuasion whose efficiency has been proved for thousands of years in the relations of parent to child. What I loved about Jimmy was that he allowed me to express forbidden impulses, secret wishes and fantasies. He seduced me because he did not have the conflicts that I had. As a leader he wiped out my fear and permitted me to feel omnipotent.

I met Boyle a few times during those years, but I never got to know him (if anyone ever got to know Boyle, which I doubt). My presence at the Gateway, and in my brother's life, was tolerated at best (though I did make a documentary of its workings, my first ever Super-8 film, since lost). The only time I remember Boyle showing an interest in me was when I got punched in the face coming home to my apartment on a Saturday night. It wasn't a serious attack, but I told my brother about it and soon after he showed up at my apartment with Boyle. Boyle sat in my leather armchair and leaned towards me with a steely look. He wanted to know what the "cunt" looked like, and pressed me to tell him everything I could remember. Apparently the only time Boyle took notice of me was when I presented him with an opportunity for violent revenge; I knew what he had in mind and was not averse to it, but I couldn't give him much satisfaction, and it was a fruitless visit. Still, it perhaps gives some indication of how much Boyle had really changed as a free man.

While I was working on this last segment, I received an email from the young friend already mentioned (the one who watched snuff footage as an adolescent), about the BBC TV show "Sherlock." He mentioned that the title character reminded him of me and had an enemy named Sebastian Moran (an underling of Moriarty). When I told him what I was working on, he pointed out that Sebastian Moran is a minor character in Alan Moore's comic book series *The League of Extraordinary Gentlemen*, with its cast of intriguing dandies. Moran was a secret agent assigned by MI5 to create a criminal empire through which the government can control the criminal underworld. *The League of Extraordinary Gentlemen* had come up in a project I'd been working on in 2013 about the writer and alien abductee Whitley Strieber, called *The Prisoner of Infinity*. The context had been Strieber's mysterious 1968 sojourn in London, which weirdly intersected with the notorious gangster brothers, the Krays. It was an odd coincidence to arise at that particular moment, since I was writing about how my brother had been (literally, as it turned out) in bed with the Glasgow (ex-)mafia. Both Strieber and the Krays had had connections to The Pheasantry, a famous 1960s hang-out on the King's Road, Chelsea, just a few blocks from where my brother lived in the 1980s. (Oddly enough, the house in Yorkshire which we moved to after my brother moved to Chelsea was also called the Pheasantry.) *The League of Extraordinary Gentlemen* featured a character who had been hanging around the London Pheasantry in the late 60s, called David Litvinoff, and Litvinoff had been described as "a living link between the various contemporary, queasily cohabiting underworlds of criminality (boyfriend, or at least sometime arm candy of Ronnie Kray), showbiz (the *Performance* filmmaking/art scene connections) and psychedelic occultism (probable sideline in good acid)."

The "living link between the underworlds of criminality, showbiz, and psychedelic occultism." Dandies in the underworld. My brother was certainly into all of these things to varying degrees. He hung out with Genesis P. Orridge in his teens and claimed to have robbed a church with them (allegedly they put a curse on him for making off with the most coveted of the spoils), and his fascination for criminality included writing letters to the Kray twins and to the notorious Moors murderer, Myra Hindley.

> Better still, it had been revealed that she and Brady had killed *far more children* than was originally thought ... Sarah [Boyle] had been advising the pair for years to come clean. [Hindley] was a vicious torturer. But my letters still began "Dear Myra."
> ... Naturally, my sympathies were with the criminal rather than the victim. They were so much more glamorous. Besides, Jimmy had told me: "It takes two tae make a murdah, ah'm telling ye. Thirs are born fuckin' victims, born to have thir throats cut."

While assembling this material, I found a 1999 *Guardian* article about Jimmy Boyle that mentioned that, in 1967 (just before he was arrested), Boyle "was on the run in London and under the protection of the Krays." According to my brother, Boyle worked with the Krays before that too, during the 60s and possibly earlier. The Krays were known to use Scottish "thugs" to commit murders for them.

There's a passage in my brother's book that had caught my

eye when I was working on *Paper Tiger*:

> A pedophile friend of Grandfather's, his face riddled with cancer, once took a shine to Brother [that's me]. Brother, as a child, had one of those faces of marvelous beauty which stopped strangers in the streets, so a pedophile invited into the family circle could hardly have been expected to be indifferent.

Paper Tiger was written before my brother's death and before the Jimmy Savile scandal broke in the UK in 2012, something I also discussed in *The Prisoner of Infinity*. Savile was from Yorkshire, where my brother and I grew up and where Peter Sutcliffe, the notorious Yorkshire ripper (whom Savile knew), stalked his victims during my teen years. A television "icon" of the period (roughly the equivalent of Dick Clark in the US), I grew up watching Savile on TV on the kids program "Jim'll Fix It" and on "Top of the Pops," which I frequently saw with my brother.

Savile's long career in sexual abuse was only made public after his death, and his victims included not only children and teens but convalescents and even (possibly) corpses. Some 214 criminal offences were recorded, with thirty-four rapes reported by twenty-eight police forces. What was more striking even than Savile's sexual activities was the fact they continued for as long as they did, despite at least six investigations (the first in 1958). Apparently Savile's activities were not only tolerated but actively facilitated by high-ranking officials in the police, medical establishment—Savile had free access to hospitals and morgues—and other institutions, including the BBC, where Savile worked. Savile started out as a dance-club owner, a scene monopolized by gangsters, and as a celebrity he enjoyed surprising political connections, including to the Royal Family. (According to David Icke, who wrote about Savile's activities years before they came to light, Savile was a procurer of children for sexual use by the power elite.) Savile and the Krays reputedly partied together in the 60s (sex parties called "Pink Ballets") and were almost certainly involved with supplying children to pederasts via Haut de la Garenne (among other locales), the notorious Jersey children's home where human/animal remains were found and children were allegedly tortured and sexually abused. In her diary, Myra Hindley mentions that she and her partner, Ian Brady, frequented dance halls where Savile DJ-ed in Manchester in the 1960s. In 2012, the *Daily Telegraph* reported that Savile bragged about being friends with Ian Brady. For his part, Brady, who grew up in Glasgow before moving to Manchester, boasted about being hooked up to the Glasgow mafia and associating with the Kray brothers. His claims were dismissed as "fantasy" by the prison psychiatrist. Yet Savile did run dance halls in Glasgow in the 1960s and 70s (as well as in Manchester and Leeds), which puts him in the same place and time with Boyle (as well as the Krays), and possibly with Brady and Hindley.

And there's more. Glasgow was also the place where PIE, the Paedophile Information Exchange, was founded in 1975 out of the Scottish Minorities Group. PIE was affiliated with the National Council for Civil Liberties (a cause my own family were certainly sympathetic to, if not actively involved with); its view was that children should be free to have sex with adults. Pedophilia, they argued, was simply a sexual preference, like homosexuality, and shouldn't be discriminated against. Their aim was to lower the age of consent to four or simply to abolish it altogether. PIE's members, "mostly educated and middle-class, were good at finding 'progressive' academics—some useful idiots, others rather more sinister—to fight their cause." For example, one leading member of PIE was also director of education at the National Institute of Social Work, leading to recent claims that child abuse involved "an Establishment conspiracy, with 'rings' of powerful abusers, including Cabinet ministers, protecting each other." Although many of PIE's activists went to jail and the group was disbanded in 1984,

> a climate was created where the abuse of children became acceptable [such as in] a hard-Left London council, Islington, with thousands of vulnerable children directly in its care. In the Eighties, an official inquiry found, Islington's children's homes were riddled with abuse, sex and paedophile rings. Dozens of sexual predators worked for the council and were, found the inquiry, protected by misplaced "equal opportunities" policies which enabled them to cry "discrimination" if anyone tried to rein in their activities. [*The Daily Telegraph*, 21 Feb 2014]

The implication of all this is that fields generally thought to be worlds apart—in this case organized crime, serial murder, pedophilia, popular entertainment, and Leftist social reform and civil liberties—were all working together, not just in Glasgow but all over Britain. It was a small, dark world, all right, one which I had no inkling of as a child but which was disturbingly close to the world I grew up in. My sister even had Jimmy Savile's autograph when she was a teenager—allegedly my father had procured it for her after a chance meeting with Savile on an airplane! I found out later that Savile claimed to have a phobia of flying. As the head of Northern Foods, my father was a highly respected businessman with political connections, so he might well have run into Savile in less neutral circumstances. Savile did a charity walk over several days from John O'Groats to Land's End in 1971 (the year he was given an OBE and became "Sir Jimmy Savile"); according to Savile (in his autobiography *As It Happens*), Northern Dairies (as it was known at that time) provided him with his food for the hike.

Like Alec (who started the family business), my father was a liberal and a socialist, ideologically at least, a fact that didn't prevent him from building a multinational corporation. My mother often described my father as a "sex addict"; at the very least he was a philanderer who had repeat affairs and went to prostitutes. As I wrote in *Paper Tiger*, there was no shortage of sexual libertines hanging around our "family circle" (this was the 60s and 70s) and evidently a predilection for young boys was no reason not to be included. As far as I recall, the incident with the "pedophile" which my brother recounts took place at our grandfather's house, which was probably also where I first met Jimmy Boyle. I have no memory of the pedophile, only how the story of his clumsy attempt at fondling me under the table was told with amusement by my parents. Was this a one-off incident or were such tendencies covertly indulged in our family circle — even perhaps seen as somehow "progressive"?

I don't remember much at all from my early childhood, so it's no surprise I don't remember this incident. It's as if those early years have disappeared into a black hole. My brother also has referred to something in his early past that he has no memory of, something "terrible" he thinks happened in the house we grew up in: "a foul octopus from whose tentacles [he] would never quite escape."

An Invisible Antagonist

"God is the Overpowering Tyrant (*al-jabbar*), and a human being who manifests this name without qualities that modify and balance it will be a monster."
—William C. Chittick, *The Sufi Path of Knowledge*

At the age of twenty, after a sojourn in New York, I moved to Edinburgh. All my friends and my sister had moved there, almost as if my brother had led an exodus. My brother and I began to develop a kind of friendship for the first time. We would drink champagne and smoke cigarettes and talk till two in the morning. He was obsessed with Ernest Becker's *Denial of*

Death, a book which Boyle had recommended to him and which became a lifelong passion for him. He wanted me to read it; I tried but found it lacking in spiritual dimension. (I was just starting to get into Castaneda and Jung.) I didn't know it until much later, but this was a turning point in my brother's life. As he recounts in his book, he had been having sex with Boyle and other women (often in threesomes) for years when he walked in on his wife and Boyle having sex in his kitchen. He had only married Evlynn, so he claims, after both she and Boyle pressured him into it. During this period he describes suffering a nervous breakdown and attempting suicide by jumping off a cliff. Because my brother exaggerates, embellishes, and invents so much in his memoir, however, it's often impossible to know what to believe, and no doubt he intended it this way. Despite its "tell-all" flavor, my guess is that his memoir leaves out a lot of material that was either too painful or too compromising for him to talk about. But I think that something changed in him during this period. He divorced his wife and quit the Gateway (though he continued living next door for several more years). Partly due to alimony, he was in financial difficulty and began playing the stock market, eventually making himself a millionaire. (Again, this is if his own account is to be believed; it possible, in light of everything, that this was a cover story for more illicit activities.) Apparently he took after our father more than he cared to admit. Ironically, or symmetrically, it was during this period (1991-3) that disaster struck for me, in the form of intolerable heartbreak, and I closed down my former life, threw away my inheritance, and went to seek oblivion (if not death, at least destitution) in Morocco (where, curiously, Boyle lives today).

I went to see both my brother and sister before I left; I didn't tell them where I was going, only that I was going somewhere I knew I would be treated badly and that I might not return. I still remember the stricken look on my brother's face as we said goodbye outside his little cottage. We both knew we might never see each other again. I had no clue I was leaving him in such a desperate condition, however. He never talked with me about any of those things.

A few years after my disappearing act, while I was in Amsterdam, I decided to get back in touch with my family. I had no way of contacting anyone, and the only thing I could think of was get hold of my grandparents, Alec and Susan. Unlike other family members, I knew they would still be listed at the same address as always. As it turned out they didn't live there anymore: they had both died. I managed to find my sister's number and we met up in Amsterdam. A few months after that, I met up with my brother in France. He rented a car and drove us to Pamplona, Spain, where I'd ended up after Morocco and where I planned to set up living again. On the drive, he told me about the love of his life, Rachel, and how she didn't like sex. I suggested, with typical lack of tact, that any woman who didn't like sex hadn't found the right man to awaken her desire. ("If Jesus Christ came onto her, you don't think she'd be into it?!" was probably what I said—ironic, since Rachel was a Catholic.) My brother was understandably furious and I offered a heartfelt apology. I still remember how he patted my knee reassuringly.

A couple of years later, in 1998, he visited me in Amsterdam (where I was then living) with same said love. In the interim, I'd committed the error of sending him some chapters from an early draft of what eventually became *The Lucid View*, my pseudonymous treatise on occultism, ufology, and conspiracies. He had been ruthless in his dismissal of it, calling it insane and adding that Rachel, his not-quite-girlfriend who wrote for *The Times*, insisted it would never get published. In Amsterdam, I pointed out to my brother that Paul Bowles, whom I'd spent time with in Morocco, and William Burroughs, whom I'd corresponded all-too-briefly with just before he died, had both been encouraging about my writing. My brother was scornful. He wanted to know why their opinion counted for more than his.

The other conversation I remember having was when I told him—and Rachel, since she was there too—about the last time I'd watched *The Texas Chainsaw Massacre* and how I'd had an erection throughout the film. My brother didn't seem surprised, he only wanted to know if I'd masturbated. I told him, truthfully, that I hadn't. What's interesting to me about this memory is that, not only was it the first time I'd spoken so openly about my strange predilection, but that I'd done so with a beautiful woman present. I knew that my brother wouldn't think less of me; on the contrary, as a fellow deviant I knew he would enjoy my confession. I also knew, apparently, that anyone who was trying to have an intimate relationship with my brother was unlikely to be shocked by anything I could say.

On our last Amsterdam meeting, I gave my brother a book I'd just read called *Remembering Satan*, about experiences of satanic ritual abuse. The book tried to make the case for the memories being false but I wasn't convinced, and I'd stuck some photocopies in the back of the book taken from another book, by Alex Constantine, describing hard evidence (animal bones and the like) which supported the stories but which had been suppressed, the accounts dismissed by mainstream media as "false memory syndrome." I told my brother that I wanted to write a screenplay based on the book and asked him to look after it. A few weeks later, I received an email from a total stranger with the subject line "Remembering Satan." They had found the book (with my name in it) in a hotel room in Amsterdam!

Shortly after this meet-up (this would have been Christmas 1998), I called my brother from my sister's house in England. He told me that both he and Rachel had found me insufferably arrogant. I was surprised—I thought we'd had a pleasant time together. I questioned him, challenged him, and finally told him I didn't accept his opinion. I remained calm and if anything my tone was reconciliatory, and definitely not aggressive. He told me he didn't want to have anything more to do with me and hung up. I never really understood what had turned him against me, but in the light of all the other stuff, I wonder now if the subject matter of the book might have triggered him. I always believed that my brother was dismissive, even contemptuous, of my interest in satanic conspiracies and occultism because he simply didn't know enough about it. In the years since his death, however, I have started to wonder if it was because he knew *too much*.

*

Shortly after our falling out, in March of 1999, my brother's "Flowers of Evil" exhibition opened. I attended the event, and though we avoided each other throughout the evening, at the end I hugged him. "Fly high, my brother," I said, meaning it as an Icarus curse. I moved from Amsterdam to Guatemala a few months later, and I began taking powerful hallucinogens with an ex-junky turned shaman. In April of 2000, on my 33rd birthday, I performed Elvis' "Trouble" on stage, dressed in black. A young guy from El Salvador supported me on bass guitar. After the performance, for reasons unknown to me, he fell to his knees in front of me on the street and cried, "Hail Satan!" A few hours later, I was driving home with a friend when I lost control of my vehicle and came off the road. The van flew through the air and landed in a dry river bed, and my face hit the steering wheel, hard. My friend was unhurt but I very nearly lost all my bottom teeth (they are still loose today), and I was eating through a straw for a couple of weeks after. I was convinced at the time that my accident was due to my being cursed—as well as my runaway ego (my own Icarus Syndrome).

Sebastian had himself crucified in August that same year. We still weren't speaking, but he told me later that, while he was going in and out of consciousness, during or immediately after the crucifixion, he realized he had been unfair towards me.

Shortly after that we resumed speaking. In October of 2000, two and a half months after the crucifixion, I took a large dose of extremely powerful, synthesized DMT and had what I later called my "red pill experience" — when I also got to see (maybe) what it's like to die. The same night, in the midst of sleep, I underwent a series of visions. One of these visions was of receiving a call from my mother and being told that Sebastian had shot himself in the night. As was well-known even then, my brother kept a loaded gun by his bed in his apartment in Soho (as well as the thirty-six human skulls on the wall). It wasn't for protection from burglars but, according to him, in case he ever had a sudden desire to end his life. In the vision, I imagined him waking from a nightmare in a frenzy of terror and, only partially conscious of what he was doing, reaching for the gun and firing a bullet into his head. In my vision, his suicide not only ended his own life but effectively destroyed our family, since my mother was devastated by it and it seemed unlikely she would ever recover.

I'm not sure if it was before this or soon after that he told me, but my brother had been sleepwalking; he had even gone so far on one occasion as to call his dealer, go to a cash point, and get money out for drugs while still asleep! I was convinced the vision was a warning, and I booked a flight back to England for the end of the year. I didn't tell my brother about my DMT vision on this trip; since he virulently rejected anything that smacked of "mumbo jumbo," and since he considered suicide a perfectly honorable, even "manly" path, I knew that my concerns might not be well-received. Somehow I did manage to persuade him to unload his gun, however, probably by pointing out that, if he was sleepwalking, he was also capable of sleep-suiciding.

In late August 2001, a year after the crucifixion and three weeks before the World Trade Center collapsed, I moved back to England and my brother and I began to see each other regularly; it was always in Soho, on his home turf. I was still having regular visions after my "red pill experience," and shortly after returning to the UK, while staying with my sister, I had a vision in which I was surrounded by dead people. One of them warned me, "Your family is in danger!" I pushed the ghost away because I already knew this. When I visited my brother at his apartment, I looked and saw that the bullets were back in his gun. Eventually I worked up the courage to tell him about my vision of his death. He admitted that the dream was worrying.

I kept a journal during this period; what follows is taken from two entries from late 2001:

The first time I met up with my brother, we were both morose in different ways. I had admitted to him that I felt zero interest or desire for anything at all, and that everything had lost its appeal, or at least its attraction. I told him it wasn't depression, for me (as it was for him), but a sort of coming of age. I was recognizing the illusory emptiness of the world, I said, and I believed it was a necessary wisdom to attain before undertaking any worldly pursuit. Sebastian was in a similar but very different place. Since his crucifixion, his dreams had been dying one by one, just as mine had ten years earlier when I went to Morocco. The difference between us was that, where I had faith, he did not.

"Even if God exists, I don't believe in Him," he said. His position was very consciously a "Satanic" one. He chose isolation over connectedness.

The next time I saw him, I was finally able to say the things I most needed to say. I told him of my vision of his death and that he mustn't forget that he was loved, and needed. I said that his destiny was a great destiny and not to back away from it or his "Muse might turn into the Furies." I admitted I was afraid I'd been meddling of late, and that I had backed off because of it, but that I didn't want to lose him. Losing him would be like losing a limb, and I wanted to see the glory trail he would blaze if only he could overcome his demons, once and for all. I urged him to make a decision soon.

"If you really want to kill yourself," I said, "go ahead and do it. But if not, get rid of that damn gun and stop fucking around and face up to the fact that you are a great soul, with great things to accomplish."

It was difficult for him to respond but he seemed to appreciate my saying it. I was pretty sure that not many people, if anyone, ever talked straight to my brother, free from bullshit. And I was equally sure that not many, if any, understood where he was at or what he was faced with. I understood it perfectly. I believed I could help, and that I would help, if he would let me.

A month or so later, we got into a heated discussion at his apartment. It was prompted by my spontaneously quoting from a magazine, *New Dawn*, which had just published my article on *The Matrix*. The article that came immediately before my own was called "Nothing's Shadow" and was about "The contemporary relevance of the Samurai." I quoted a passage on the feminization of the male to my brother:

> A man is only truly a man to the extent that he does not act to be attractive. This is the Black Hole of male consciousness from which masculinity can never emerge. When a man does something, even a good thing, in order to be attractive, he creates the invisible antagonist to an honorable existence that intrinsically must be selfless. He instantly becomes dishonorable, living in a lower domain. It sucks the life out of him like salt on a snail. It is acting from the outside rather than the inside.

It didn't occur to me while I was reading the passage that it might be construed as a direct assault on my brother's chosen vocation as a dandy and a poseur. That was how naive or unwitting a foil I was to him. And of course that was how he took it.

"I couldn't disagree more!" he said, and then launched into a sincere but shallow attack on the phoniness of "the contemporary relevance of the samurai." He insisted they were just peddlers who happened to be selling immortality, or whatever it was, rather than mouthwash. Unconsciously, I realized that I had chosen that particular quote in order to challenge my brother's already shaky sense of identity. Fortunately, since I had done it innocently enough, it didn't lead to a clash of egos (though it came close) but only to an impassioned discussion that, in the end, brought us closer together. But it was definitely touch and go for a while. My impression at the time was that my brother simply refused to accept the notion that anyone could be different from himself or could act with anything but the most vain and self-serving of motives. He scorned the idea that any of us could be truly indifferent to the opinions of others or could ever act for something other than personal gain. I was arguing just that, and only when he accused me of having impure intentions myself, and I freely admitted it, did he mellow.

"That's all right then," he said. Apparently he had seen it as a contest between our respective egos, which I hadn't intended it to be at the time (not consciously). I found the conversation exasperating, and was struck—not for the first time—by my brother's fierce insistence on human impurity and imperfection, his desire not merely to accept it but to glorify it; and how, in the process of glorifying human impurity, he despised and dismissed all sincere bids towards perfection. At the end, he wound up quoting himself quoting Nietzsche, and though it was a good enough quote (about the illusory nature of virtue as just an aspect of the will to power), I responded by saying that Nietzsche wasn't much of a role model, since he had died a raving syphilitic. At that point we left the flat, still debating.

I was acutely aware of the possibility that a real argument was brewing between us, but I was also determined not to pussyfoot around my brother anymore. It was a fine line between not giving up my own ground and being actively aggressive and storming *his*. But somehow we managed to walk that line. It was a fascinating couple of hours, during which we shook hands on two separate occasions. The first time, my brother commented, not for the first time, how I overvalued my talents while he undervalued his. He suggested we might become one person.

"We could conquer the world!" I said.

"Sounds great," he said. "Shall we shake on it?"

A little later, he accused me of wanting everyone to be like me. I admitted it, and joked, "Everything's Jake." I then paraphrased Shakespeare: "If a newborn baby had infinite power, it would destroy the world. If you could do anything you wanted with the world, Sebastian," I said, "I get the feeling you would destroy it."

He laughed and during that jolly moment I added: "I, on the other hand, might just be foolish enough to try and remake it in my own image."

He remarked how, whenever anyone tried to create heaven on earth, they ended up taking the world to hell. "So what I think," he said with boyish glee, "is that we should try and create hell on earth!"

I suggested that we shake on that too, and we did.

Beyond our twin-horned pact, what I found most gratifying about our talk was that, for the first time, I was able to declare to Sebastian my spiritual allegiance, of having surrendered to God, without flinching or stammering. I had said casually to him that I felt like we were both on the verge of success. Rather than let me finish what I was saying, he pounced on my remark and demanded to know what on earth I expected to happen, what I had up my sleeve, and so forth. I refused to bite and merely stressed that I felt ready for success, and that it was God's will. Then I added, "If it doesn't happen, then obviously it's not God's will; so that's OK too."

He laughed at me and said, "You can't lose," with irony.

I said, "But that's exactly right. When you surrender your will to God, you can't lose!"

Only moments before that, as it happened, Sebastian had

accused me of *hubris*. My brother consistently has trouble with what he perceives as my extreme over-confidence, even arrogance, and I knew that he felt threatened by any suggestion of my being successful. Yet strangely enough, he didn't have any problem with me declaring that I had surrendered up all personal desire to the will of God, even though it was the most outlandish and "arrogant" claim of them all. (And also the idea he had railed against earlier, in relation to samurais.) This one all-important statement actually met with his calm acceptance, and even tacit approval. In which case, I wondered, perhaps all the other areas of friction and conflict between us were but failures to communicate? Were they just the inevitable rubbing together of egos as a shared unconscious struggled to recognize itself? Above all, Sebastian could see that I truly did have something that he didn't have, something he wanted; not self-confidence, much less talent, but simply happiness. And my happiness stemmed from one faculty alone that he did not possess: the ability to surrender.

A short time after our meeting, making what I could tell was a big effort, Sebastian told me that he had appreciated my past concern and my efforts to straighten him out. He said that he had realized he had been dancing with death, and that he didn't want to do it anymore. The mere fact he made a point of speaking about it seemed to indicate that something had shifted.

Crucifixion-As-Revenge Mission

"A lifetime of neglect had left me seething with a lust for revenge."
   —*Dandy in the Underworld*

Initially I ended this chapter with a description of my brother's crucifixion (I almost typed "crucifiction") and my bold attempt to interpret it psychologically. It didn't work; the chapter seemed to grind to a halt and just lie there, dead on the road (or cross). The crucifixion was my brother's crucial fiction. It was the lynchpin of his myth, the thing that held it all together, that kept the fake narrative (the mask) in place. He very carefully defined the terms of any discussion about it, and I was unwittingly going along with those terms, even in my attempts to break it down and psychoanalyze it. Maybe it would be better not to talk about the crucifixion at all, to let it be conspicuous by its absence? But somehow that isn't quite possible, either. Everything that has come before, in this chapter, is an attempt to create a new context for that defining act in my brother's life. So what was that act?

My brother went to the Philippines to have himself crucified as part of a yearly ritual which the Filipinos perform, a tourist attraction but also a rite of passage for the most devout Catholics among them. Some years earlier, a Japanese man had filmed his crucifixion and sold it on the S & M market, and since then the Filipinos didn't allow outsiders to be crucified. My brother managed to "persuade" them to lift the ban, not only to let him participate but to film it too. In his memoir/novel, my brother writes that:

[The Filipinos] took a lot of convincing. I had to prove that I was an artist, that art is less a pastime and more a sort of priesthood; that, though we talk of religious art, art is itself religion, a devotional act offered to some transcendent aim. They eventually agreed to allow me to stage my own private ceremony. I was to be the first Westerner to take part in the event, known as "Karabrio."

The book's tone here, and throughout this chapter, is uncharacteristically serious, even reverent. Yet my brother neglects to mention, in the above account, that what really convinced the Filipinos was money: he bribed them.

Before the ritual, he recounts his intense discomfort, waiting to be crucified while wearing nothing but a loin cloth: "I wanted to be invisible, to close my eyes and vanish I wanted to make the whole world disappear just by refusing to look." During the ceremony, the support under his feet (only the hands are nailed) gave way and he fell off the cross, so instead of being up there for the usual time period of half an hour, he remained on the cross for less than five minutes. All this was captured on film by the artist Sarah Lucas (who once used Jimmy Savile as the model for a "Toby-mug figure" of Richard the Lionheart). After my brother falls off the cross:

I was inconsolable. I had been humiliated. There was no question in my mind. I had lost. I had been rejected by a God I didn't believe in and he had thrown me off the cross for impersonating his son, for being an atheist, and for being a disaster. I had made a complete fool of myself. I was going to be a laughing stock ... I'd yearned for a blaze of glory. I'd got a blaze of ignominy instead. I had failed ... It was only the next day that I started to feel a quiet pride—not arrogance, but pride, that I had been through it. I had survived and I had this wonderful thing to work with. It gave me a rare and intimate knowledge of myself and my subject. It centered me and made me feel humble. It was as if I had this warm and cozy room within me, wherein a strength and a secret lay, like a clandestine lover, but the lover was myself.

There is no mention here of what my brother told me, that "If that was death, there's nothing to worry about." As a message, apparently it was too life-affirming (and God-affirming) for what he had in mind. Instead, Sebastian found a way to reconcile himself to the embarrassment of falling off the cross: "without the accident, I realized it would not have worked so well ... It came like a shock. Disaster, it seemed, had been transformed into art." The film was eventually shown publically in London (followed by a chat with the writer Will Self), and my brother did a series of paintings. When the art failed to find a backer, he was "devastated. I felt even more vulnerable than I had in the Philippines. I had shown the world the unpainted Sebastian, the raw material, and it had been dismissed." In the end he decided to exhibit it himself. The paintings were poorly received but the crucifixion event turned him into a local celebrity. I was living in London during this period (late 2001-2003), and I contributed to my brother's PR machine by writing a glowing piece for the exhibition, about art and self-sacrifice.

After the show, Sebastian read all his press avidly. "I had to find out who I was, a shaman or a showman." He acknowledged that "the paintings were the weakest part of the show. But I have always spelt art with a capital 'I.' But did *I* have the airs and graces of a genius and no talent? The real truth is, I'm not actually interested in art ... Producing art is essentially conservative." After this, he used a line he got from Carlos Castaneda via myself. This is the one and only time in his book where my influence shows up unequivocally, and it is in the key context of his *rationalizing his failure as an artist*. "The secret," he writes, "the key, to being a warrior in this world is: leave no traces."

Over these critical months, as his celebrity as a self-made artwork increased, he lamented that

> I used to have everything that I wanted. Now I was on the point of getting everything that other people wanted—which wasn't nearly so interesting ... Isn't it better to be an anonymous celebrity than a famous non-entity? Where once I was a universe had I become a mere star—maybe a black hole?

A couple of lines later, however, and without any explanation for the sudden change of heart, he asserts his happiness: "I was finally happy. I'd done my bit for art—I'd stopped making it. Jesus was crucified to save humanity. I had been crucified to save my career. In my opinion neither of us had had much success."

This is the second time in the chapter my brother compares himself to Christ. The first time, he describes Christ as "the ultimate dandy," and adds, obliquely and rather creepily, "style is a way of buying people rather than things."

So what did my brother *do* in 2000? In the baldest terms, he bribed the Filipinos (presumably government officials) to let him participate in a religious ceremony, during which he was stripped almost naked and his hands were nailed to a cross of wood while his associates filmed it and took photographs. He then used the footage as a means to become famous. This—the element of self-promotion—would be the obvious difference between what my brother did and the Japanese man had done before him when he sold the footage of *his* crucifixion to the S & M market. My brother sold his own little "torture" movie to the art world and of course that was considered more tasteful and prestigious, more "authentic." But in the end (I found myself wondering *for the first time ever* while writing this piece), what was the difference? If my brother had done what he did under any other pretext than that of a "method artist"—that license for obsession—wouldn't his actions have been seen as either crassly opportunistic or insane, or both? They *were* seen this way by some people, of course, but somehow my brother successfully framed the event so that it was invariably the squares—the Christians and moralists—who were the most audible naysayers (and who would want to be lumped in among them?). When Mel Gibson's *The Passion of the Christ* came out in 2004, Sebastian reviewed it, or reviled it, for *The New Statesman*. If memory serves, he referred to the film when talking to me as "pornographic." I wouldn't know where to begin sorting out the layers of irony in his position, except to note that the original meaning of pornography is "writing about prostitutes"—something my brother did with more persistence and passion than probably any public personality in recent history.

After his paintings were dismissed by some critics, Sebastian reacted in anger and sent one of them a turd (his own) inside a Tiffany box—a fairly well-known "occult" method of cursing one's enemies. In *Dandy* he wrote of the act: "Revenge and the desire for it has a negative effect. If you're hurt by somebody, then you're controlled by that event. If you go into revenge mode, you're still at the mercy of that event." Reading between the lines of his memoir—and knowing what I know about his past, as an insider—that could pass for a reasonable summation of Sebastian's life, or at least for his motivation and modus operandi as "an artist."

After he was stripped naked, both literally and figuratively, for the crucifixion event, my brother began to assemble his full dandy armor, which eventually included preposterously tall top-hats and sparkling nail varnish. Now that God had publically rejected him (or thwarted his suicide mission), it was as if he suited up for a full-scale war with the deity. Like Travis Bickle with his elaborate gun-mechanism and his Mohawk, here was a man who was ready to *stand up* and take on the world. And as with Travis, the actions of a desperately alienated soul, of a God's lonely man projecting his demons onto the world and firing blindly at it, were greeted as bona fide heroism.

In its obituary of him, *The Guardian* compared my brother to Van Gogh, Caravaggio, and Rembrandt! I like to think he would have cackled gleefully from beyond the grave at the grotesqueness of it. A much better comparison, I think, is from a Kris Kristofferson song called "The Pilgrim," which Betsy quotes to Travis in *Taxi Driver*. She might just as well have been speaking of Sebastian as Travis.

> He's a poet, oh, he's a picker, he's a prophet, he's a pusher
> He's a pilgrim and a preacher, and a problem when he's stoned
> He's a walking contradiction, partly truth, partly fiction
> Taking every wrong direction on his lonely way back home

Sebastian Horsley, R.I.P.

Mother Bondage, Ancient Bloodlines, Cultural Plutocracies

[*Trigger Alert: If you have reason to suspect sexual abuse in your past, or if you are especially close to this subject matter, please approach the following chapter with caution.*]

"My dear Jake, the other brother. Part warrior, part stargazer, part gambler, part crusader, part plunderer, part violator, part martyr, we two are one. As ever, Sebastian."
— Inscribed to author, in hardback *Dandy in the Underworld*

To once-was Sebastian,
Writing this has been a bitch. I just wanted to finish my own "book" on the right note. And as usual I bit off more than I could chew. But something good has come of it.
    I now see more clearly that it's a mistake to regard you as either a corruptor or a victim of corruption. What I see, am starting to see, is that, whatever you did, whatever you turned yourself into, you were only trying to survive. You saw a corrupt world and learned to match it, to love it, as well as you could, as the only way to be accepted by it and feel safe within it. I hope that doesn't sound patronizing, but on the other hand, fuck it. Truth has no temperature.
    What happens when someone turns their lovely, soulful sweetness and beauty into a commodity and a currency for trading with the world? Using charm and charisma to be a success—that's show biz! But if innate virtues are turned into commodities, they can no longer be experienced as innate, as belonging to us or being an intrinsic part of us. They become extensions, adornments, like clothing or jewelry, and hence part of the lie you worshipped. (Or did you, or did only want to see if worship could turn a lie into something real? And what did

you see?)

When you traded your soul for the world's favors, how could you continue to believe that your soul had any real value? The Faustian bargain begins with self-rejection, trading in one's soul for the world is choosing external over internal reality (remember the piece about the samurai that enraged you?). Those who master the art of self-rejection are the "stars" of this world; the rest of us look to them with envy and admiration for having succeeded where we have failed. It's a beautiful irony, don't you think?

You wouldn't have agreed while you were alive—"Sebastian" wouldn't have agreed. But now you are all "Soul," now you have discovered that the soul is real, that it can neither be traded nor corrupted, that it cannot ever be diminished by the things we do to the body and that it is never lost, only unfound, that, like the Philosopher's Stone, its value isn't decreased for being buried and despised, now you know all of that—if you do—what do you say?

I just hope you are able to say some of it through me. You were the canary in the coal mine of the underworld that we were both born, or vomited, into. You showed me the way ahead and not simply the way not to go; if only it were that simple, but I have no choice but to continue where you left off, because we are truly one. But you showed me the way to let go of the illusion of "the world" while there's enough life left in me to survive the loss of that, of every dream, every adornment, every vanity, every lie. To surrender to my soul before I am crushed by it.

The words run dry. I will miss you until I die. The darkness of your sparkles is slowly becoming visible to me. I see you now as you are. I am beginning to see your light.

Now be at peace,

Your brother.

Tragic Paradox

"Nobody knows what a man must undergo in order to be free.

Every sorrow, every anguish, every indignity must be experienced if you are to render these things powerless to disturb you ... An artist inhabits the depths of pain and self-loathing like fish inhabit the sea. He breathes disgust and melancholy as lesser mortals breathe rancid air. In such tainted thoughts and racked emotions is our purpose and purity assured! Learn as much as you can while in Hell, Martin, because our time in Paradise is always short."

—Lucien, *Beauty Fool*

In 2003, shortly before publishing *Matrix Warrior*, I made a digital feature film called *Beauty Fool* in which I played the small part of Lucien. Lucien was based undisguisedly on my brother. (I think I even plundered his letters for some of Lucien's dialogue.) In Lucien's only scene he tells an anecdote to Martin (myself, played by Bruce Mackinnon) about how he tried to impress a girl by playing Russian roulette with himself, whereupon she leaves in horror. It was based on an account Sebastian told me, but it's an archetypal story, with all the usual suspects: self-destruction, sexualized violence, the "wounding" (or banishing) of the feminine, and the "show biz" (exhibitionism) of Lucien's "performance." Lucien (a name our mother almost gave Sebastian) played the *role* of a suicidal artist in a misguided attempt to seduce the girl (connect to his *anima*), and instead drove her away. (I wonder if, in the real-life incident, my brother ended up doing drugs alone after the woman left?)

I found acting in the scene—playing the role of my brother playing the role of a suicidal artist—extremely difficult, but with enough takes and some careful editing it made it into the finished film. My brother came to the "premiere" (the first and last screening of the film), and stayed just long enough to see me in the role of him. He never told me what he thought about it. I never asked.

257

*

"It is a tragic paradox that the very qualities that lead to a man's extraordinary capacity for success are also those most likely to destroy him. [W]e must be willing to jump into total emptiness and nothingness and travel in the direction of our fear. The ultimate terror is of being adrift, abandoned ... One's ability to cope with these darker elements will determine the heights one will reach."

—Sebastian Horsley, private correspondence to the author

In 2004, in an attempt to free himself from his heroin addiction, my brother took ibogaine. He wrote a piece about the vision he'd undergone during the twenty-four-hour "trip," including a moment when he and I met in the air and switched heads. In his account of the vision, he admitted to "sibling rivalries carried to some pretty nasty and petty extremes"; but now he realized that "the war was over." I never did ask him to clarify what he meant by "nasty and petty extremes" (and as it turned out, the war was anything but over). We never talked directly about his mistreatment of me as a child, but it seems inevitable he remembered more about it than I did. In those days it hadn't yet occurred to me that his mistreatment of me might have included a sexual element. I do remember how, in 2007 or 2008, we got into an argument about whether sticking a penis into a baby's mouth would be harmful to the baby. He didn't think it would be, I thought he was crazy. I found the argument deeply disturbing, and in retrospect it sowed an ugly seed for a jungle of dark imaginings.

Just before *Dandy in the Underworld* came out, in August of 2007, my brother and I had another falling out. We were in Soho, sitting at one of his favorite outdoor cafés, and he began talking about how we were both "mediocrity on stilts." I objected to being included in his self-disparagement. He replied by insisting that I would never be great, wasn't a "genius," and would never be happy until I faced up to it. I got angry and he stood up and warned me not to raise my voice to him. We made up immediately, but when I got home it was still rankling. I wrote him a very earnest letter and sent it by ordinary mail. It was a few days before his book launch. He replied by email saying that he hadn't read my letter and didn't plan to. Bringing up personal issues right before "the most important event of [his] life," he said, was the height of insensitivity. He finished by saying that he didn't have time for falling out with anyone, by which he meant, for making up with me. At the book launch, he stood around in his red suit while people lined up to congratulate him; I avoided him. This time our falling out didn't last long, however, though I don't remember how it was patched up. Probably I just decided it wasn't worth holding a grudge with my brother, since he was so good at that.

Funnily enough, during the time we weren't speaking, I came the closest I have ever come to "making it in Hollywood": an independent production company in New York expressed interest in my script about Sam Peckinpah and, for a very brief time, it looked as though they were going to find a way to fund it. For several weeks, on either side of my brother's book launch, I was convinced I was finally about to "break in" to Hollywood. My brother never knew about it however, because, by the time we were speaking again, the deal had fallen through.

The tragic paradox of the artist was a double helix in which we were both bound. Fame and worldly status was instilled in us from an early age as the goal of goals. Our parents had no religion and reserved their highest respect for the *intelligentsia*. This was especially true of Alec, my paternal grandfather, who especially admired political "great men," was actively involved in social reforms, and who published a book about traveling through Russia in the 50s (and self-published poetry later in life). My father also wanted to write but wasn't able to. Since he conveyed to us, in very clear terms, that this was the currency he valued the highest, it's no wonder if both his sons went through so many contortions, trials, and tribulations to prove themselves worthy of the Horsley standard. We were striving not so much to be the man our father wanted us to be (he never expressed *any* desire for us), but the man *he failed to* be. That would also have been the man *his* father wanted him to be. And not just his father, either.

The Will of the Mother

"Shallow are the actions of the children of men
Fogged was their vision since the ages began
And lost like a lion in your canyons of smoke
It's no joke."
—Marc Bolan, "Monolith"

2008 was the year it all began to come unraveled for my family. Our mother was ill for well over a year—suffering from indigestion and vomiting after meals—before she was finally diagnosed with stomach cancer in 2009. By then I had moved to Canada to live with my wife-to-be. When I heard about my mother's diagnosis, I booked a flight back to England. Before leaving I decided—with a mixture of wild intuition and psycho-logic—that I didn't want to be included in her will. I didn't want to be dependent on her in any way, and I hoped that a clear gesture to this effect might help facilitate her recovery. My plan was to ask her to give my portion of the will to my sister and niece; naively, I was hoping my brother would offer to do the same once he heard of my grand plan. I hoped that, together, we could demonstrate to our mother that we were self-sufficient, autonomous men, no longer in need of her support, and that this might somehow give her a new lease of life.

Sebastian was on the verge of major success. His book had

sold well and the rights had been bought (by Stephen Fry) for a film adaptation. The team behind *Jerry Springer: The Opera* were discussing doing a show based on my brother (after they did one on Anna Nicole Smith). In contrast, my sister was a single mother struggling to survive as a psychotherapist; giving the money to her seemed obvious—especially knowing that my brother spent most of his money on prostitutes, drugs, and clothing. I told them both of my decision while we were walking on Hampstead Heath. Although my brother was calm, he said he thought it was an unfair decision on my part and that I ought to split my portion evenly between him and my sister. I told him he was "an upright man" and didn't need his mother's money. He said he thought my action was "divisive." By the time he left our mother's, he was visibly brooding. It was the last time I saw him alive.

After I returned to Canada I heard from my sister that he had given her an ultimatum: either she refused to accept my gift or she would no longer have him for a brother. The news came as a shock but not a surprise. In the later years before his death, my mother and sister, as I saw it, were in constant fear of invoking my brother's wrath. He would shut them out completely if they failed to support him, no matter how outrageous or self-destructive his behavior became. My mother rarely gave him a reason to do so, but my sister had been warned by him on several occasions, and had always backed down in the end. Until now. I learned from my mother that Sebastian believed I'd done what I'd done out of anger for his mistreatment of me as a child. Nothing of the kind had occurred to me, and yet I never attempted to set him straight (I was too angry with him, on the one hand, and I saw it as pointless, on the other), and a year went by in which I chose not to call him or email him. Instead I tried to work it out in my own psyche, making podcasts and writing and even consulting an astrologer. I wrote *Paper Tiger* in March of 2010 and had it printed up in May. I sent a copy to my brother;

it was in the mail when he died.

As in my vision of ten years earlier, I heard about my brother's death on the telephone, not from my mother but from my sister. Though I'd been predicting it for years, it came as a terrible shock. It seemed impossible that someone so alive, so full of passion, intelligence, rage and ambition, could be snuffed out so abruptly and so easily. His death occurred a few days after the premiere of the Soho stage production of *Dandy in the Underworld*. He hadn't liked the play or the way he'd been represented, and told *The Independent*: "I'd rather be crucified again than sit through that. I knew I was obnoxious but I never knew how much." (Perhaps he'd had a similar reaction watching me playing him in *Beauty Fool*?) Predictably, he managed to go out with a quip. His famous "last" words were: "They say seeing your doppelganger is an omen of death, so I got quite excited about that and thought, best get my coat on."

*

I flew back to England for the funeral. By the time I arrived I discovered that a program had already been drawn up, as for a stage performance, with Stephen Fry as the main speaker, and that I wouldn't be allowed to contribute. Sebastian's affairs were being managed by his girlfriend of ten years, Rachel Garley, who would inherit his estate, and Ivan Mulcahy, his manager. I heard from my mother that it was Mulcahy who provided the heroin which caused my brother's death (I haven't substantiated this, however.) I also discovered that I was perceived by my brother's "people" — those close to him outside of his family, almost all of whom he'd met in the last ten years of his life — as persona non grata: they didn't even want me at the funeral. Apparently Mulcahy and Garley saw me as such a villainous presence that they even tried to stop me from visiting my brother's body at the funeral home, and it was only through my mother's intervention that I managed to do so.

I was afraid to see the body, but at the same time it felt essential to do so. Plenty of people I'd loved had died—my best friend from my teenage years, my stepfather, my brother-in-law, my brother's ex-wife, my father—but never anyone so close to me. And because I was always traveling, always away, I'd never seen any of them after death.

My brother's face was deep red. It had chalk on it from a casting that had been made for a death mask and he was wrapped from neck to toe in white linen. His black hair was thick and wiry and he looked like a doll. I kissed him on the lips and wept. There's nothing that can compare to seeing the lifeless body of someone you have loved your whole life. There's nothing to be said about it. It was the sweetest devastation, love that tears the soul. I can still feel it now. I will feel it until I die. That was my only real goodbye to him in lieu of the fiasco of his funeral—but it was enough.

The Mask of the Beast

"I think Freud is right in that a son who is worshipped by his mother will never doubt himself. But a contentious father can undo that. And the virtues of a dead father—his very identity for that matter—are limited only by the mother's imagination. The best kind of father is a dead father."

—Malkina, *The Counselor* (edited scene)

In 2010, I had never met Mulcahy and had only encountered Rachel Garley a few times, and never for any length. At the time my brother met her she was a famous "Page 3 Girl" (topless model in the British tabloids). Though she wasn't actually a prostitute (*The Guardian* had to print a retraction recently for having suggested otherwise), she certainly had an affinity for the lifestyle. Soon after they first met in 1999, as my brother recounted in his memoirs, Garley gave him a Christmas present of five hundred pounds and told him, *"I want you to go to Amsterdam and fuck a different whore for me each day."* She wanted him to phone her every time he fucked one. My brother had been clean for a few months, he writes, and his lusts were running high, so he followed her instructions avidly. He describes going from prostitute to prostitute before giving Garley the gory details. "[A]fter a week," he writes, "I was growing jaded," whereupon Garley tells him she wants to buy him "something *really* deviant." He then reports having sex with an old woman; allowing for exaggeration, the woman was roughly the age our mother was at that time. "I was disgusted with myself," he writes. "I looked down at the old carcass. It wasn't her that I hated. It was me. This was my fate." After that, Rachel tells him, "You have two days and one hundred pounds left. I want one more story. Something special." At this point my brother's writing becomes more colorful.

This time the brothel was a dungeon surrounded by churches ... I had been given a password to get me through the pearly gates ... I wanted hardcore. I was taken into a dark chamber ... The dregs of human bodies dragged themselves around me. This was the shambles of human life. The wrecks of carcasses salvaged from the genetic battlefield ... And in the far corner, lying on a bed in an alcove, lay a beautiful amputee. She had no arms. And no legs. She was my choice. We came together in our coupling, flailing my four limbs and her four stumps like some giant insect. What on Satan's earth was I doing? I looked down at her. *There's so much to say, but your eyes keep interrupting me* ... This was a woman who needed someone to feed her, to pick her up, to clean her. I had fucked her.

In late 2003, I saw a photograph of this grisly coupling, of my brother inserting his erect penis into a dark-haired, legless, armless woman. Not only had he fucked her, apparently he'd arranged to have himself photographed while doing it, then used the photograph for a greetings card, had the words "If you're happy, clap your hands!" inscribed on the back, and sent it to family, friends, and assorted others. He sent it to our mother, and as we commiserated over it I had a moment of hope when it occurred to me that the image might be a fake, photoshopped to shock. When I spoke to my brother, however, he denied it. I expressed my dismay and told him I thought it was a kind of black magic. "I don't see it that way," was all he said. Only later, when I read his account, did I discover that it was *exactly* how he saw it:

> You need deep resources of character, resilience of mind and spiritual stamina to make of decadence a virtue. But this was vicious. I had thought that the soul should be made monstrous. That to let this happen one must assume the mask of the beast. But was it a mask? Or had I become a beast? The idea was horribly exhilarating.

My brother was an offender; that was his chief delight and, to one degree or another, it was behind most of what he did in the public realm. He loathed anyone who identified as a victim. His defense of what he did with the amputee in Amsterdam was: "She wasn't a victim. She was a warrior." It was painful for me to read that because I knew he'd adopted the term "warrior" from me, in one of the scant ways in which he ever let my influence show. Ironically, considering that his philosophy was that "everything is permitted" and that only clucking liberals and other "losers" were offended by anything he said or did, my brother was forever taking offense, at least where his family were concerned. He experienced me expressing my individuality (as in the case of our mother's will) as an intolerable affront to him, a wounding. From what I observed of him in those final years, the more "offensive" he became—the more he demanded the world's attention, like a mischievous child—the greater his success and the more quickly he took offense at anyone who questioned or challenged him on his path to "glory."

If Sebastian wanted to take moral turpitude as far as it could be taken, "to turn decadence into a virtue [and] make the soul monstrous," it's hard to imagine that illegality would have presented an obstacle. Going to prostitutes and taking drugs was not something he could get arrested for confessing; but what else might he have been involved in that he *couldn't* talk about, not only because of legal consequences but also for fear of reprisals from those involved? Were there things he was sworn not to tell anyone? I can only imagine, but my imagination goes a lot further than anything hinted at in his memoirs (though I think he did hint at it to me, even if I didn't realize it at the time). I can also imagine that, if there *were* things he couldn't talk about, things he was ashamed of but also, in his strange, dark fashion, proud of, how irritating that would have been for him. In this context, maybe the incident with the amputee, and his choice to rub everybody's nose in it, was a way for him to really shock people, to horrify them and see how much he could get away with (children do it all the time), without admitting to anything illegal or seriously compromising? When you have a secret password to enter a sex dungeon in Amsterdam guarded by dwarves, there's probably a whole lot more on the menu than amputees...

*

Sebastian winds up the account of his Garley-directed initiation on an improbably positive note: "In reality, the whole experience had softened my heart. In some funny way the brothel is the home of spirituality. It is almost like you go to there to pray." Though there was almost certainly some truth in this for my brother, my experience of him was not of a man whose heart was growing softer. Nor could I see his sinister Christmas jaunt as he saw it, as delightful proof of his new woman's imagination and soulfulness, of her willingness to let him be his own man and never to put any claims on him.

> I flew home to Rachel. She cooked a cheese soufflé for my return—and it rose. *I was no longer afraid of her*. And she noticed the change in me. If treated circumspectly I am domestically pliable ... I had found a girl for whom there are no rules for the exception. I worshipped the air she walked on—and if you *really* worship a woman she'll forgive you everything ... For the first time in my life I was happy with a woman. Lovers generally want to share the loved one's thoughts and to keep them in bondage. They say "no strings" and then fashion a noose. Never again. I was free for ever from the damp, dark prison of eternal love. [Emphasis added]

It's hard for me to imagine Garley frying an egg, much less cooking a cheese soufflé—my brother's favorite as a child, a dish our mother continued to make it for him as an adult, especially when he was depressed. Apparently he'd found in Garley the least likely candidate imaginable for a mother surrogate. Why did he say he no longer feared her after performing his strange ritual for her? My brother claimed he wanted to avoid all emotional entanglements with women, and Garley certainty accommodated that desire. He described dandyism as "a form of self-worship which dispenses with the need to find happiness from others—especially women." In his memoir he quips, "Sex hasn't been the same since women started to enjoy it," then adds a few lines later: "I remember the first time I had *real* sex—I still have the receipt."

The ritual act he underwent to gain his "eternal freedom" was having sex with a prostitute with no arms or legs to hold him while acting *under the direction* of a woman he "worshiped," whose *will* he now embodied, becoming the plaything of her imagination. In Garley, did my brother find himself not so much a lover as a handler? And our original handler is our mother.

A male whose libido has been hijacked and crippled by the possessing mother and the absent or abusive father—what choice does he have but to express his sexuality through violence? Becoming potent with a strong, liberated woman is not possible, because the experience of his own powerlessness is too great that the threat of being devoured paralyzes him and makes him impotent. Rape, or some sort of enactment of it, is the only way *through* that paralysis for him.

In *Dandy*, my brother gives his own brief meta-commentary on the enactment with the amputee: "I had grown up with cripples. I went through a period in my twenties when I was terrified I would get the same disease as father. I wanted to attack life for what it had dared to do to him—and to us all."

The desire for revenge *on* the father is conflated with the desire for revenge *for* the father—but in both cases, the act is the same. Baby wants to fuck.

The Wolf Within

"I too found my inner child some years ago—and had an abortion."

—Sebastian Horsley, 2004, private correspondence

I learned some surprising facts before my brother's funeral. In his last months, my brother had fallen in love with someone and was thinking about breaking up with Garley. Actually, he had been thinking about it on and off for years. (I remember reading his Tarot as early as 2002 and he was thinking about it then.) I also heard from my sister that Garley and Mulcahy were sexually involved, though only as "hearsay," and whether their alleged affair began before my brother died was unclear. If such an affair did begin while he was alive, it would be an almost exact replica of his previous betrayal by his wife and Jimmy Boyle, which itself was probably a reenactment of when I came along and received our mother's favor and he was pushed out of his primary position. The circle returneth in to the self-same spot.

All of this is hearsay and I could be wrong about Garley, and about everything else. My worldview is highly suspicious at best, paranoid at worst. Rightly or wrongly, I have come to believe that my brother was being groomed for success before he died, and that his groomers may not have been limited to the people he hired for the job but may have also included lovers and "friends." It's possible that part of his grooming *required* his being on drugs, since junkies are a lot easier to "handle." If show business is politics, then no one makes it to a position of influence without being carefully "managed" first. Maybe my brother was seen by agents or agencies as unreliable in the end, and was turned into a sacrifice instead? Or maybe I am trying to make sense out of something too big to understand, and only succeeding in turning it into non-sense?

Another thing that came out after my brother's death was that he may have been alone in his apartment for as long as two days before his body was discovered. For some reason, though Garley had the key, and though Sebastian hadn't been seen in all that time and people knew he had relapsed, apparently she hadn't gone to visit him (or if she had, hadn't reported it). Even more disturbing, somehow, was the rumor I heard that Mulcahy had managed to sneak into my brother's apartment, after his death, and steal one of his ties, a gaudy pink number which Mulcahy wore to the funeral. In *Rosemary's Baby*, Guy Woodhouse (John Cassavetes) gets his break as a Hollywood actor by stealing a rival's tie, a tie which is then used in an occult ritual to strike the rival actor blind. Why had Mulcahy been so intent on wearing my brother's tie? What did it symbolize? To my already seriously disturbed state of mind, it hinted at Shakespearean intrigue and a simmering, *Macbeth*-style brew of witchcraft and murder. These were the people closest to my brother when he died. How was it possible that he had ended up so utterly alone?

*

A few months before my brother died, I was reading a book called *Programmed to Kill*, by Dave McGowan. The book was about how many of the most well-known serial killers might be part of a large, hidden network of activity involving military, police, and high-ranking government officials. It was the same network Savile appeared to belong to, and Peter Sutcliff, Brady and Hindley, the Krays, and maybe Jimmy Boyle (though I didn't know this at that time). While I was reading the book, it felt as if I was hearing my brother's voice in my head, telling me what rubbish this all was. I became preoccupied with how his influence over me went so deep, and with why I felt it especially strongly whenever I approached these kinds of subjects. My preoccupation led to a series of podcasts, and eventually to writing *Paper Tiger*.

There was something else. A few months before we fell out over the mother's will in 2009, we'd corresponded by email about Ted Bundy. (I just did a search for the emails but found nothing either from or to my brother; it's as if our correspondence never happened). In the exchange, my brother expressed his admiration for Bundy's "efficiency," citing as an example how Bundy had escaped from jail several times. I was disturbed that he would have anything good to say about Bundy, and in an attempt to challenge his peculiar idealization, I pointed out that Bundy might have had help, that there was evidence that many of the most notorious serial killers hadn't acted alone. One of the things my brother admired about these sociopathic types was that he saw them as defying the social, moral code of behavior and acting as "true individuals," a depressingly Ayn Randian point of view. (Rand wrote about her admiration for William Edward Hickman, who dismembered a twelve-year-old girl named Marion Parker in 1927). My brother responded to my suggestion by saying that he'd read "ten" bios of Bundy and that I was being "sloppy." I doubt now if there even *are* ten bios of Bundy, but who the hell reads ten books about the same serial killer? (This didn't even strike me as odd until my wife pointed it out.) When I read *Programmed to Kill* later, I found evidence that Bundy *had* received help escaping from jail, as well as evidence that he wasn't a lone agent. By then my brother and I weren't speaking, however, and never would again.

Listening to those podcasts four years after I made them, while writing this chapter, I realized that, in my attempt to make sense out of my brother's life and death in the context of my own psychological development, I'd been digging in the exact same dirt, and uncovering many of the same worms, as I was now. Now I had some extra pieces and the picture was clearer and more compelling. It was also darker, but still essentially the same picture.

Even now I find it hard to believe there could really be anything to these connections, yet somehow it's even harder to dismiss them as "coincidence." At a certain level of the game—as Westray warns the counselor—there *are* no coincidences, only the resemblance of them. My brother met Genesis P. Orridge as a teenager; he was friends with David Tibet of Current 93 and was an obsessive-compulsive who performed rituals all day long to keep bad things from happening. He wrote letters to Myra Hindley and the Krays, had sex with Jimmy Boyle, had himself crucified, frequented S&M dungeons in Amsterdam, and experimented in every kind of sexual depravity he could afford—and that's only what he admitted to. Though he would never have called himself a satanist (that would have been far too pedestrian), he invoked the name of Satan frequently; the thirty-six skulls on his wall and his increasingly Jack the Ripper-esque wardrobe were unmistakable occultist *chic*. I never talked about any of this with my brother; for example, I never asked him what sort of experience he'd had with the occult. There were certain subjects which he expressed only contempt for, and in such cases his contempt would also be directed at me for being stupid enough to believe in those things. I was intimidated into silence.

Whether or not he was, I was certainly drawn into the world of the occult and am still trying to extricate myself from it, psychologically at least. This week, I was listening to audio tapes I made twelve years ago, in March of 2002 (just before I wrote *Matrix Warrior*). At that time my nervous system was messed up from using too many psychedelic drugs and I'd become convinced, at a semi-literal level, that I was an avatar of "Lucifer." (I wasn't a Satanist either—I believed Lucifer was the original and lowest emanation of God, or something of the sort.) On one tape I remark with great enthusiasm how, the same day I initiated a series of rituals, my film career officially began. The film project was called *The God Game*, and it fell apart a month or two later, or rather, transmogrified into *Being the One*, a staged documentary or improvised fiction about my being the world destroyer-savior. This coincided exactly with my brother's crucifixion event (May 2002, the same weekend *Spiderman* opened). In fact, I was handing out tongue-in-cheek fliers to the guests (unbeknownst to my brother) with the words "The Antichrist Needs Funding" emblazoned on them, hoping to raise money for the film. It sounds like cheap fiction, and it's obviously not a coincidence that, immediately after playing Lucifer/the One, I played my only other film role to date, that of Lucien/Sebastian. I was consciously embodying the very same "energies" which I was unconsciously trying to exorcise.

*

Now, as I'm finishing up this book about how I was seduced by pop culture, clearly *none* of this is coincidental. These family patterns extend not only across generations but across blood-lines. Apparently my family was at least close enough to the hub of that wheel to have been sucked in by its centrifugal momentum. Digging around a bit on the Net revealed that my grandfather did more than aspire to be part of the *intelligentsia*, he was a co-founder of the Hull branch of Bertrand Russell's Committee of 100, and a founding member of the Hull Fabian Society. The logo of the Fabian Society is a wolf in sheep's clothing, and it is commonly associated (by David Icke, Alex Jones, and other researchers) with Orwellian (and Huxley-esque) agendas of social engineering. (After quitting the Fabians, H.G. Wells denounced them as "the new Machiavellians.") The Fabians were behind the creation of the Labor Party, the London School of Economics, and *The New Statesman* (which my brother wrote for, briefly), among many other things. Tony Blair is a current member, and Russell Brand is currently advocating their ideas to the masses—a curious detail because my brother saw Brand as a rival, and it's easy to see why (They were both upper class British drug-users, sexual experimenters, and humorists who wrote their autobiographies around the same time. Brand has a messianic complex, my brother had a Luciferian one.)

One of the founders of the Fabians, George Bernard Shaw, spoke publically on the need to eradicate all non-productive members of society, and Alec's pen pal Bertrand Russell was well-known as an advocate of eugenics. In my grandfather's day, Fabian Society members advocated the ideal of "a scientifically planned society" which included "eugenics by way of steril-ization." I never heard my grandfather talk about such ideas, but then why would I? I wasn't part of the club. The Hull branch of the Fabians was established in 1943, with sixteen members including a committee chaired by my grandfather. (Its main activities included organizing public meetings, "Brains Trusts," and film showings!) Apparently my grandfather followed closely in Russell's footsteps; like Russell he was an aristocrat who spoke out for the common man yet had next to nothing in common with him. (As far as I know, he rarely if ever mixed with the lower classes—not counting his prison visits.) Alec also cofounded the CND party (the Campaign for Nuclear Disarmament) and when I was a child he used to give me a pound whenever I wore their badge. Naturally I wore it every time I saw him and took it off as soon as I'd left, though it must have taken hold in the end because I took to wearing it to school (until I got threatened with violence by a Neo-Nazi). If Alec didn't think twice about bribing his own grandson to support the cause, it seems likely he extended those same principals into his workplace.

While the causes he seemed to support might have appeared to be socialist, for the good of the common people, a closer look at history shows that at least *some* of these sheep were wolves in disguise. Alec went to Oxford in the 1920s, and immediately after was set up in Nigeria as District Officer (the pivot of Britain's Colonial Administration throughout the Empire). He was the Sheriff of Hull in the early 1950s, and visited the Soviet Union in 1954, a time when even getting in wasn't easy. Among his life-long pals were Jacob Bronowski (*The Ascent of Man*), who worked for the Ministry of Home Security during World War Two (i.e., he was a spy), and Baron Eric Roll. Roll was appointed Professor of Economics and Commerce at University College, Hull, with the backing of John Maynard Keynes, the famous economist and (not so famous) pederast. This would have been around the time my grandfather met Roll. Roll worked for the Ministry of Food, went on to become director of the Bank of England, and between 1986 and 1989 acted as chairman of the notorious (among conspirologists) Bilderberg meetings.

The more I looked into my grandfather, the more evidence I

found that he was a *player*, a man with great social influence and grand visions for the future of humanity combined with some dubious ideas about how to implement it. By most accounts, he also had some questionable personal characteristics: both my mother and father referred to him as a bully, and he was involved in some sort of financial scam later in his life that entailed robbing pensioners of their savings. From what I've heard, Alec deeply resented his own father for leaving his money to Alec's brother. My father, Alec's firstborn son, told me he hated Alec up until Alec died. Sebastian, also a firstborn son, hated *his* father and likewise there was never any reconciliation. Apparently this was the legacy passed down to us. My brother died trying to live it down, or live *up* to it (a bit of both), and now it's fallen to me to shake off the legacy of deception and abuse, both the sheepskin and the wolf within.

As terrible as much of what my brother did and/or got involved with undoubtedly was, underneath it was a desperate struggle to escape from that familial octopus of "pent-up violence and depravity" (as he called it). I realize now that he was doomed to failure, just as my own attempts have been. You can't escape a value system by resisting it without making those same values stronger. The Horsley standard of a cultural elite or *intelligentsia* elevated individualism above all other values while paying lip service to socialist ideals. My brother's attempt to individuate from that family value system (and from the social matrix that spawned it) entailed a ferocious embodiment of individuality (dandyism) taken to pathological, Randian extremes. The reason it became pathological, I think (in both our cases), was that, the more we tried to extricate ourselves from the family mold, the more we reinforced and affirmed it and the stronger our identification with it became. It was a Yorkshire finger trap: the harder we pulled against it, the more fiercely it gripped us.

In my own experience of him, the closer my brother got to his coveted celebrity status, the more frequently he relapsed into drug use, the further out of reach he was, the testier and touchier, the more easily offended, and the more tyrannical he became. As part of this downward spiral, I think he surrounded himself more and more with unappealing characters, fawners, exploiters, handlers, groomers, enablers. I think he did this *somewhat* consciously, but I also think, like the counselor in *The Counselor*, he was naïve about the forces he was aligning himself with. Sebastian's self-awareness was matched by a Herculean capacity for denial. He fought every step of the way to live an unexamined life but it was a losing battle. It was as if, the more clearly he saw himself, the harder he had to work to erase the evidence of that *seeing*, and the more elaborate his stage magic and dandyism, his sorcery, had to become. And when he really saw it—the *doppelganger*, and how he had remade himself in his (grand)father's image—I think it was literally the death of him.

*

When I read this penultimate chapter back to my wife, she felt it was too disturbing, that readers wouldn't be able to sympathize with me, much less my brother, that they'd be too horrified to process such material and would turn away in disgust. Certainly I never meant for this book to end up sifting through such dark waters or dredging up such rotten remains. But at the same time, I was looking for the ghosts of my past, and one of the main leads I had to follow was a strange, adolescent predilection for simulated scenes of rape, torture, and violence. I might not have expected to find so *many* body parts, but I couldn't have thought I wouldn't find anything at all. The danger is that I will fall into the same trap which Michael Powell stumbled into with *Peeping Tom*, and unconsciously turn the reader into an unwilling receptacle for my confession.

Why would anyone want to hear about this sort of thing, this unremitting darkness that lurks behind a tawdry sheen of glamor? I am certainly aware of how crazy much of it sounds. I don't know if there's any reality to any of it or if it's evidence of an unbalanced mind seizing on connections in the world to try and make sense of damage done in *here*, by my home environment. But I don't think there *is* a clear dividing line between the psyche and the world, between one's family and the larger structures of social, political, and occult control "out there." Not in my case, at least. Maybe my reader has a greater luxury of distance, in which case you may wonder why I felt the need to bring you so close to this fire. Wonder away.

Both my brother and I were driven—at a deep, unconscious level, due to deep, unconscious trauma—to become players on the world stage, celebrities, culture makers; at the same time, we were driven to embody "Luciferian" energies. My brother took it further. He was the firstborn son of the firstborn son of our grandfather. He inherited the throne. He embodied the satanic majesty of celebrity in a way that let all the wild contradictions show. He let the mask become the face. His scarlet velvet suit and matching top hat was like an open mockery of those hidden masters whose favor he was courting, and with him the Fabian crown of our grandfather became a Jack the Ripper top hat: the wolf *without* sheep's clothing. I was more torn. I've been compelled since adulthood to bust open the Ickian conspiracy, to pull back the matrix-veil that's been drawn over our eyes and get to the truth of the world. At the same time, running parallel to this drive, fueling it and being fueled by it, is my desire to become a writer, a filmmaker, to conquer "Hollywood," to join the ranks of the spell-casters who keep the veil in place and who work day and night to maintain the deception that prevents the sleepers from waking. To join the cultural plutocracy.

My brother got close enough to the flame to be burned up by it. My warnings fell on deaf ears because he couldn't believe them. Why would he believe them when I was dancing around the same flame he was? Maybe I got it backward, and everything he did was meant as a warning for me. If so, it worked. I am backing away from the flame. I am starting to understand the secret benefits of "failure."

The Glamor Magic of the Hollow Man

"I'm not constrained pretty well by anything. The tough thing in life is ultimate freedom, that's when the battle starts. Ultimate freedom is what it's all about, because you've got to be very strong to stand for ultimate freedom. Ultimate freedom is the big challenge, now I've got it."
—Jimmy Savile, 1991

To individuate is to make conscious the contents of the unconscious. To integrate what's integral to the psyche and let everything that's alien go back where it came from. That "sorting of the seeds" process is what this book is supposed to be. I've been trying to identify the internal structures implanted in me by my cultural and family conditioning. These structures have imprisoned my libido through a combination of dissociation and sublimation. They have shackled my life force to misguided "creative" (worldly) drives, turning a simple love of life into a license for obsession. Once those internal structures are fully seen they begin to dissolve. If I can trust my own experience, this results in a corresponding lack of libido and ambition or purpose while the life force is redistributed. No longer trapped inside the head and the cock and balls, the soul begins to move into the total body where it belongs. I call this process genital disorganization, or, to subvert Travis Bickle, "One of these days I'm gonna get *dis*organized."

Why have I become so preoccupied with Jimmy Savile while working on these last two chapters? With his outrageous outfits, big hair, ostentatious jewelry and unique public persona, Savile was a *dandy*. He even occasionally wore top hats, like the Child-Catcher in *Chitty Chitty Bang Bang* (a film we grew up on in my family), a character who in retrospect seems to be an archetypal portrait of Savile. Although my brother certainly wouldn't have ever consciously used Savile as a role model, it would be difficult to overestimate Savile's influence on both of us when we were growing up. Savile was not only a national icon, he was a local celebrity, a Yorkshire man (he even met our father), considered for several years to be the single most influential man in rock and roll. This was the world—pop music—which my brother was most drawn to in his youth. His first—and I think most enduring—goal in life was to become a pop star in the glam rock style of Marc Bolan. Unconsciously, my brother may very well have been imitating Savile, and not just his dandyism. Flamboyance is a great cover for deviance, and one of the most disturbing things about Savile was how open he was about his psychopathic tendencies. Here's just one example of his hiding in plain sight from an interview he did for the Process Church magazine, in 1969, "The Natural Life of Jimmy Savile":

> I find it more difficult to destroy morals these days than ever before in my career, or maybe it's because I'm using the wrong "After-shave." ... I would say that I am highly moral during the day, and even higherly [sic] moral during the evening, but of course we won't say anything about night-time, because that is when all the real wolves like myself rise from the darkness and leap about causing mayhem left and right.

Allowing for the difference in generations, the quote could be mistaken for something my brother might have said. And if this wasn't enough to ring alarm bells across the country, other articles in the magazine (the "Sex" issue) covered rape and necrophilia. There are countless other examples, both of Savile's brazen behavior and of his bragging about the things he got away with. He joked about his sexual predation on TV and got big laughs for it. He even admitted to it in his autobiography! How is it nobody said anything? It's the glamor magic of the hollow man; surface sparkle deflects the world's gaze and prevents it from seeing the shadowy presence that lurks behind it. Seen and not seen. Although Savile and my brother were very different *types*, I think my brother practiced the same method, the same glamor magic. The proof for me is that the person closest to him in all the world, myself, took as long as I did to recognize that my brother, slice it however you like, was a practicing Satanist!

What does it mean to be a Satanist? There's another process that constitutes a kind of *false individuation*. It entails taking subli-mation and dissociation to such extremes that a person can separate from the collective (family and society), not by owning the contents of the unconscious but by *disowning* them. This is the process I think which my brother was fully and tragically consumed by, in his open (self-)worship of "satin and Satan." It requires widening the split in the psyche created by early trauma through a continuous re-wounding. Repeated, ever-worsening acts of "depravity" cause the soul to withdraw in horror and leave the ego to its own devices. Better to reign in hell. By this method, we can create and maintain a constructed, surface reality that's like an image or shell of our true being. When a celebrity soaks up the adoration of the masses he or she finds identity through it and becomes an *image*, an icon; they become a container which external, worldly energies move into and possess. This is a shadowy realm in which the ego can completely divorce itself from the life of the soul, and so gain total control over the physical world. Jimmy Savile was the *über*-celebrity—gangster, pop star, philanthropist, royalty by proxy, sexual predator and psychopath; his every whim and desire was met in the moment it arose, and so his desires grew increasingly insatiable and aberrational. He enjoyed "ultimate freedom."

Isn't this the dandy ideal: proof not that God is a man (as my brother liked to quip) but that Satan is a raging infant, forever sacrificing its own image in order to live on indefinitely *as* image? Isn't this the bid for immortality by selling the soul to the devil? Having looked for the first time unflinchingly at my brother's life and death, I think now that he wasn't joking when he said that he'd aborted his own inner child. That was the stark and awful truth of it, though I wasn't able to hear it. (Significantly, he wrote it to my partner at that time, not to me.) My brother was trying to come clean about what he was doing with his every act of distortion, to come clean to get clear, to escape the octopus that only wrapped itself more tightly around him in response to his every thrashing. He laid his insides out for the world to see, but no one saw. They only saw the image, an image which is now the empty shell he left behind.

Rest in pieces.

The Dissolving Artist

Or: This Book Will Self-Destruct in T-Minus 20 Minutes

When I wrote *The Blood Poets* in 1999, I wanted to write a mammoth tome about movies and to use them as a vehicle (a Trojan Horse) to look at the larger picture, a picture most easily (maybe too easily) summed up as "the occult conspiracy of the unconscious." Fifteen years later, I set about to write a little book about movies, using them as a window into my own psyche and a way to better understand my past and my trauma. By the time I was finishing the book, I wound up staring at the very same picture as in 1999, only this time from a position of direct, personal experience. I was like a dog who'd been chasing his own tail without realizing it. Apparently I'd gone so deep undercover that I'd forgotten I even *was* undercover. I'd been programmed to remember my mission and the trauma *was* the programming. Eventually, by trying to get to the bottom of my own psychic wounds, it was foreordained I would start to uncover family bones. I was muckraking not because I wanted to but because the muck was in my own backyard, and because it was the only way to see what was there and get anything *done*. (Next month I'm due to buy a very run-down house and set about salvaging it; so this is more than just a metaphor.)

The second title I had for this book (after "Confessions of a Movie Autist") was "The Disappearing Artist" (a deliberate homage to the Lethem book that kick-started this one). By the time I'd fallen down the rabbit hole of the last two chapters, I knew I needed another title. Maybe that's proof that the artist has disappeared in the act of writing the book, an act which has entailed one insult, uncovering, and disillusionment after another. Maybe "dissolving artist" would be more apt—as in a fantasy that's dissolving in the corrosive battery acid of truth.

What's the fantasy? That being an artist is something noble, lofty, or heroic. What's the corrosive truth? That artists are just people, and at least some of them (I suspect most if not all of them) have made a career out of lying, also known as perception management. They are spinners of illusions, driven by the wild conviction that fantasy is not only better than reality but the only thing that can get *rid* of reality. But at what point did reality cease to be good enough?

Ground Zero

"You can't reclaim a thing that changes as you touch it."
— Jonathan Lethem, *Amnesia Moon*

While I was working on the last chapters of the book, several related incidents occurred. I read two exposés of Clint Eastwood (one by Sondra Locke, his ex-lover and co-star, the other by Patrick McGilligan); Philip Seymour Hoffman died of a heroin overdose at 46, the same age I was at the time, and a year younger than my brother was when he died; the story broke around Woody Allen's alleged sexual molestation of his daughter, Dylan Farrow, when Dylan wrote an open letter describing her memories of what happened. She began the letter with, "What's your favorite Woody Allen movie?" Eastwood and Allen were two artists I have loved (or "loved") since I was a teenager or even earlier. Now I was faced with the question, what if these artists were also morally deficient men who abused their power in ways that would cast them as villains in any of their own movies? What if they were the opposite of how I'd perceived them to be? Did that make their "art" part of the cloak behind which they'd concealed their true natures and activities (like "Sir" Jimmy Savile)?

I probably shouldn't write about them in the same sentence, however, since Allen's shady behavior remains in question, while

Eastwood's really isn't. The two books I read made an unassailable case against Clint as a controlling, vicious, vindictive, vain, power-hungry, raging, spoiled infant in the form of a "legend." Yet Eastwood was also my first real role model—after my brother—and the first "man" (image of manhood) I ever looked up to. That's testimony to the power of art—or of fantasy. I was seriously misguided, and it took me more than thirty years to face up to the fact. Eastwood's drive was to be "number one," to be the most successful movie star in the world; then, once that goal was firmly established, to be recognized as a great artist and filmmaker, a great *man*. He pulled it off not so much by becoming a great artist (even his best films are overrated) as by mastering the *moves* of a great artist and by wooing critics and public until the illusion was complete. He did it by sheer force of will and charisma, and by surrounding himself with the right entourage.

Lastly, there were the revelations about my grandfather, an elitist who posed as a socialist, and a bully who presented himself as a philanthropist—a wolf in sheep's clothing. He made sure that all his sons (he was less interested in his daughters) went to Oxford. If he did belong to the Fabian Society and the Committee of 100, it's a safe bet he would have wanted his sires to join the social reform agendas too. I suspect that my father didn't, at least not consciously (he took over the reins of the family corporation, which may have been part of the plan); but his two brothers were quite active in the fields of social reform and philanthropy. It was often inferred around our family that our grandfather's values were hypocritical; now it was starting to look less like hypocrisy than duplicity. Imagine growing up being indoctrinated with values by someone who wasn't practicing those values and who never really intended to, but who was only using them for other, undivulged ends. How crazy would that have made my father—and by extension myself?

If being an artist—like being a "radical" socialist—is a license for obsession, then obsession for what? Politics is show business and show business is politics. In these realms (those of the world), art is a means and not an end and the end is always the same: personal empowerment, sourced in a powerful, infantile need to feel *safe in the world*. And the power, once attained, is invariably abused. If men like Woody Allen or Eastwood, or my grandfather, or my brother, abused their power behind the scenes while making "art" (or social reform) to conceal their real nature and turn moral emptiness into sensitivity, humor, insight, philanthropy, even compassion, what's wrong with this picture? Is it a wolf or is it a sheep?

*

What's clear is that *I don't know how to end this*. I only know that I must. My brother was my other and he got the celebrity status he wanted and that was the end of him. My experience of him was that, the more he became the person he wanted to be, the more he identified with his public persona, the less *himself* he was, the less present, the less loving or *real*. He undertook the process of becoming a self-created *image* consciously. He became a dandy and joked that the clothes made the Horsley, that he was an authentic phony because he *knew* he was a phony and because there *was* no real self apart from whatever fantasy figure he could cobble together. Since Sebastian did not exist, it became necessary to invent him. He was seen as a one-of-a-kind, a unique entity, but to me, the Sebastian the world saw was like Frankenstein's monster, a collection of old body parts—Oscar Wilde, Francis Bacon, Quentin Crisp, Marc Bolan, Johnny Rotten, Gene Simmonds, Byron, Baudelaire, Nietzsche, Aleister Crowley, Genesis P. Orridge, Jimmy Boyle and, yeah, Jimmy Savile—stitched together and animated by a bolt of lightning. Uniqueness is only recognizable—as separate from aberration—when it's familiar enough to cater to people's fantasies. Underneath it all, my brother was a lovable rogue, and losing sight of that only proved the victory of the subterfuge, of the dark enchantment—of which, in my view, he was less perpetrator than victim.

My brother magnified a neurosis common to all artists driven to enter into a new, heightened form of existence in the public eye, as public figures. It's the inverse of a meaningful pursuit, and the proof was that the end of all his self-invention was the oldest, dreariest outcome of all: self-destruction.

The real goal of art is to disappear into the work, to become a *process* by which the unconscious (soul life) becomes conscious and the divine moves into form in the world. The early Chinese masters spent years preparing to paint their masterpieces, years of *inner* preparation, before the brush ever touched canvas; and when they were done, they never even signed their names to the work. The idea of bringing something of transcendental beauty into the world for the spiritual improvement of others is a world away from the idea of creating to receive credit, to gain status. If the artist's ego is involved in the creation process, how can the finished work allow others to see past their own egos? Isn't all we end up with a turd in a Tiffany's box?

The idea of *being* an artist is oxymoronic. I've spent my life trying to join a club that not only will never have me for a member, but which I would never want to belong to.

*

Late February, 2014. While going over the manuscript before sending it to the editors, my wife and I watched *Inside Llewyn Davis*. The timing was acute, because the film (which we both loved, and which is about a brilliant folk singer unable to make a living by singing) questions the widespread, and totally unfounded, assumption that "talent will out." This idea is probably particularly American but I think it's pretty much everywhere nowadays: the idea that if you are sufficiently talented, determined, and dedicated to your craft, eventually you will achieve recognition because history sorts out the "players" in a kind of cultural selection process, so the cream eventually rises to the top. The obvious fallacy of this assumption is that it proves its own phony premise, because any talented individuals who *don't* make it will be unknown to us. All the bodies are buried.

In the film's centerpiece, Llewyn (Guatemalan actor Oscar Isaac) travels all the way to Chicago with a heroin addict in the backseat (John Goodman), and plays a song for a producer, played by F. Murray Abraham. Like all the songs Llewyn plays, it's deeply vulnerable, raw, and from the heart. Llewyn plays from his whole body, he doesn't seem *able* to hold any of himself back. He makes eye contact with the producer—a man he's just met and who hasn't shown a glimmer of warmth toward him—as if he was singing to his beloved (or to his father, who he sings to later). There's a pause after he finishes the song, during which the producer's expression betrays nothing. Finally the producer says, "I don't see much money here."

It was the exact same message the world had been giving me for the last twenty years. After watching the movie, I realized how it presented a far more nuanced demonstration of the old cliché about artists with integrity refusing to sell out. Having integrity, selling out or not selling out, wasn't a *choice* but the result of a person's nature. There's a particular kind of artist who can (loosely) be compared to the autist in the neurotypical world, the highly sensitive, vulnerable type who's dedicated to bringing out his or her innermost, the stuff of soul. Trying to bring such open, raw vulnerability into the world of show business, and to achieve worldly success by it, is an agonizing ordeal for these types of people, and it leaves only two options: either the artist eventually becomes discouraged and withdraws, as Davis seems ready to do in the film; or he or she adapts to survive. An artist who learns to develop a less authentic, raw, vulnerable kind of expression, who learns to push down that innermost part of them to keep the world from seeing it, as my brother learned to do, can develop the toughness needed to endure the insensitivity of the show business world. This applies to any kind of artist, and to every other field of human endeavor too. To succeed in the world, a person not only needs to develop enough insensitivity to let themselves be exploited, they have to learn to *like* it. Eventually, they have to learn to exploit *themselves*. Only once they have aborted their own inner child—made their confirmed kill—can they enter into the cartel and become *made men*.

Watching this tender, pitch perfect movie, finally, finally, the penny dropped: failure was the healthier option. This present book will come out and, as with the last seven books I've published, it will be ignored by the mainstream press and change little or nothing for me on a surface level. It will cross the sky like a comet in the dead of night while the world sleeps, and only a handful of insomniacs will ever see it. That's all it needs to be. There's no need to climb the mountain. I need to be down in the dirt, where the stone is buried. I will find my home at Zero.

To keep one's soul, the world cannot be gained. It's the world that loses.

Mount Hollywood

"You ascend the sacred mountain of God, not so the world sees you, but so you can see the world."
— Francis Bennett

Once upon a time, movies were the equivalent of shared, "tribal" experience. We gathered together in dark movie theaters, like primitives around a fire, and immersed ourselves in a collective story. Not quite the same, however, because, while the experience was shared, it wasn't interactive. All eyes are on the screen and in a movie theater we don't interact with, or even acknowledge, the crowd. We slip in and shuffle out with our eyes down. The experience of watching a movie, even as part of a theater audience, is an *internal*, passive experience, one that has "naturally" evolved in our current time into a private one, as more and more people watch movies on their TVs, computer screens, and smartphones. As the image itself becomes progressively smaller, it moves closer to the body itself. The next step is watching on Google goggles. If this movement continues—as I think it must—eventually the images will play out *inside of us*. If movies are our collective dreams, projected outward into the world, at a certain point the projection boomeranged. Now it's moving closer and closer to entering inside of us, until the movies play out on the screens of our retinas, or even inside our minds. The manufactured, external reality will then have become internalized, and our inner life will have been replaced with nonstop advertising. We will have been colonized.

This may be why movies seem to be becoming less and less of a social phenomenon, and it may also be one reason *The Counselor* was rejected, since it referred to social realities without any of the nostalgic sheen that makes them palatable as *entertainment*. If the experience of people in the modern world is becoming more and more "autistic" (in the limited sense), cut off from social reality, from the external world, at the same time we are being more and more bombarded by signals *from* that world. It's as if Nature (via human intelligence) has spawned its own artifice, its own matrix, and lured us, using the oldest, must trusted lure of them all (power and pleasure), to draw us in and close the pod doors behind us.

This may be why many of the more socially relevant movies of recent years (such as *The Matrix* and *Fight Club*) are about being lost in fantasy worlds. *The Counselor* was about what the pod-world looks like when we wake up *inside* it. It shows in clear, unequivocal terms, why no one *wants* to wake up: because the extinction of all (false) reality is something no amount of resignation can encompass.

The desire to escape into a disembodied state of being is common to (what we can observe about) autism, moviegoing, and heroin addiction. In the opening scene in *The Counselor*, the couple is seen wrapped up in white sheets, making love, hidden from the world. They have withdrawn into the surrogate womb of "love," a fantasy bubble akin to the sleepers in the *Matrix* pods, to a junky floating inside a heroin daze, and to a moviegoer completely absorbed by images on a movie screen. This dream of disembodiment is the desire to return to immersion inside the mother's body, to be swallowed up—but also made "real"—by the mother's imagination. Not to live fully means never having to experience death. In the words of Woody Allen, it's how we get to not "be there when it happens."

For the counselor, living was being in bed with his woman, everything else was just waiting. That bubble of blissful womb-life was the only kind of life he knew. It was the same for my brother, with his whores and heroin, and it's the same for me. Look closely enough and you may be surprised to see it's the same for everyone. We are all movie autists of one sort or another. It may be time to drop the movie—the false narrative—and embrace the autist. When the counselor lost the "object" of his fantasy-desire, his bubble burst and he was torn screaming from the womb of mother-dependence, into life. He was utterly alone but he was awake. Only once you are willing to die can you start to live.

*

In the family environment I was born into, it was difficult to find a real connection to anyone, a way *into* the world. My mother was drunk from conception on (she was even drinking during my birth, which was chemically induced). My father wasn't around much and when he was he was either on his way to being drunk or already there. My brother was so badly wounded by the time I came along that he was in no condition to guide me through the surreal and violent landscape which I'd landed in. Instead, he was actively hostile towards me. (There's a photo taken when I was probably only a year old in which we are glowering at each other.) My sister was the firstborn and our father's favorite, and she certainly tried to provide an island of sanity for me to retreat to, and to act as a surrogate parent, but that too came at a price. The point of this recap is, I've been trying to *connect* to the world ever since I first came into it, and in that struggle movie stars became living symbols for the "gods" (parents, and older siblings) who were out of my reach. They existed on a higher plateau and they seemed to *understand* the world, even rule over it. They were where *the real action was*. They had the power (so I imagined) to usher me into an understanding and experience of myself that would make sense of the terrifying chaos—that would *validate* me. Because my drive to connect to Hollywood was fueled by an unconscious desire to get the connection I couldn't get as a child, of course it was a failure. After thirty years of trying to get the gods' attention, Mount Hollywood remains indifferent.

But something *has* changed in those thirty years, and that's that I no longer believe in the reality of "the gods." I now know that celebrities are no more perfect or superior than my parents or siblings were. In fact, I've gradually reached the opposite conclusion. I have begun to see Hollywood as a mafia-cartel run by criminals, murderers, rapists, and sexual predators (I am starting to think the same about my own family too!). This may be an overly jaded, compensatory view, as when we go from seeing a partner as a goddess/god to seeing them as a whore/beast. It may be no truer than my previous, naïve view. There does seem to be more evidence for it being true than not, however. Not just the Jimmy Savile disclosures, or even the Woody Allen charges, but many other stories (such as those pertaining to Corey Feldman and Corey Haim) suggest the Hollywood "casting couch" is not only fundamental to how the business operates but that it includes children too. Randy Quaid's recent "episode" was most compelling to me because the media framed it strictly in terms of his being crazy, even though what he was claiming (that there was a Hollywood mafia that used stars the way traders use currency, and that managed not only their careers but even their deaths in order to exploit their commercial potential) seemed totally plausible to me. As I was prepping this manuscript for publication, charges of sexual abuse were filed against Bryan Singer, director of *X-Men* and its sequels. *The Uncanny X-Men* was a comic book I grew up on and even one I associated with my adolescent, awakening sexuality (via a crush I had on Marvel Girl). Isn't that how the Child-Catcher operates—by disguising depravity as magic?

What better hunting ground for the wolves to mingle with the sheep than the land of glamor magic? It's as basic as instinct— sharks go to where the biggest fish are—and this natural, if tragic, affinity is between not just art and exploitation but also between creative people, social reformers, and the worst sort of human predators. They instinctively flock together, driven by shared traumata. It's in the nature of trauma to replicate itself, not only via fantasy but via actual re-enactments, acts of depravity for which the fantasy serves a threefold purpose: as a lure, a snare, and a cover.

This book isn't an exposé; at least it didn't start out as one. Whatever levels of depravity the real Hollywood might sink to, the one thing I know for sure is that I'm never going to participate in them. I have my brother (and more recently my sister, who has recently shown symptoms of the same family glamor magic virus) to thank for helping me to see that.

So what happens when the dream dies? One of two things: either we die with it, or we survive and find out what the world looks like—outside the pod.

The Only One Here

Also in February, I was contacted by a young Brazilian who had read some of my writing and wanted to share his own experiences of early trauma. He had come upon my blog via an occult forum, he said, specifically a thread about the occult writer Kenneth Grant. He had found the scanned letters which Grant wrote me, in 2002-3, while I had been living in London, embarking on my film career and lobbying as the Antichrist. He was particularly struck, he said, by Grant's advice to me to "abandon the illusion." I remembered the letter well, it was dated April 28th, 2003, and was in response to an interview/article I'd done with Liz Wu (my partner at the time) for *Fortean Times*, in tandem with the release of *Matrix Warrior*. Grant wrote:

> You are now in a position to quit the Sphere of False Knowledge (Daath) and move on to the City of Pyramids, which means that you should invoke a period of quietude and stabilize a dearly won insight into the non-phenomenal nature of "reality" … Why do you not see that there is no one besides you? Why all the histrionics? Why have you not understood, clearly, that THERE ARE NO OTHERS? Look at the "Tree," man—the Supernal Triangle beyond Daath (false knowledge) is shouting at you to awaken from the dream of attempting to make "others" see the Light—when there are no others to see it. All else is playacting, and that is exactly what you seem to be bent on doing … OK, let it all come out, and enjoy the show—but you will be the only one in it and enjoying it; there really ain't nobody out there, to know or not to know.

In *The Counselor*, Jefe tells the counselor something similar:

As the world gives way to darkness it becomes more and more difficult to dismiss the understanding that the world is in fact oneself. It is a thing you have created, no more no less. And when you cease to be, so will the world.

I hadn't been able to receive Grant's counsel back then. Was I ready to receive it now?

*

I know how this book began; but how is it going to end? My brother, Sebastian, used to say that the goal of art was "to get rid of reality." In the first chapter of this book I quoted Jonathan Lethem: "I asked works of art to bear my expectation that they could be better than life, that they could redeem life. In fact, I believe they are, and do. My life is dedicated to that belief." A few months ago, when I started this book, I shared this belief—or thought I did. Now I see that life has dragged me, first kicking and screaming but lately just groaning and muttering, 180 degrees *away* from it. Art is ideology because art aspires towards ideal forms (it started with Plato), so what we really need, I think, is for *reality* to get rid of the cultural spell of "art."

In my days as a student of the occult, I read a succinct parable from Rudolf Steiner. Steiner said that ancient Man (back in the Garden) was able to see the workings of the Gods, the natural and divine forces, as they worked *through* him. Because of this ability to *see*, there was never even the slightest possibility for Man to go against the divine workings because he was inseparable from them and knew it. The only problem was that Man didn't have free will, because free will depends on the illusion of being separate from the divine. Enter Lucifer (also known as Prometheus), who decides to set Man free and make of him an independent agent. To do so, Lucifer makes Man blind. Now Man experiences himself as separate from the Gods, but also as cut off from the divine, isolate, cast out of the Garden, fallen. In order to make up for stealing Man's sight, Lucifer gives him a compensatory gift of imagination. If he can't see the divine workings, Man can now at least *imagine* them. Outer vision is replaced by inner vision.

Lucifer's idea was for the imagination to provide Man with a way to rediscover the hidden nature of reality and eventually reconnect to it and regain access to it. The catch was that having imagination meant Man could fool himself (and others) into imagining *a false order of reality*, one in which he could remain "free" (isolate) and lord it over. Man could "choose" (though he would never know it was a choice) to reign in Hell, the realm of the imagination, of art, ideology, culture, rather than serve in Heaven, reality. That's why Blake said (of Milton) that all artists were "of the devil's party."

Reigning in Hell is a game that never gets old because the nature of the game is endless reinvention. So elaborate and sophisticated is this matrix-free-will-playground-hell that even the very elect have been fooled—we fooled ourselves. The most skilled in the game—the most endowed with Luciferian vision— imagine the gods for the rest to worship, giving them idols to bow down to and relieving them of the need to imagine their own place in the cosmos while simultaneously making them subject to other imaginings, to the false gods of magic, religion, science, politics, and art, all provinces of the *intelligentsia*. Artists and reformers are seen as the high priests of culture whose job it is to administer to the masses. In such a world, the only thing that seems worth imagining is a place in the ranks of the culture makers, the illumineers, the Luciferian elite: to become a creator of idols and escape the ideological enslavement of the peasant class. Now the advertising, the imagined idols of mass culture, are everywhere, leaving no space for new imaginings to happen. The movies stole our dreams—but it began long before "flickers" were invented. It began with the word. So that's how it will end.

"I've seen it all counsellor, and it's all shit. It's all shit."

How to write a book about how it's all shit—all reality excreted out as ideology—without adding to the excrement? There's really no way, is there? But there's no need to kill the messenger: he already committed *hari kari* with his pen. I am a suicide bomber and this message is set to self-destruct. I only hope I can take a few of you with me.

*

During a July morning of 2013, I had the following dream:

I am walking with my brother Sebastian. He is talking about making it to the top of the mountain. The mountain represents freedom, enlightenment, but it is also a real energetic "space." We are both headed there, but it's impractical for us to climb together. We must go separately and meet again only *if and when we arrive at the very top.*

He describes something about yoga and the nature of true self/no self. I comment how it's strange how one can know these things in theory, but still not understand them until it becomes *experiential*. With a powerful outrush of emotion and tears, I say that I can no longer tell the difference between being totally fed up with myself and just giving up, and the state of self-realization.

"It's the same for me," says my brother. There's happiness both in the realization and in the agreement.

He says he doesn't want to go up the mountain only to get a bunch of gifts and take them back down again, to his old life and self. He is determined to go *all the way*, to let go of every last one of the trappings of the false self, forever.

We embrace and I tell him how much I love him. He expresses the same.

After a moment I awake, and the dream dissolves.

How Did We Get Here?

Last Words from the Land of Disenchantment

The original subtitle I had for this book was "How Pop Culture Saved My Life." By the time I'd written it, it seemed like a misrepresentation of the facts.

The first person to read this completed manuscript was Jonathan Lethem. It was definitely a first for me as a writer to have so illustrious a reader at such an early stage. But besides providing a jewel for the rusty crown of my ego, what was it worth? If a tree falling in a forest with no one to hear it means there is no sound, it follows that, the finer the ear, the more resonant the sound. Literary merit is in the eye and ear of the beholder. The act of observing the experiment affects the outcome.

This book has been an experiment from start to finish, but the outcome of it only becomes clear when and as the observer reports his or her observation. The author is the primary observer, of course, but he is the very opposite of impartial. Mr. Lethem has kindly stepped up as a *transitional character* existing in the liminal realm between "objective" observer and engaged subject. In fact, Mr. Lethem *is* a character within this narrative— a bit like a Schrödinger's-tiger under the city—albeit not to anything like the same degree as the author is (or was—since hopefully this is my post-fictional self speaking).

Mr. Lethem's observational response to the work you've just read was gratifying. When I asked him for editorial suggestions, he tentatively indicated that I might try and bring the narrative back to the same or similar ground on which it started, a "circling around at the end, from the devastating personal revelations in the latter third to their being examined and parsed according to some of the framework from the earlier portions."

This struck me as sound counsel, from both within and without the narrative—Mr. Lethem being an outsider who was allowed (or rather dragged) *in* to the post-fictional framework and so became an insider (or is that vice versa?). In fact, his comment caused me to remember a passage I had taken *out* of the book, from around the halfway point:

> There are at least two kinds of journey: ones when we know where we are going, for how long, and why; and ones that are open-ended, that take us into wholly unexpected realms and maybe off the map entirely. These are usually known as "quests." I'm trying to write this book as a quest. A quest for identity or, better yet, for a realm beyond identity, which is the only place to find truth. To write that sort of book means not to know where it's going. Only that, if I'm following the clues as I find them, eventually they'll lead me to "the body"—at least if I stay alive long enough to uncover it (there are guardians whose job is to ensure I don't). At one point or another, a quest becomes a solitary journey. We can only make it so far accompanied; the final, crucial steps have to be taken alone. At a certain point, then, the reader and I must part ways and we will find ourselves alone.

Apparently this is what happened, and Mr. Lethem, in his intuitively tentative or tentatively intuitive way, was indicating the fact. Since I don't wish to leave the reader wandering forever across the wastelands of my unraveled narrative non-/post-fiction, I will endeavor to throw down a few markings by which he or she may stagger, or crawl, out of the labyrinth I have created, before the book is closed forever.

*

A couple of weeks after Mr. Lethem's suggestion—having

decided to wait patiently on some internal guidance to guide hand back to page and keyboard—I had a dream that pointed towards a possible conclusion. This was after two or three extremely immersive weeks exploring the dark and conspiratorial under layers of my family history, an exploration which resulted directly from writing this book and which took me almost instantly beyond it. In the dream, I was with Dave Oshana and he was telling me that I needed to be careful due to my tendency of seeing life as a point-scoring, reward-and-punishment system. Come death, he warned, I might die into that perspective and have much self-punishment to endure. I wondered aloud where I'd adopted such a belief system when I hadn't even been raised a Christian and had never believed in Heaven *or* Hell. Oshana's response was something along the lines of it having been conditioned into me from the earliest possible age via cultural artifacts (such as movies and comic books). I had an "Aha!" moment, and it occurred to me that I had what I needed to write the last chapter of the book.

Entertainment is instruction, instruction is ideology. The Judeo-Christian values of good and evil, heaven and hell, right and wrong, reward and punishment (as *The Counselor* shows) are so deeply embedded into western culture that we adopt them as if instinctively, regardless of the specifics of our family background, just like the air we breathe (as it happens, the root of the word *conspiracy*).

In the dream, I started to draw a diagram of a soul entering into existence via a vortex of some sort which was created at the moment of conception and which sucked the soul into it, like a whirlpool dragging a leaf underwater. I put a speech balloon next to the descending soul inside which I wrote the words "My God!" This was the first thing the soul thought as it was pulled (for the umpteenth time?) into earthly existence. The words were not the words of a prayer but came from a song which I first heard in my adolescence. They were followed by the words,

"What have I done?!"

Whether the soul incarnates into a "beautiful house" or a "shotgun shack," for the rest of its life it wonders how it got there. After much wondering, at a given point, it realizes that this world is *not* its beautiful house, *or* its beautiful wife, but that it only *looks* like it. And throughout it all, the days go by.

*

Water dissolving, and water removing; there is water, at the bottom of the ocean. Being born into culture is like being a fish born in the ocean. I've never been without it or outside of it so I can't imagine an existence independent of it. All I *do* know with any confidence is that, as in the song, something went terribly wrong.

Talking Heads' "Once in a Lifetime" was released as a single in late 1980, when I was thirteen. I remember it well because I saw the video on "Top of the Pops" (the show started by Jimmy Savile, though by then he was no longer a regular host). When I saw it, I thought, "Who the hell *is* this guy?" It was a few years before I bought the albums, but with his demented preacher act, David Byrne got my attention. Another reason I remember that time so clearly is because, a couple of months later, John Lennon was shot. While I watched the images of him and Yoko on TV (also on "Top of the Pops") to the accompaniment of his new song, "Happy Xmas (War is Over)," even though I was far from being a fan, I cried. The song went straight to number one, of course. And the days went by.

How do I know that something went terribly wrong? Call it existential ennui. From as far back as I can remember, I couldn't *get* no satisfaction. Well-being, contentment, happiness were all things that had to be *earned*. They were not a natural state to be enjoyed. They required the right shirt, the right cigarettes, a cultural stream of "useless information" to "fire my imagination." That was how it was for me, ever since the first bite of that apple, when what seemed so innocent, ended it all.

*

If pop culture saved my life, it was only in the way morphine might save a sickly infant: by turning it into an addict for life. I never grew out of the need for the dissociative fantasy of fairy tales because I associated them with life-saving values—the source of goodness, a reward for a life of suffering, like grace to a Christian. The fairy tales we tell ourselves as adults perpetuate the insanity that surrounded us as children and that made us need fairy tales to begin with. My parents didn't partake of the opium of the masses (they were anti-religious)—they took their opium straight: sex and alcohol—but the end result was the same: they got to blot out the pain of trauma, to stupefy their senses and retreat into a "blissful" fog of forgetting, a womb-like quasi-existence of all-reward and no-punishment. Limbo is the state that souls who aren't ready to die enter into and that souls not ready to be born end up in. A twilight zone where reality and fantasy overlap and cancel each other out.

He wonders if he too might have made a similar mistake.

When movies became my escape from the endless confusion of childhood, they became the "reward"—happiness earned—for the sustained nightmare of living. (To this day I still look forward to the weekend when I can "veg out" with a movie—a completely irrational routine, since I have no job and choose my own hours to write in.) Earthly existence is little more than a Job-like trial of suffering to determine if we are worthy of life everlasting in the Hereafter. The Heaven that has to be earned through the renunciation of the body is called limbo. It's a dissociative realm in which "the days go by," endlessly, where nothing ever happens, nothing changes, and nothing is real. Rinse and repeat. Groundhog Day. A once in a lifetime deal, while stocks last.

And yet. Where the sickness is, seek the cure. Cold turkey may not be an option. Shock the system too much and it will die. Sometimes babies need morphine to survive. Pop culture in homeopathic doses might be "just all right with me." *This book is culture too.* Songs and movies and comic books reveal the nature of the no-satisfaction sickness even as they spread it. They are like sleeper agents inside the Matrix that appear to belong to the same system which enslaves us but which secretly (sometimes even to themselves) serve a deeper, higher agenda. They carry microscopic doses of the truth that will someday set us free.

*

One of the little details I found out while uncovering the conspiracy of my family history was that A.A. Milne, the author of *Winnie the Pooh*, was an agent for British Intelligence. Interestingly, I'd already found this out without knowing it, while reading selections from Christopher Robin's memoirs. I learned from these that A.A. Milne was remote as a father and unable to really connect to his son while Christopher Robin was growing up. In fact, Milne was *too busy writing*! (And perhaps secret agenting?)

The stories I grew up on of Pooh and the hundred-acre wood were the products of Milne's compensatory fantasy life of being a father *and* a child. Apparently it was too painful, too unsafe, for him be a flesh and blood father and connect to his son in real time, to play with him in the forest or throw sticks off the bridge with him and see which came out the other end first, or any of the things he turned into such warming, haunting fiction. Instead, he created a surrogate childhood for his son—and for a million other children—by imagining for *himself* the childhood he never had and the fathering he could never give because he never got it from his own father. Milne's idealized version or fantasy-matrix of childhood was of course an enormous, transcultural, multi-generational success, and it is now owned by Disney, Inc.

I wish I could just let those two paragraphs speak for themselves; I think they really say it all.

I also think the more mundane facts "trump" the whole question of whether or not Milne was a secret agent, writing children's books as part of a vast social engineering agenda to infantilize and nostalgize the minds of millions and create an enchanted forest in which part of us would remain forever tapped, along with a boy and his bear, "dancing" like flies frozen inside amber.

The Ickian horror stories of Child Catchers (*Chitty Chitty Bang Bang* was written by British Intelligence agent Ian Fleming; the movie was probably the most beloved of my early childhood) — like Jimmy Savile procuring sex slaves for the reptilian elite (or Hollywood predators like Bryan Singer — or Woody Allen?!) — are really just the cover story, for those of us who like our fairy tales in the form of *cinema verité* (or video nasty), for a far deeper and more heart-wrenching horror: that of a billion fathers who couldn't love their sons — who "immortalized" them as fantasy projections of a non-fiction narrative, and turned them into the playthings of a godlike, fallen imagination.

Yet despite it all, even *because* of the melancholic sickness and heartbreak at its center, Milne's excretory fantasy delivered the cottleston pie I needed, inside the vacuum of my own godless universe. I might not have had a father; but I wasn't the only forsaken son.

The lost boys are everywhere. Seen and not seen. Same as it ever was.

Postscript: The Last Word (from Our Sponsor)

May 23, 2014, Berlin

Dear Jasun,

First, let me express my gratitude, after all, for what I know risked seeming an imposition, and must have been for you a bizarre gamble: your involving me in your manuscript at such an early point in its composition. Encountering myself wandering in your labyrinth before it was even constructed has been disconcerting, unnerving—a plunge into the state of *mise en abyme*, even—and I wouldn't have missed it for the world. Needless to say (but important to get out of the way; I'll raise this in order to expose and expunge it) you've tickled my vanities; that *The Disappointment Artist* could call forth this ferocious twin seems to me one of the greatest compliments a book could be paid. Elsewhere, your chapter on *Chronic City* feels seminal enough I wish I could retroactively include it in the pages of that book, as an exegesis committed by one of its characters. Or I could write you into a chapter, have you spend an evening with Perkus Tooth, forced to listen to the Rolling Stones' "Shattered" a few dozen times. But perhaps that's simply an urge to seek revenge for the way you've engulfed me here in your book? My situation addressing you reminds me of a gesture in one of my favorite memoirs, by Philip Roth—*The Facts*. At the end of that book Roth's autobiographical mouthpiece, Zuckerman, writes him a letter, accusing the preceding chapters of being merely a stunt fiction, another product of Roth's elaborate machine for manufacturing artistic meaning by pretending to reveal his life. Here, I'm as much your character as Zuckerman is Roth's, and it's generous of you to let me try and talk back to the book that includes me. I wonder if you'll really give me the last word?

Well, in that case, in place of a thousand last words, in place of the entire book I could be tempted to write in reply to your reply to mine (We have to get off this carousel somehow!), I'll offer a bit of recommended reading. Like a magnet, or black hole, your book has demonstrated the capacity to draw other texts helplessly into its space. As Borges said of Kafka, the best books create their own lineages and predecessors, out of formerly unrelated texts. Yours, for me, has roped together, among other things, Adam Phillips' *Houdini's Box*, his superb study of the famous escape artist and how he stands for the escape artist in all of us, wishing to astonish others and also to disappear; Edward St. Aubyn's *Patrick Melrose* novels, which seem to me emblematic of the human capacity to transform family abuse into sheer sensibility—for better and for worse for the sufferer!—and, most of all, Laurence Rickels' *Spectre*, an analysis of the morbid undertow of deferred grief animating Ian Fleming's James Bond novels. From the last chapter of that book, which concerns Fleming's son Caspar—an eventual suicide—as played out through one of your own surprising talismans, Ian Fleming's *Chitty Chitty Bang Bang*:

"Originally invented for his young son as a bedtime story and then written down while convalescing from his first heart attack … *Chitty-Chitty-Bang-Bang* emplaces the gadget love of the Bond world up on the screen within a family's relationship to its magical car… the car is technically the father's prosthesis, but its magical qualities—its uncontrollability and independence—represent as separable the object relation to mothers and all others. As a happy medium for the father's relationship to his beloved but neglected son, this story separates out its transmission from its inheritance …"

And so on. Congratulations; your book is large enough to contain us both, and a whole lot more. Zuckerman told Roth: *don't publish*! I say: *do*!

Sincerely,

Jonathan

zer0
books

Contemporary culture has eliminated both the concept of the public and the figure of the intellectual. Former public spaces – both physical and cultural – are now either derelict or colonized by advertising. A cretinous anti-intellectualism presides, cheerled by expensively educated hacks in the pay of multinational corporations who reassure their bored readers that there is no need to rouse themselves from their interpassive stupor. The informal censorship internalized and propagated by the cultural workers of late capitalism generates a banal conformity that the propaganda chiefs of Stalinism could only ever have dreamt of imposing. Zer0 Books knows that another kind of discourse – intellectual without being academic, popular without being populist – is not only possible: it is already flourishing, in the regions beyond the striplit malls of so-called mass media and the neurotically bureaucratic halls of the academy. Zer0 is committed to the idea of publishing as a making public of the intellectual. It is convinced that in the unthinking, blandly consensual culture in which we live, critical and engaged theoretical reflection is more important than ever before.